ROBIN MUKHERJEE

THE ART OF SCREENPLAYS
A WRITER'S GUIDE

creative ESSENTIALS

First published in 2014 by Kamera Books,
an imprint of Oldcastle Books
PO Box 394, Harpenden, Herts, AL5 1XJ
kamerabooks.com

Copyright © Robin Mukherjee 2014
Series Editor: Hannah Patterson

978-1-84344-200-4   (Print)
978-1-84344-201-1   (epub)
978-1-84344-202-8   (kindle)
978-1-84344-203-5   (pdf)

8 10 9 7

Typeset by Elsa Mathern in Franklin Gothic 9 pt
Printed and bound by 4edge Limited, Essex, UK

*For Tony Dinner – mentor, friend and
lasting inspiration to so many writers.*

*And to all my students over the years,
from whom I have learned so much.*

ACKNOWLEDGEMENTS

Many hands made this work. I can mention here only a few. Most immediately, my thanks to Hannah Patterson for challenging me to write this book, and to Anne Hudson for her meticulous and insightful editing. Thanks also to both of them for their unstinting support and enthusiasm. Then, of course, my appreciation to Ion, Frances, Claire, Clare and the whole team at Creative Essentials whose energy and enterprise made this possible. I have been lucky enough to work with some wonderfully talented people over the years, all of whom have added something to my own efforts. Much is owed, meanwhile, to that small band of theatrical adventurers, many years ago, gathering to talk, experiment, and study the art. Their continuing friendship remains invaluable. Finally, thanks to my family for their unmitigated support, and enduring patience.

CONTENTS

While the main laws of strategy can be stated clearly enough for the benefit of all and sundry, you must be guided by the actions of the enemy in attempting to secure a favourable position in actual warfare.

Sun Tzu, *The Art of War*

INTRODUCTION

Overheard in a café:

GIRL 1
(Munching on a cake)
So I was like, 'You know, I'm just saying, you do that – yeah? – and it's gonna come down, like, really hard on you.' And she was like, 'Wha'? What's it to do wiv you?' And I says, 'But it's Neil, you know, he's like my bro' in he?', and she was, 'Huh? You and Neil?' I says, 'No, I said he's like my bro', yeah?' And then she goes...
(Sits back, folding her arms)
...'Oh, I see.'

GIRL 2
You and Neil?

GIRL 1
Well... yeah.
(Giggles)
Just the once.

Girl 1 might not have known it, but, in her construction of narrative and portrayal of character to evoke a moment and convey a point, she was writing a script. If you had asked her (which I wouldn't have dared), she would probably have acknowledged that she was telling a story. And, much as the grammatical purist might question her use of language, I couldn't help feeling a sneaking envy for the skills with which she commanded the attention of her audience. It's possible that she was a recent graduate of some intensive course in scriptwriting, or that the bookshelves of her bedroom sagged with voluminous tomes on the subject. But I doubt it. I'm sure she watches TV and possibly the odd movie, but the question is: without a formal grounding in the art of dramatic composition, how was she able to tell a story? Moreover, why would she want to? And why was her friend so captivated – apart from a personal involvement with some of the circumstances and our perennial fascination with scandal?

Girl 1 knew what she wanted to say (in between mouthfuls of pastry). She understood the central characters, and she was possessed by the emotional content of her tale. She needed only to let these dynamics operate to provide the entertainment her friend so enjoyed. Of course, there is a leap from the act of conveying an anecdote to the finessing of a professional screenplay, but the elements remain the same. Beyond formatting issues, structural niceties, editing of dialogue, and authentic character construction, our natural understanding of storytelling is enough to get us a long way, from title sequence to end credits.

Like anything, a story unfolds according to a mix of creativity and knowledge; which is to say, its need to exist and the form by which it can function. Story is, by nature, a structured phenomenon, just as any event worth relating has a pattern of sorts. We know quite a lot about character, because most of us are characters. Dialogue is speech, and we use that every day. So the place to look, for both the creative energy and knowledge of form, is not some extraneous template, but the material that you're bursting to express.

I am, of course, assuming that you have material to express. You might have picked up this book because you like the colour of its binding. The chances are, however, that you have stories, or a sense of the presence of stories, and you want to have a go at shaping them into a script. If you're simply hoping to try your luck at becoming a professional scriptwriter because the money sounds good and the parties look fun, then either find something else to do that might reward your labours with more alacrity or have a scout around your psyche for a story. You won't get far without one.

It may be, however, that you have already written something. And that there was something about it which jumped out at you, crackling with vitality, while something else crouched in a corner refusing to join in. Maybe your plot convulsed into knots around the midway mark. Or your central character never got beyond slouching around in an existentialist angst more interesting to him than to anyone paying good money to watch it. Or you sat back at the end of your efforts to realise that you'd written about everything except the thing you wanted to write about. You've gone back over it. You've tweaked and nudged, deleted and added, but the more you struggled, the worse it got. And when your manuscript thudded, finally, into the corner of your room, it might have joined a pile of previous thuddings.

And now you're asking why. Why didn't it work? Why does the story sag and the dialogue sound leaden? Why does that heart-pounding finale you spent 86 pages building up to fall flat? These are good questions, because they indicate that you understand story and recognise that what you've written doesn't quite match up to the intrinsic, natural, even commonplace sense of narrative so integral to our human sensibilities.

In this book you will find many questions. Sometimes there are more questions than answers. And when there are answers you should take them only as indicators pointing out some possible places to look. Do take the time to ponder the puzzles. In the end, every writer will find, feel and frame the answers in their own way, in their own terms, according to the infinite variety of nature and experience. This is important because your writing should be yours, not somebody else's. The answers you find will come from the knowledge and the creativity that reside in you and you alone.

So let's begin our journey. Our destination is the moment when a story unfolds on the page in front of you, vividly, beautifully and surprisingly, because that is the only way it can. You're not struggling to find the words. You're struggling to keep up with them. You're not putting speech into the mouths of characters. They're telling you what they want to say. And they're saying things you didn't even know you knew. You've probably had that moment. And you want it again. It's what keeps most writers that I know writing.

ONCE UPON A TIME
IN YOUR HEAD

It is said that fish have no awareness of the water in which they swim, although one suspects that a change in temperature, consistency and condition would send a shiver through their scales. The water doesn't just support them, it informs them; which for a fish, predatory or otherwise, is likely to matter. The principle here is that the medium in which they move is so ubiquitous to their existence that, unless they're dragged out of it, they never think of it as an entity separate from themselves. (Whether or not fish think about anything at all is not a question into which we shall digress.) In the same way, it can be argued that we are so surrounded by stories, so supported and informed by them, that we hardly notice their existence as anything separate from us.

From as early we can remember, there will have been stories. We might have heard them told by our parents, or grandparents. We might have pondered the squiggly lines in picture books, waiting for someone to read them out. There's a good chance that they greeted us on our first day at school, and smiled from the shelves of a classroom library. Throughout our lives they will have marched across television screens, not just in the programmes flagged up as 'drama', but in news items, sports reportage, idents and ad breaks. We might have pursued them in cinemas, or theatres. We will have unfolded them across the pages of a newspaper, and pored over them in books.

Stories provide some important services. They're a device to keep the kids quiet, tell us about the world, shape the way we think, and make us buy things. Good marketing tells us not simply what a product does, but how it fits our 'narrative'. More powerfully, perhaps, stories uphold the great belief systems. Moses didn't just announce the Ten Commandments, he staggered down the mountain with them. Prophecy without a bit of thunder and lightning is merely prediction. And it's a dull sermon without parables. Getting your message across, therefore, whether it's a tin of beans or the meaning of life, needs story.

So we know what stories are. And, even if we listen to them without much concern for the technicalities of narrative structure, we know a good one when we hear it.

Before we proceed, a cautionary note. If fish only understand the presence of water once they're out of it, so we need to step outside of story to perceive its workings. And, like a fish out of water, this can be an uncomfortable experience. In the long term, as aesthetes rather than ordinary consumers, we may develop a different kind of appreciation for good material, but we become harder to seduce.

I was startled once, on a research visit round a Russian mortuary, to see a pin-up calendar in the staff lounge. How, I wondered, can anyone spend their tea-break leering at a human body having just spent the morning slicing them up? Surely there's a moment when you know too much of the grisly innards ever to be enchanted by its outward form. But as writers we need, like pathologists, to step beyond our sensitivities, past the obvious charms of a bikini-clad drama posing for our dubious pleasure, to a deeper kind of beauty. After a while we will find that what makes up story, that finely tuned, powerful assembly of dramatic elements, is as beautiful as the story itself.

Consider the following questions (you might have asked them already). Although unnecessary for the average consumer of story, they do help us to see past the pin-up. Dig in a little. Try to get an eye on that great sea of stories in which you swim on a daily basis – in which you have swum for as long as you can remember.

- Why do we want or need stories?

- Why are stories to be found through all ages, across all cultures, from the most 'primitive' to the most 'developed'?

- Why are storytellers among the first to be silenced by totalitarian regimes? Are they a threat? To what? How?

- What happens to a conversation when somebody starts to tell a story?

- What happens to us when we hear a story?

- On a personal level, are there stories that have moved and changed us?

- Why do we connect with stories from childhood right through to the end of our days?

- Do we recollect stories from an early age that have stayed with us?

- Has a story ever changed the way we think about something?

- Has a story ever changed the way we think about ourselves?

- Can we imagine a life or world without stories? What would that be like?

Apart from pondering these myself (anything to put off actually writing!), I have occasionally offered them to writing groups. Here are a few of the most frequent responses, a list which is not intended to be definitive. Before reading on, take a moment to jot down, or think about, your own answers. Return to the questions from time to time – especially if you're feeling tired, or jaded. It may take you back to why you wanted to do this in the first place. At the very least it will open your eyes again to the extraordinary power of this art.

STORIES TELL US ABOUT THE WORLD

Thus *Downton Abbey* gives us an insight into the machinations of an Edwardian country house. *Lincoln* opens the door to a crucial moment in history, the ramifications of which we might otherwise not fully acknowledge. Through various movies and TV shows, we can find ourselves observers of the world of boiler rooms, hedge-fund trading, the English Civil War, opium dealing, the low-rise projects of Baltimore, and space stations. Aficionados of medical dramas could probably, after a season or two, perform an accomplished Heimlich Manoeuvre or tracheotomy. Fans of courtroom series might be tempted to conduct their own defence – although this would be inadvisable.

The stories we watch or read enable us to peek into corners of the world from which we might normally be excluded. And we are inquisitive creatures. Our progress and survival, both as individuals and as a species, depend on it. In this way, stories maintain the narrative of humanity, a tradition as ancient and vital as the epic poem and the wandering troubadour. It's also fun to spend a little time vicariously walking the beat, or in the company of notorious people, or standing up for liberty in some far-flung colonial outpost.

STORIES TELL US ABOUT OURSELVES

Shakespeare described story in terms of a mirror in which we can see all that's good in us, all that denies the good, and the prevailing ideas which influence our thoughts and actions. Thus, story can reveal to us the great virtues of courage, trust, loyalty, dignity and so on, along with their shabbier cousins of spite, envy, cowardice, arrogance, etc. When Gordon Gekko, in *Wall Street*, said that greed is good, echoing a potent idea of the day, we saw past its glitter to the tawdry consequences of uninhibited avarice. When Dr King Schultz decided to shoot Calvin Candie rather than shake his hand (*Django Unchained*), we were invited to ponder the fine balance of integrity and self-preservation.

'Story' derives from a word related to 'wisdom'. Wisdom necessitates some degree of self-awareness. It is this attribute of self-awareness, of reflection, that distinguishes us from the other animals with whom we share (often not very well) our eco-system. It is an idea built into the very name we give ourselves as a species. *Homo sapiens* means a thinking man, with 'sapiens' related to self-awareness. Story, then, is not just a tool that we use, but essential to who we are. This might go some way to explaining why tyrants burn books and, eventually, the people who write them. It also elevates the role of story from idle diversion to the realisation of our identity and function as human beings.

RITUAL AND THE COLLECTIVE EXPERIENCE

We pride ourselves on our individuality ('I am not a number'), but there is a pleasure to be had in the subsummation of our sometimes brittle singularity into the collective strength of a greater good. Which is why we congregate sometimes, as pigeons do and pandas don't, in sports stadiums, places of worship, and cinemas. In *Hitchcock*, Anthony Hopkins, playing the eponymous hero, stands outside the auditorium listening for every gasp and shriek. His film *Psycho* has transformed a roomful of fidgeting bodies into a group of people sharing a single, collective sense of terror. But this could equally be a sense of joy, or wonder, or any other human emotion. Aside from moments of crisis, our feelings can often be muted, generalised, and woven so closely with a host of other emotions that we hardly feel moved at all. In the auditorium, those feelings, amplified through shared experience, can be savoured afresh, however old or cynical we might have become; feelings like momma used to make. That is the power of cinema, and a large part of its delight.

Television brings us together in smaller units, but can still be shared beyond the family sofa through social media, water-cooler camaraderie and a general buzz. It enables us to connect with the Zeitgeist, to be more than an inconsequential mote in a pitiless universe. The function of the writer is to provide the ritual, the moment, the mechanism around which the many can gather into one. Put simply, when watching a play, movie or TV show, or when listening to the radio or reading a book, we are not alone.

STORIES SPEAK FOR US

I sometimes joke that there are three perks to being a writer. The first is the parties. The second is that there is no such thing as a bad experience; only story material. The third is that you get to poke about in areas of the world closed to people who don't normally belong there. I have sat in the backs of police cars, in the fronts of ambulances, roamed the corridors of a prison, talked to soldiers, nurses, rescue workers, specialist lawyers and engineers of various descriptions. Of course, you have to clear your credentials, but once you're through the door it's quite astonishing how willing people are to talk. They do so because we all need to be heard, to be validated. The forces of oblivion are as potent as the forces of creativity, and if we don't all teeter on the edge of disappearing for ever, perhaps a residual panic at being left behind while the tribe moves on haunts our most primordial instincts.

Blackbirds sing for various reasons: to sound the alarm, declare their territory, announce the dawn, and call for a mate. The human repertoire might be more extensive (or the same, but more nuanced); nevertheless, even those who are not 'writers' will know the occasional urgency of a necessary message.

Sometimes it's straightforward enough: Man Overboard, Officer Down, Help. These aren't statements to be refined, reordered or calibrated for delivery. But a child running in to tell Mum of a slow worm in the bushes is also driven by need. We know this imperative. Its expression requires no effort. In fact, we have no choice but to tell it. Our words, gestures and intonation are animated by its passion, and just as the blackbird has no choice but to sing, so we find ourselves not commanding, but at the command of, language. At this level of communication, there is no question of technique, or room for doubt. This is a great place to write from, if you can get there. You get there by having something that needs to be said.

A particular instance of communication might pertain to individual circumstances, but communication itself belongs to us all. The survival and progress of our family, tribe and species depend upon the swift delivery of message. It might be a cry of 'Fire!'. It might be some profound consideration of an intellectual detail. But it runs like a stream through our genetic imprint. It is a part of being alive, written, like the song of birds, into the package.

TALKING OF INTANGIBLES...

You can't measure love, courage, trust, jealousy or rage – except, perhaps, by their influence upon our actions. You certainly can't bottle or tin them. So how do we experience them?

We only have to be barged aside in a queue to understand the meaning of 'fair play'. A parking ticket issued when the yellow lines were obscured by litter can leave us in no doubt as to the importance of justice. And if the concept of 'Truth' can have philosophers, scientists and theologians beating each other over the head with academic papers, we know it's uncomfortable to lie, and we appreciate honesty when somebody offers it.

Stories can evoke the great intangibles without the penalty of a parking ticket, or the hazards of an actual firing squad. By conjuring an aesthetic representation of the real world, they provide an opportunity to experience its material from the safety of our seats.

At the same time, we can savour, through stories, subtle experiences for which there isn't a word, or for which no single word will do. This is what distinguishes stories from essays, academic analyses or sermons. The latter can speak of these matters. Story invites us to live them.

This is why the great stories can never quite be pinned down through analysis. It is also why different people experience the same piece in different ways, or why the same person might experience it differently at different times. Their meanings are so deeply rooted, sometimes beyond the boundaries of language, that they can shift, at any given time, according to the contours of our inner landscape. The storyteller may strive to guide that inner landscape, but only up to a point. The release of powerful writing invites the participation of its recipient. Sometimes even the writer cannot express the meaning of the piece except by the piece itself. What drives the communication is the intuitive sense that it needs to be.

FUN

Drama is also playful. In fact, you might have noticed that a play is called a play. So it should delight, surprise, startle and perhaps even creep us out.

When my son was about six years old I took him on set to watch a bit of filming. This was a Sunday morning on the streets of Bristol and the scene involved an undercover police officer chasing a bag-snatcher across some traffic lights, nearly getting hit by a vehicle in the process. The local police had been informed and we were able to control the lights as needed. Gloriously, a police car from an outside district was passing through, stopped at the lights and observed the chase. They swung round the traffic, hit the siren, and chased down the two actors, one of whom turned to them and said, 'It's alright, officer, it's just pretend.' At which point they noticed the camera crew.

My son understood this. Pretend is what he played with his friends. What thrilled him on this occasion was that all these grown-ups spent their professional lives behaving like kids. When a teacher asked him, not long after, what his dad did for a living, he replied, 'Being Silly.'

So can a serious thing be silly, and a silly thing be serious? Why do children play and some people never grow out of it? I'll leave you with those! Just remember that drama has an element of joy about it. It should be fun. Sometimes stories are used to teach a lesson, or raise an issue. I once used a medical character to berate the government about health privatisation. Useful as a diatribe can be at times, there comes a point when it's no longer drama. Play, in the end, is for the sake of play. And if recent research suggests that children swing on swings to develop the balance mechanism of their inner ears, that's unlikely to be on their mind when they're doing it.

ENTERTAINMENT

By 'entertainment' we mean holding the attention. That attention is always somewhere. Often it's sauntering around the catacombs of twisted neuroses, deepest fears, petty anxieties and minor worries.

Our responsibility, as writers, is to rescue the audience from all that plagues them. In our care, they can be free for a few minutes – or ninety. If you lose their attention, even for a second, it leaps back to the mortgage, the homework, the boss, the athlete's foot and the cat's fleas. Which they'll blame you for. Just for that moment, you are the pay rise they didn't get, and the snotty memo they did. Lose their attention, therefore, at your peril.

ETC

Food has an obvious nutritional benefit but it can also bring people together, celebrate a special occasion, provide a treat, and so on. The more complex an object, the more functions it can fulfil. Story, as we shall see, is a highly complex, multi-functional artefact. I have only jotted down some of the more usual responses to the question, along with a little rumination of my own. Populate your own list. Add what I might have missed. Embellish or adjust any of my suggestions. But keep the questions alive. Your answers, or your emphasis among the many answers, might change over time, but they can help to power your writing. When a script gets knotty, or flat, or snarls at you from the desk, and your motivation, however much coffee you drink, is inexorably ebbing away, remember the importance of this art. Remember what writers do. We entertain, delight and enchant the otherwise burdened brains of our fellows. At our loftiest heights, we are there to validate, enrich and develop the most profound human sense of self. That's our job. We sing for the species. It isn't your decision to write. And if ever you're feeling down about it, consider what drives you to speak the speech. Perhaps you didn't choose that story, there, sitting on your desk, mulling around in your head. Perhaps it chose you.

SO YOU WANT TO **BE A WRITER**

Another question that I've sometimes put to groups is: why do you want to be a writer?

It's a little unfair because, personally, I'm not sure that I ever have. And when people ask me, 'What do you do?', I'm a bit embarrassed to use the 'W' word.

This may not be the case with you, and it doesn't really matter that much, but, if you want to 'be a writer', you're asking for so much trouble that you really ought to examine the proposition before being so reckless, or so foolish, as to act on it.

When I first went to visit my mentor at the BBC he asked me what else I did. After I stared at him blankly, he said, 'Well, do you have any other skills, training, vocation or profession apart from writing?' I said I'd studied law. 'Become a lawyer!' he exclaimed. 'But, if you choose to disregard my advice, let's talk scripts.' It was only later that I understood why he'd asked that. He was happy to help me as a writer, but he wanted to absolve himself of responsibility for any suffering that might result from the pursuit. You embark on this road at your own risk.

So have a little think. Why do you want to be a writer? Do you even want to be a writer? What the hell is a writer, anyway? We've already established the role of writers in the grand scheme of things, and quite a role it is too. But what is the daily life to which you might be consigning yourself? How do writers operate, live, breathe, feel? Are there common patterns, or familiar rigours, or typical lives? What do you think it entails? There are no right or wrong answers here, just realistic or delusional. What is it that you have in mind?

If you have an image of what a writer is, prod it from various angles to see if it stands up to scrutiny. I met up with an old school friend a few years back, who had become a policeman. I was just about to remark how nice it must be to know that you're actually useful to the world on a daily basis when he looked up from his pint and said, 'You know, I really, really envy you your life.' When I pressed him on it, he said he'd seen an advert a long time ago with bohemian types lounging around in dappled sunlight, sipping aperitifs (which were the object of the ad), and had always dreamed that, one day, he might be on that grassy knoll, smiling gently as somebody recited a rhyming couplet they'd spontaneously conceived. It was a far cry from shifting drunks out of shop doorways on the mean streets of North London. But how accurate is that view of the literary existence?

OK, I might have had a 'Dubonnet dream' of my own at some point, but the reality is hard graft. It's the blank page, the idea that collapses after days of toil, the client who wants two irreconcilable things in the same piece, the mysterious executive lobbing in notes that destroy everything about the script that matters to you. It's actors reading the script for the first time in the taxi on the way to the shoot. It's directors who change things just to stamp their egos on the screen. It's a phone call at seven o'clock on a Friday night asking for a 'quick rewrite' by Monday morning. It's the long, lonely trudge from the railway station to the script meeting and the long, lonely trudge back. It's forgetting why you ever wanted to tell this story, but the hell with it: they're expecting delivery three hours from now. 'Have you ever wondered why our offices are located on the first floor?' asked my first television producer on my first television show. 'It's so the writers don't hurt themselves too much when they jump out the window.'

Of course, it has its moments, but dismiss for ever, right now, any lingering vestige of the bohemian dream. It is not a soft option, easy life or genial cruise from inspiration to red carpet. The red carpet, FYI, is coloured by the blood of all the agonies you went through to get there. And, even when you hold the prize up to a barrage of flash bulbs, what's on your mind, mostly, is the next project, which might have hit a tricky spot. A few weeks after we'd had a standing ovation at our premiere, one director said to me, 'You know, when that happened, I should have inhaled more deeply.'

So if it's not about a leisurely working life, the vanity of seeing your name in lights, the glory of an award ceremony, or even money (there are easier ways to get that), what is it? What do you have left? You might want to take a little walk around the room at this point to rearrange your dreams, but, when you get back to the desk, be prepared to pursue the question, since your life could depend on it.

I'm not saying these dreams aren't valid, or that we don't all succumb to them from time to time, or that we don't feel a rush when all or one or some of them become real. I'm just suggesting, humbly, that they might not be enough to sustain you through a long night's rewrite, or the disappointments that might come your way, or past the many hurdles that will present themselves, from idiot executives to the more personal demons of self-doubt and despair. There has to be more. And, if there isn't, you're more than likely to drop out when the going gets tough. Most people do.

Perhaps unsurprisingly, the answers to the question 'Why do you want to be a writer?' begin, eventually, to resemble those answering 'Why do we need stories?' The urge exists. Some are content merely to share anecdotes over a pint. Some will keep a blog, diary, or pen-friend. But there are those who choose it as a life. Our reasons may change on a daily basis, or according to the vicissitudes of struggle. The following are among the more common answers offered by various groups to whom I have put the question.

- **Revenge on all those who didn't take us seriously at school.** Seriously, this one rarely crops up, though a few people have admitted that it lurks around the fringes of their nobler motives.

- **To make sense of the world.** Writing is a way of processing the mad mush of experience into harmony; or of finding harmony within the dissonance of the day. Writing makes music out of noise.

- **To process our feelings.** This is similar to the point above, but with a more therapeutic emphasis. This is writing as a cathartic exercise. It is beloved by diarists and bloggers but has its place in the highest echelons of the literary pursuit.

- **To address our questions.** By writing we can explore the perplexities of experience.

- **To record our experiences.** So they don't just parade past our momentary gaze into the oblivion of meaninglessness.

- **Because some things just need to be told.** For ourselves and for others.

- **For fun.** (Don't forget this one.)

- **Because it's your job.** Of course, if that's how you earn your keep, you'll be at the desk bright and early on a Monday morning. You don't wait around for inspiration, because neither do your bills. Although the distinction between the words 'professional' and 'amateur' is taken largely to mean 'paid' and 'hobby', the former actually signifies the taking of a vow. We profess, at a very deep, hopefully irrevocable, level, our commitment to the art. So we don't quit when it gets difficult. We don't even quit when we're not enjoying it. Personal enjoyment isn't the point. 'Amateur', on the other hand, means we do it for love. It's fun. As indeed it should be (see above), even for the professional. But the amateur might give up when it stops being fun. And this is a very different motivation from the one which keeps you staring at the page, pen in hand, late at night, wrestling a line of dialogue into shape when the mind and body ache for sleep.

- **'It's what I was made for.'** We have already considered how humanity, like most species, needs to declare itself. We have even given a special place to the act of self-reflection in the self-aware animal. In a complex society, the various roles that maintain the proper organisation of the community become specialised. Some are drawn to medicine, carpentry, teaching, cooking, engineering and so forth. In the same way, we all need writers, but we don't all need to be writers. There are those for whom it is a particular vocation. It comes with their sense of being. It is wired into them. This might be you. It isn't something to worry about. But if you wrote from an early age, or told stories as soon as you could talk, there is a very good chance that you have a kind of calling. The stronger that calling, the more resilient you'll be when engaged with the challenges of the industry. And you will write, and write, whether or not anybody else believes in you. If it really is your calling, then console yourself with the notion that eventually, inevitably, somebody will.

The industry, with its call-sheets, administrators, catering wagons, deadlines and budgetary considerations, doesn't much care why you write. The *Guardian* newspaper recently announced its media awards categories, which included the usual 'best actor', 'best director' and so on, along with 'best line of dialogue' and 'best scene'. The lines and scenes, evidently, either wrote themselves or are best credited to the people who spoke or shot them. For the *Guardian*, which presents itself as something of a literary rag, the writers simply do not exist.

Nevertheless, our private, personal, and possibly ever-changing reasons for putting pen to paper are to the media what plankton is to the petroleum industry: different in form, essential in nature. Without your need to make sense of a disturbing experience, explore some question that nags a hidden crevice in your consciousness, or delve into your psyche for those emotions of which polite people do not speak, there would be no writing, television, cinema, directors, actors, costumiers, award ceremonies or celebrities. They all depend on you, your experiences, your peculiarities, your discomforts and your dreams – whether they know it or not.

Most writers, when I've pressed the question, usually admit, finally, that they don't want to be writers. They just want to write – and not even in a general sense of wanting to sit down somewhere and scribble for a living. They want to write because they have something to say. To put it another way, they've found something that wants to be said and they need to write it, here, now, as soon as they can. It demands expression with a vehemence and urgency they are powerless to deny.

So what is this substance, this material which, once you get hold of it, or it gets hold of you, won't leave you alone until it's out there, written down, on a page, for the benefit of your own personal quiescence and the pleasure of many? For want of a better word, we shall call it 'Stuff'. It is the experiential matter, the raw material of writing. Get that, and nothing can stop you.

STUFF

WHAT IS STUFF?

The word 'Stuff' means material, substance or fabric. Although this might seem less tangible in a work of literature than, say, the wood of a tree or the waters in a lake, we know it's there because we can experience it.

Stuff also means 'text', but we're not just looking at words on a page. The Stuff we're concerned with lies in what those words are about.

As writers, it is our source material. It is, in a sense, what wood is to a carpenter. All of your skills, ingenuity, passion and dreams are nothing without it. And just as a carpenter needs to understand wood – where it comes from, what it's composed of, the different types, their virtues and limitations, how to shape and frame it – so the writer needs to get to grips with the Stuff of drama.

Stuff originates from experience. It starts with the senses. And, being of the nature of experience, it follows that every waking moment of every single day is awash with it.

Much of it, of course, we hardly notice. If you look back over the day, the week, or even further, you may become aware of large tranches of time that left no residue at all. These are the most mundane, the most unremarkable types of moment which, necessarily, yield the least Stuff.

Some moments, or the details thereof, are memorable only as long as they need to be. Where did I leave the car keys? What time is the train? Some are simply a part of our organisational imperative.

Where do I live? What's my job, again? And some are stuck in the mind, it would seem, only to annoy us. Did I *really* say that? This isn't Stuff, but data. It serves a purpose and helps us to function. It doesn't necessarily produce great writing.

Take a moment to glance back through time, starting with now. Did anything happen to you at any point that struck you as interesting, unusual, or in some way remarkable? Hopefully you won't have to look too far. Once you've found something, grab a pen and write down, in a paragraph or two, just enough to cover the salient details. What happened, when, in what context, who was involved, what did you say, see or do? How did you feel about it at the time? How do you feel about it now? If nothing strikes you as remarkable, at least go for something memorable. You'll know it's memorable because you can remember it – even if it's just yesterday's breakfast, or putting the bin out.

What you have just done, of course – assuming you did it – is write. Which, for any writer, is a good start. Now ask yourself why you chose that moment. What made it remarkable? Perhaps it had some kind of emotional resonance. It might have been sad, comic, poignant or scary. Perhaps it told you something, said something about the way you see the world, who you are, what anything is. It had meaning. Meaning is what distinguishes a remarkable moment from a mundane one. Meaning means 'to make known'. And what it makes known is some territory of human experience.

An aspiring writer once complained to me that his life was so comfortable that he had nothing to write about. I replied that he hadn't been looking. You don't need trauma to write, just a good eye. In some ways, life itself is a trauma: we arrive screaming and leave reluctantly. That, in itself, is worth writing about. There are many writers who can yield sublime Stuff from the minutiae of everyday life. Mike Leigh and Alan Bennett are obvious examples. In the hands of a writer like Bennett, a biscuit under the sofa can evoke metaphysical conundrums that make Nietzsche look shallow. Personal crises might provoke serious reflection, but look closely enough at even the most ordinary moment and you will find questions to ask, mysteries to unfold, the gentle presence of Stuff.

A few years ago, one of the major returning TV series decided to crack this whole coming up with ideas thing through a focus group. They plied a room of 'ordinary people' with alcohol and asked them what they were worried about. The focus group noted their primary issues as a lack of social cohesion, failing educational standards, the state of youth, and an overall increase of fear within society. When the drama executives triumphantly presented these findings, one of their writers said that he'd got all that from his train journey that morning.

He recounted how he'd noticed, across the aisle, a young man with his feet on the opposite seats. The writer had wondered about saying something, but didn't want to cause a fuss or get punched in the face. Instead he'd squirmed through a series of feelings from guilt, to outrage, to fear, and back again. Then he had noticed other passengers going through much the same, at which point something interesting happened. The writer began to wonder what was going on in the young man's mind: where he came from, what drove his anger, his hopes and fears, what he was saying by this act of defiance, and what the writer, along with all the other passengers, might have looked like to him.

The writer hadn't just demolished the point of the focus group, he had come up with real Stuff, from his own experience, which no amount of secondary research could ever match in depth or quality. The key is in that view from the subject's eyes. Just for a moment the writer stood in the shoes, or sat in the seat, of the young man with an attitude. Anger, resentment, challenge and alienation are known to all of us at different times and to different degrees. The writer knew them, and could find them, and could empathise with the young man. From that moment on, he had something to write about.

Writers are, by nature, people who test and savour their experiences. This makes them attuned to the world around them, to the Zeitgeist, to the ideas of the day, to the subtleties of human behaviour. It's why so many of them are socially awkward, self-doubting neurotics! Words on the page are merely the product of that. We might more commonly be defined, categorised or recognised by the act of scribbling, by the pages we produce; but that scribbling can only follow from our reflections. And our reflections can only be as good as the stuff it comes from. Your writing starts, therefore, not with dreams of glory but from what's in front of you, your experience. How you read that experience is up to you. And how you choose to convey it will be in the gift of your artistry. But that you do read it is the inescapable source of all your writings. The absence of Stuff, put simply, is nothing to write home about.

So let's take a look at the nature of this material, of Stuff. What exactly did the writer connect with in that moment on the train?

There are three components here:

One is the simple architecture of the circumstances: a train, a journey, a young man with his feet on the seat, the reluctance of others, including the observer, to intervene, and perhaps the greater social context in which all this is taking place.

But there is also a sense of meaning: social cohesion or a lack thereof, the indifference of youth and timidity of grown-ups, fear, courage, and so on.

Thirdly, there is the act of observation which, in some ways, is an act of interpretation. The circumstances could be seen as comic, tragic, disturbing, etc.

We are probably familiar with the concept of theme. Often these are indicated by a whole load of Big Words, like Love, Justice, Loyalty, Greed, and so on. But these are words only. The realm of theme can be too nuanced, layered and textured to be pinned down by one or more of these thunderous indicators. The key remains with experience itself. The more richly layered, or textured, that experience, the richer the writing which comes from it. Even if we're writing about the experience of someone else, we need to find those areas within our own that will give us a personal insight into the meaning. For that reason we don't necessarily have to come up with the Big Word (except to pitch it, maybe). We just need to feel its authenticity in the realm of our own observation. It will sit at the heart of our drama. Its Stuff will be the material with which we work. So let's see how that works in practice.

IN SEARCH OF STUFF

IF YOU GO DOWN TO THE WOODS...

I was lucky enough, a few years ago, to hear a wood-carver talk about his morning forays through the forest in search of material. He described the early mist lingering over the low shrubs, of not quite knowing if he was going to find anything at all, of picking up a piece of wood and turning it around in his hands to see if it was useful, interesting or beautiful. He described the quickening of his heart when he found something perfect, either for what he was planning to work on, or because it gave him a new idea. He called himself a 'wood-botherer', and his works were exquisite. Sometimes, if I'm early enough at the desk, I'll think of him as the sun rises over the trees, out there in his wellies, leaning down to pick something up, turning it around, cold and damp in his hands, studying, feeling, assimilating; the day's artistry beginning to flow, potent and sure, from that very moment.

Like a piece of wood yielding its possibilities to the wood-botherer, our moments become 'Stuff' when they reveal a truth, or truths, which can be communicated to others. This might be some cataclysmic event. It might be a biscuit under the sofa. 'Drama' has come to signify 'big' or 'in yer face'. A flower arrangement rarely becomes 'dramatic' by virtue of its modesty. But the true Stuff of drama is potency of a different order (although exploding helicopters might get your audience's attention). There is a beautifully crafted passage in Virginia Woolf's *To the Lighthouse* where Mrs Ramsay contemplates a dull errand to the shops. The dullness is entirely from Mrs Ramsay's perspective. For the reader, her contemplation of dullness, and her steps to alleviate it by taking Charles Tansley along, is full of pathos and a kind of urgency to find something real and permanent amidst the transience of life. It is a dramatic moment, and all the more so for challenging dullness head on.

A few years ago I got into conversation with an illustrator, after which we agreed to exchange contact details. He flicked through the little sketch book he was carrying and, unable to find a blank

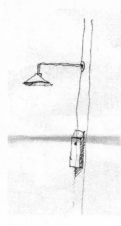

sheet, scribbled his email address beside a drawing. What struck me was how many things had caught his eye. A box on a post – which I would have passed by without a glance – gave him a shape, a form, a pattern of light and dark, a little quirkiness, a tiny puzzle, a nugget of story. And, of course, he'd sketched it. His notebook holds the Stuff of his art and you'd never catch him without it.

There are good reasons for keeping a notebook, for making your own, more literary, sketches as you go about your business:

- **The first is that, if you see something or have an idea, you won't forget it.** I am often amazed, when going through my own book, how the slightest detail of a tiny moment can provide the basis for an entire story, even if, at the time of jotting, it was so unremarkable that it might have been forgotten a moment later.

- **The second is that you become more observant.** You practise seeing and therefore start to see more. At the same time, you train your mind and heart to absorb and organise, sift and consider. You start to look like a writer, by which I mean your eyes tune in to the existence of Stuff (not that you've bought a beret or hang around all day in your dressing gown). My illustrator friend wasn't just collecting, he was practising. With every sketch his eye refined, with every twitch of the pencil he became a better communicator.

- **The third is that, the moment you write something down, it takes on a creative life.** The notebook is less of a memorandum than an organic process. It is as much a thing in your mind as it is in your hands. Noting something down has already begun the process of reflection. That reflection joins all the other reflections jostling around in the book, in your head. They meet up, flirt, move away, pair up and sometimes breed. A bit of idea joins another bit of idea. Years may pass. Suddenly you spot something else, and that partial, half-formed, semi-gestated notion looms out of the swamp to devour it, to merge with it. And now it's a whole thing; maybe the seed of a complete story, maybe a moment to further a scene, or a tiny detail in the background of a character's speech. But it will have an authenticity and conviction which comes only through experience. You haven't just thought it. You've felt it. And making your audience feel it, too, is what the writing is all about. The writer doesn't walk from idea to idea, but allows them to fester in this swamp, soup, compost heap – however you like to think of it. And you never know when something will crawl out, or stand up, ready to be written. But it's a joy when it does.

Not every writer keeps a physical notebook. And sometimes it wouldn't be appropriate, or practical, to make a note even if you had one handy (I'm thinking of dinner parties or windsurfing). But every writer goes into the woods to gather. In fact you can't avoid it. You might be walking along the streets, or sitting in a café, or doing your day job, or arguing with a salesman, parking attendant or friend. But you see something, pick it up, turn it over in your hands and, if you think it looks like Stuff, you take it home with you. You can use it immediately or, as we've said, save it for later. You can add it to material or wait for material to join it. It doesn't matter. But you have Stuff. And that matters enormously. In fact, without it you are about as useful as a wood-botherer without wood. Which is to say of no use at all.

I was invited to give a talk on story at an esteemed educational institution. Taking a bit of a risk, I decided to illustrate my points only with the Stuff I'd gathered on the journey there.

A few miles into the drive, my sat nav began to disagree with the directions I'd been emailed. My first instinct was to disregard the sat nav. After all, the organisers knew the roads from direct experience. But there is something naggingly, even menacingly, insistent about an instruction repeated over and over again in exactly the same tone of voice. In the end I succumbed to the mechanical. It added 20 minutes to my journey.

So now I was running late. And, of course, a lollipop lady had to stop the traffic while a bunch of ambling school kids, oblivious to my haste, sauntered nonchalantly across the road. But I recognised that nonchalance from my own school days. And it made me think about myself at that age, my dreams of youth, the life I thought I'd lead and my life as it was now. We don't know where we'll end up. What did those kids dream of? What would they become? The car hooting behind me let me know that the road was now clear.

I arrived, fortunately, with enough time for a quick dash to the gents before presenting myself, serenely composed, to the assembled gathering. What is it about hand dryers? Why do they always cut off before your hands are actually dried? And why won't they then come on again until *they're* ready?

So there I am, flapping my hands, trying to get the sensor to reactivate, the clock ticking; my hands, meanwhile, have dripped water on to my trousers. So now it looks like I've peed myself. Great. One hundred and fifty people who should be nodding at my pearls of wisdom will instead be thinking, 'Has he actually peed himself?' Plus my hands are clammy. And the organiser wants to shake them. So he'll think: 'Not only has the speaker peed himself; he's obviously terrified. The man's an incontinent neurotic.' But is that how I wish to be perceived? Of course not. I want to be thought of as dignified, assured, reasonably cultured, and amiable in a non-obsequious way. But wait a minute. Is that what drives me? Do all my efforts in life revolve around wanting to look cool? Am I really that shallow, that narcissistic? They'll see through me in a second. That's why I hate giving talks. Why do I keep getting myself into these situations?

So I had plenty of Stuff to talk about by the time I took to the stage. What interested me was that the audience laughed in most of the right places. The point, of course, was not to relate anecdotes, but to explore these moments for Stuff. The sort of things I've described happen all the time. That simple dilemma of going with the sat nav or the organiser's advice hardly seems remarkable at all. But what if you simply heighten the stakes? Do I take my platoon along the gully as my commanding officer insists, or go with the suggestion from a local with intimate knowledge of the area? Do I sing the song my producer tells me to sing, or the one I believe in? Mr Bean, meanwhile, might have nailed the hand-dryer gag, but there are plenty of stories left to be told of feeling foolish, awkward and inadequate; not to mention those moments when a character gets some uninvited glimpse into the febrile machinations of their inner demons and recoils from them, as enlightened as they are appalled.

....

MORE **EXERCISE**

Go back to the writing you did for the last section. Look through it. Dig into it. See what the Stuff is. Now turn yourself into a character, going from first to third person. And add a little turbo. Change the context. Increase the stakes. If you were going into a grocery shop, go into a starship, or a war zone, or a casino. If you were driving to the shops to post a letter, put your character on a journey to find the Ark of the Covenant, or the Holy Grail, or a hidden treasure trove, or a lost love. Just play around. Get a feel for toying with Stuff. Turn it around in your hands. Smell it.

If the moment you wrote about doesn't allow you to play like this, find another one. If you like, take the examples from my journey to the college. Reflect on childhood and the passage of life; on how we fight to present an image of ourselves that may or may not be true. Consider what it is to contend with conflicting advice. Mess around with it. What story can you find? Which themes are suggested?

We started out by saying that what distinguishes an ordinary moment from a dramatic one is that the dramatic reveals meaning. The more we look, of course, the more meaning we can find in increasingly ordinary moments – just as the illustrator's eye was caught by a simple box on a pole. In the end, perhaps, there are no ordinary moments. Everything reveals something. By this equation, there is nothing, in the end, that isn't Stuff. But what you choose to see, turn over in your hands and pop in your pockets for later is up to you.

....

RESEARCH (THE ART OF FORAGING)

If most of the Stuff we collect is stumbled upon during the usual activities of our daily life – with the occasional cataclysmic event flying round the corner to smack us in the face – it is perfectly respectable to engineer situations for the sake of Stuff-hunting. An obvious example would be travelogues. A travel writer who doesn't travel to the places they're writing about is unlikely to write anything either useful or convincing. But a travel writer doesn't just wait for an opportunity to present itself. They book the flight and pack a bag. If you find that Stuff isn't chucking itself at you, or if you've become so numbed to your environment that you can't see it for trying, organise something.

It helps to have a production company or broadcaster behind you, but, if not, just try your luck. You'll be amazed, as we said earlier, how helpful people are to writers. It's because we can tell their stories; through us, they can be heard. But there are many situations open to the public which can be full of Stuff-gathering opportunities. Volunteer somewhere. Do charity work. Speak to your neighbours. Travel. One writer I know worked for the RSPB for a summer, showing school children round a bird sanctuary. Her YA novel featuring swans is now available in all good bookshops.

This sort of research provides you with different types of material.

Hopefully, you'll gather plenty of anecdotal Stuff. For instance, I now know that ambulance crews can drive at insane speeds while calmly discussing what they're going to wear that night. I know that surgeons tell jokes while cutting somebody open. And I know that soldiers don't want their daughters to marry soldiers.

You will also get a feeling for what it's like to do that job, or belong to that world. Which means you will write it convincingly, according to its own particular laws and *mores*. Part of that is knowing which way up to hold an x-ray, and it's good to get that kind of thing right. But these details are part of a deeper texture, woven into the story world, commanding, one way or another, everything that everybody within that world does or says.

I recall returning from a day out with the police in East London. We'd spent ten hours going from one disagreeable experience to another. We'd seen horrible things, and met terrible people. On the train home, I was musing on the ghastliness of the world in general when I realised how one's psychology, one's perceptions, could be warped by that kind of experience. My bristling irritation with the passengers who'd crowded out the entrance of the carriage was a perfect snarl to give my next disenchanted cop.

In my experience one tends to start off rather self-consciously, as a kind of literary appendage; but, after a while, you become a part of the team. I'm a dab hand at opening syringe packets. I've even been asked to keep an eye on a potential witness. I have helped to relocate a hip and once propped up the head of a dying man so that he could breathe his last in comfort.

If you're lucky, you'll get some real insights. When a police driver slowed down at the station exit, turned to his colleague and said, 'Here we go,' I suddenly recognised the difference between a cheery cuppa with the sarge and a world in which strangers glare as you pass by. Earlier we'd stood on a bleak expanse of darkened parkland in search of a burglary suspect. Inside we'd been talking holiday plans. That powerful sense of in and out, us and them, furnished enough material for a complete episode of *The Bill*. A three-second observation of an hour's worth of Stuff is a moment of pure gold.

If we already have material from which to write, and are busy writing it, there may still be a need to fill in some details, enrich the characters or add some texture to flesh out the story.

When writing a three-part BBC drama about army life, I spent many evenings talking to military families. While preparing a project on debt collecting, I shadowed repo men on the streets of Liverpool. The need to write a barrister gave me the perfect excuse to have lunch with one.

All of this means that you're not just cadging your Stuff from pre-processed sources, like newspapers, focus groups, or existing programmes. Instead, you are able to present fresh insights, new details and original moments drawn vividly from real experience. It will show.

This is not to rule out the value of reading. You can make anything fresh so long as you connect with its Stuff. Shakespeare drew extensively from the histories of Holinshed, Plutarch and others. *Coriolanus* differs little from Plutarch in its historical detail; but the rhythm, ideas, poetry and meaning given to the facts of mere chronology are unmistakably Shakespeare's own.

While writing a film that looked at some aspects of the Holocaust, I read many books and even spoke to survivors and perpetrators. We had plenty of Stuff, but it wasn't yet 'our' Stuff. It was documentary material that we could use or not, depending on the context of the story at any given time. If we were going to write it, and if the director was going to direct it, we needed to ask serious questions about ourselves and the people around us. We needed to get uncomfortable. A visit to Sachsenhausen concentration camp, just outside Berlin, left us speechless. So many things had profoundly affected us, among them a collection of photographs of inmates engaged in their ordinary lives before the war. We'd seen countless images of striped pyjamas, the emaciated, the hollow-eyed and the dead. But these were smiling fathers with children, wives in their homes, bakers, bankers, artists and blacksmiths. It dissolved the subtle anaesthetic of dehumanisation to reveal the true horrors of the crime. These people were us. The mists of history lifted to show our own faces in those birthday snaps, the proud shopkeepers in front of their stores, the innocent smiles of children nestled in the protective arms of their mothers.

We used that in the film, with the central character contemplating a series of simple family photos. It provided one of our most powerful moments – which I still find almost unbearable to watch. The other thing we used was speechlessness itself: the idea that there are questions to which we may not have answers. But we could only find that by stretching our attempts to comprehend the complexities of human behaviour, and its darker reaches, to their limits. That murder should have been so organised struck me as unfathomable. That people did this, undeniable. How can you square that circle? Perhaps you can't. Hovering in the discomfort of not-knowing became a central theme of the movie and allowed us to dispense with the convenience of neat conclusions at the end.

We might have stumbled upon all that theoretically, through books, but the intensity and, in its way, complexity would have been fabricated, or borrowed, and thus weaker. By allowing ourselves to be informed, moved and even disturbed, we found the Stuff of our story. And, of course, that wouldn't have happened if we hadn't gone looking.

Special trips for research opportunities will often yield more Stuff than you need for the project you're working on. One of the reasons for going around, say, with the police is to gather material for future episodes of whatever it is you might be writing. But if you're attentive – and the advantage of these arrangements is a natural heightening of awareness – you could end up with sackloads of Stuff, enough to liven a crime story you might be writing a couple of years later, or something from an entirely different genre. Good Stuff can lurk for decades before it leaps out to provide story. There is no use-by date.

In the absence of special trips, of course, we shouldn't disregard the wealth of Stuff that our daily lives can yield – although we might have to peek past the net curtains of familiarity to glimpse the seething vortex of angst and neurosis within. Being such a model of forbearance, I was having difficulty, once, writing about an impatient character. So I took a closer look. Who was that person rolling his eyes when the computer decided to beach-ball for ten seconds, or sunk into despair at the waffling person who phoned up to arrange a meeting and spent half an hour talking about nothing? By the time I'd dropped the milk while making coffee, slipped up in it reaching for a paper towel, and chucked the rest of the carton up the wall, I had learned not only about impatience but self-delusion.

You might strut around marvelling at how wonderful you are, but writing calls for a modicum of honesty. We put ourselves on the line here. Which is why most writers I know don't actually think they're wonderful at all. They see too much of their frailties and faults to be smug about it. By the time they've shared them with the world, most of them just want to hide away somewhere until all the fuss has died down.

You can sit in with the paramedics, go to memorials and read books. But Stuff is Stuff only when it sings within you, when you recognise something not just about it, but about yourself. In the absence of research trips to far-flung climes, then, take a trudge from time to time around the landscape of your own head. Prise open some doors. Venture into the basement. Open some of those boxes in the attic. You might be surprised (if not horrified) at what you find.

ADAPTATION – AND OTHER MATTERS

The subject of book or play adaptation is big enough for a publication in itself. In terms of Stuff, the question is: how do you make it your own without turning it into something else?

I have two simple principles which have proven helpful from time to time:

1. **I will only adapt a book I wish I'd written myself.** This I have learned through (sometimes bitter) experience. It has to relate to you, and you have to relate to it. It has to speak for you, because you will be speaking for it. If they're paying you enough, OK, take on a book you don't like, but good luck with that!

2. **You can mess with the narrative, the characters, the timelines, and the form, but always respect the Stuff.** Your job is not to transcribe but to recreate in another medium. You can be bold, but it has to be what it is. It has to say what it says. It might need a few tweaks or some heavy engineering, but it should arrive at the same point of meaning, with the same resonance, the same tone, and leave the audience with the same effect as the original.

It follows that you have to connect with that Stuff as powerfully as if you'd found it yourself. Where there is more Stuff than you can manage for a 90-minute script, find the Stuff that works for you. You might need to discuss this with whomever commissioned you, or the author, or both, but your honest expression of how you see it will save huge amounts of backtracking, rewrites and bickering later on.

A writer/academic contacted me recently about a paper she'd written on an adaptation I'd been involved with. Having picked out what she thought were the key scenes of the movie, those which revealed what she called the 'shadow script', she was startled to find them entirely absent from the book. Of course, what we had done was honour the Stuff, the meaning, rather than the outward form. We had to change the outward form to get closer to that Stuff. Our consciences remained clear and, perhaps more importantly, the original author happy.

THE ALCHEMY OF STUFF

So we know what Stuff is. And we know how to find it, or to recognise it when it finds us. Hours can go by. Days can go by. Then something happens. We see something. Or hear it, or feel it. What matters is that we experience it. And suddenly there's that quickening of the heart, an energy, a desire to look further, dig deeper and report our findings. In that moment, something rather strange has happened to our sensibilities. The usual confines of our personal preoccupations, cares, hopes and anxieties have taken on a universal dimension. They aren't suppressed, forgotten or denied. Quite the opposite. They are explored. Like the wood-botherer turning a lump of old tree around, we savour them to their depths. The ordinary becomes extraordinary. The personally affecting becomes something to share. The child runs helter-skelter from the grass snake under the dahlias to tell Mum. The writer watching himself watching the young man with his feet on the seat suddenly finds his personal dilemma rather interesting. It has become Stuff.

This isn't quite the same as confessional, or purgative, writing, which can be voyeuristically enjoyable to watch – if that's your thing. Storytelling is an alchemical process, by which the lead of a particular, personal experience is turned into the gold of universal expression. The dull haze of mundanity is transformed into material of value. And that, if you're hoping to make money at this game, is what people pay for.

Having got our Stuff, then, how do we shape it? How do we work it into story? How do we fire up the crucible and begin the alchemical transfiguration of our experience and observations into gold?

WORKING WITH STUFF

Not all Stuff that we come across is going to make it into our literary oeuvre. Some of it might be too fragmentary. Some of it might be more suited to the works of another. There is no harm in scribbling away on something before realising it isn't quite for you, or that maybe this isn't the place for it. At the same time, as we've seen, a bit of Stuff unusable for the moment might combine with another bit of Stuff later on. That's why the notebook, whether a physical artefact or the fermenting swamp in your head, matters so much, and why time passing and experience shifting is a part of the process. Like distillers, we might be happy to rush out this year's bottle for the demanding market, but we should also take an occasional stroll among the cobwebs of the deeper cellars where our vintage barrels, gently maturing, await their moment.

I wrote a scene for *Eastenders* in which an overbearing, hard-nosed character called Andy is facing down a more timid creature, Billy Mitchell, on the streets of Albert Square. Having been insulted and intimidated by Andy, Billy slinks away in humiliation. Andy then throws out the remark: 'Mitchell? You don't deserve the name.' Billy stops for a moment, turns, and walks back. The balance of power teeters. Billy says 'I know what I am...' and, in that moment, it is Andy who quivers.

Later on I asked myself where that scene had come from. Some of it had been suggested by the story document and the obvious narrative of the episode, but the moment could have been written in many different ways. On reflection, I found an incident from a time, 20 years previously, when I was a struggling writer/director/producer in fringe theatre. My latest production was about to go on in a room above a pub. I'd invested every penny into the venture, my last beans going into a couple of glossy posters to be hung in the bar. When I went in to give them to the manager, a slightly inebriated geezer slouching on his bar stool grabbed them from me. 'What's all this, then?' he sneered. 'We're putting on a play,' I answered, as cheerfully as I could. 'A play?' he snorted. 'Load of bollocks.' And he crushed them in his hands. The manager's advice that I leave immediately seemed the wisest strategy under the circumstances. But, as I approached the doors, I found myself slowing down. Of course I was angry at the insult, the loss of the posters, and the waste of money. But this wasn't just about me. It was about all the people involved in the production, all the effort they'd put in, and the sacrifices we'd made. It was about theatre itself, for which people have died. It was about writing, the jewel of civilisation, hard won, sometimes with blood. When I stopped at the door and turned back to confront him, I was the embodiment of the literary arts in its most terrifying form. The geezer's face changed. The pendulum had swung. The manager leapt between us and ushered me, bodily, out of the pub.

The incident had long sunk out of view but its Stuff had remained somewhere in the notebook, waiting for a character to slouch miserably away from the humiliating barbs of a superior force only to stop, question who he was, surrender the small for a more powerful identity, and turn back to wreak havoc. It gave me Billy.

The advantage of writing with Stuff is that you don't have to make it up. You just have to recognise it, collect it and let it emerge as the story demands. Because you've lived it, your characters can live it, and your audience will live it. You are not just describing the moment; you are recreating it. That this is the most powerful kind of writing may come as no surprise. But that it's also the most effortless will cheer you no end as you begin to get the hang of it.

THE ELEMENTS OF STORY

If we take a look at the Billy/Andy scene described above, we'll recognise, hopefully, that it looks, sounds and feels like a bit of drama. It has a location, characters, a narrative, themes, dialogue and so on. We also know that its provenance lies with genuine, hand-crafted, fully organic (no artificial preservatives or colouring) Stuff. And it works. As it is bound to do.

We might know from experience that not every scene we write necessarily works to begin with, at least not until we've kicked it around a bit, torn it up, started again, re-tweaked it, thumped the desk, cursed the computer and kicked the cat (not that I ever would!). Sometimes the story is good but the characters aren't convincing. Or the dialogue has sauntered on for 20 carefree pages without quite saying anything. More worryingly, it might look as if everything is in the right place but it feels kind of flat. You might have had one of those editorial notes which say, 'I really love the story, the characters, the idea and your writing style; however, I'm not quite convinced by it so go away.'

For the purposes of analysis, and practice, there is something to be said for dividing drama, the dramatic event, into constituent elements. In my experience most writers are gifted with some of these elements but have to work for the others. Personally, I can scribble dialogue for page after page without breaking a sweat, but learning to structure came only with hard labour and the sometimes apoplectic exhortations of my BBC mentor.

Drama can be taken apart in different ways, using a variety of terms. In fact, there are plenty of terms about, some of them so specialised that their only application is to the dissection of story. Let's use the following:

Theme
Idea
Narrative structure
Character
Leitmotif
Style

While each of these can be studied, practised and applied as a separate skill, it has to be remembered that the division is, to some extent, an artificial one. Just as a banana, say, can be said to consist of colour, shape, texture, smell, inside and outside, etc, we know from eating one that all of these are experienced at the same time. Where does yellowness end and shape begin? Clearly, yellowness and shape are attributes of each other. In the same way, narrative and character are integral to, and in practice indistinguishable from, each other. A character without story is not a character. A story without a character is, as we shall see, a contradiction in terms.

This cautionary note is intended to dispel a common misconception, namely that one can work out a story, bolt on some characters, chuck in a few iconic images, have a speech at the end about love or justice, and *voilà*: you've got drama. What we've seen from our exploration of Stuff is that these attributes are usually present, latent or otherwise, in the very stuff of Stuff. Our job is to unfold them from the whole, not assemble a bunch of parts ordered in from specialist suppliers. When Plotinus said that 'A work of art is not a series of details co-ordinated into a unity, but a unity working itself into detail', he was perhaps reminding us that all the outward attributes of a drama have their roots in a singular substance: its Stuff.

With that in mind, let's take a closer look at the elements we've listed. We shall find that they often blur into each other. But that, as we've said, is only to be expected.

THEME

The word 'theme' means a place or space. In literary terms, it is a territory of human experience to be explored. Thus, all those intangibles we considered previously, such as justice, love, courage, trust, jealousy and so on, are aspects of our experience, difficult to grab with our hands but known nevertheless. Arguably, the function of drama is simply to conduct this exploration so that the intangible, the theme, can be made known.

Let's explore this in practice.

TWELFTH NIGHT

I once suggested to a group of students that the themes of Shakespeare's plays are always established in the first few lines. Thus *Hamlet*, which enquires into the nature of identity and doubt, begins with 'Who's there?' *The Tempest*, meanwhile, kicks off with several instances of the word 'authority'.

In a moment of bravado, I remarked that this is because every line of the play must embody the main theme or some variation thereof, since theme is like the DNA of story. Getting carried away, I think I even cited Plotinus. Of course, somebody challenged me to prove it, so I picked up a complete works, flipped it open and poked my finger at a random line. My heart sank. It was from Act 1, Scene 2 of *Twelfth Night*:

Viola
And what should I do in Illyria?
My brother he is in Elysium.

Since a line is also its context, we read the lead-up:

Act I. Scene II. The sea-coast.
Enter Viola, a Captain and Sailors

Viola
What country, friends, is this?

Captain
This is Illyria, lady.

Viola
And what should I do in Illyria?
My brother he is in Elysium.

Which, disappointingly, looked to me like the dreariest of plot set-ups, telling us simply that Viola is in Illyria and that her brother is dead (probably). We all have to write that sort of thing from time to time. I imagined Shakespeare stopping for a moment, his poetic flow interrupted, his grand 'if music be the food of love' flourishes confounded by the stark need to tell the audience what's going on. I even heard a ghostly script editor saying, 'We love the whole cross-dressing thing, and that poem about love (although think about trimming it slightly), but could we have a couple of lines at the top of the scene just to tell the audience where we are?' Know the feeling? In a contemporary film it might read:

Viola
Dudes, where the hell are we?

Captain
Illyria.

Viola
So what am I gonna do? Me bruvver's dead.

Well, Shakespeare's opening line might be more elegant, but it has the same import, surely: a clumsy attempt to solicit narrative information. Some of its equivalents might be: what are you doing here? What are we going to do now? Why is that? Who's that over there? How long is it since we last saw each other, cousin? Why are you carrying that bag? This is cringe-worthy writing. And what about the Captain's line: 'Illyria' plus a bit of rhythmic embellishment, followed by the squeezing in of the fact that her brother's copped it. Still, it's efficient. It does the job. I was about to suggest that we chuckle at finding an exception to the rule and move swiftly on to one of Shakespeare's many tracts of timeless poetry, when something of that Billy-stubbornness came over me and I decided to tough it out. 'So what have we got?' I asked, marching purposefully to the flip chart, taking a welcome moment by the window to draw solace from the city's distant spires.

Two hours and five pages of flip chart later, we still hadn't exhausted it. So take a moment now. Grab that piece of paper next to you, and the nearby pen, look at those lines and just see if there's anything else being said; or if, in spite of the baldness of the information, there are nuances, levels and textures that lead us from simple narrative fact, via story, into theme. When you've done that, come back to this chapter…

Of course it helps to have a group who can spark off each other. And most of us knew the play, so there was a head start. If you came up with nothing, don't worry. Read the whole play at some point (or now) and have another go. At the very least, take a look at Scene One. In any case, we're learning how to work with Stuff and it can take some practice.

Here's a little of what the group came up with, although the following is intended to be neither definitive, exhaustive nor 'correct'.

Viola's collective address to the sailors instantly separates her. Perhaps she entered slightly apart, walking alone, the others giving her space. One could obviously stage the scene in different ways but there is a sweet aporia in her use of the word 'friends', as if she's bestowing that honour, or reaching out, or creating a bond through its declaration.

If she is among strangers, then, she is alone. Shakespeare could have had her walk in solo to deliver a monologue, but solitude is always more poignant in the company of others and, admittedly, she does need someone around to answer her question. In the previous scene we enjoyed a long, poetic ramble about the nature of love. We are attuned, therefore, to matters of belonging, company and isolation. Moreover, we have vicariously deliberated (via the Duke Orsino at the beginning) on questions of bereavement and mourning, with particular regard to the loss of a brother.

Simple as these few lines are, they pack a lot of narrative. That she doesn't know where she is tells us she's a stranger to the place, but also that her means of arrival was out of the ordinary; there is a clue in the presence of wet sailors. We could have had the shipwreck scene, of course, as in *The Tempest*, but this isn't about shipwrecks; it's about human bonding and the pain of separation. From the writer's point of view, knowing the primary theme enables us to choose from the many narrative possibilities; and it's generally sensible to emphasise that which serves the whole. Many a script has lost itself to the lure of digressions. That they sing sweetly may not be reason enough to divert our course.

The Captain answers her question because he has the authority to speak for them all, and it is to him that the others defer. So we know that this is a hierarchical world, and that she is, within that world, according to his address, a lady, not a wench. So she's not going to bond with these people much further, and is certainly not one of the gang, even if her use of the word 'friends' implies a shared experience.

Buried within the brevity of the Captain's reply is an assumed sense of what Illyria represents to the audience. Illyria is legendary for its wealth, its lush pastures, its fragrant groves. And, in case you don't know it, we've just understood as much from the previous scene. This is an opulent, comfortable place. People come here for their holidays. But Viola isn't happy. Why not? Because what joy is there to be found when her brother is dead? She is in mourning. She is bereft. And what did we get from the preceding scene? Olivia rejecting the providence of a gorgeous world because she is wrapped up in the death of her brother. So this is about moving on from death. And it raises several questions. When do we 'move on' from bereavement? And how do we reconcile the incessant demand that life go on with our profound need to remain true to the beloved?

These are powerful issues, especially for anyone who might have gone through a close bereavement. The play was written about five years after the death of Shakespeare's son, aged 11. His other children would have grieved, presumably, as would he. *Twelfth Night*, then, is a sweetly comedic play, with light-hearted banter and hilarious characterisation, about death, loneliness and getting over loss.

Finally, 'Elysium' is a classical reference, which not only shows us Viola's social background, but puts a shade (no pun intended) on her understanding of death. Her brother hasn't ceased to be, but is in a different – not entirely disagreeable – place. So this isn't about the tragedy of death so much as the burden of loss.

The themes, even in these few lines, are complex, rich and finely calibrated. They also strongly echo the myth of Orpheus with which Shakespeare was familiar. As we shall see in our section on structure, this particular classical paradigm has had a powerful influence on the literary tradition to which we belong, and cuts right to the centre of our understanding of drama. The scholars in his audience would have nodded knowingly. The lines achieve this fragrant evocation of profound themes in perfect harmony with the simple delivery of narrative information: Viola has pitched up in a strange country, helpless without the protection of her brother, and bereft without his love and company. As with Orpheus, her journey is to find a different, deeper understanding of the love she seeks.

One could carry on discussing those few lines and continue to find rabbits wriggling at the bottom of the hat. But it's instructive to note that, on stage, they last only a few seconds. If we were to slow them down, as in fact we have done, we would find that there are many minutes', even hours', worth of Stuff in there. Between those lines, and even within the lines, there are movements of thought and emotion, of story and theme, that develop, progress, confirm and move on again. It's up to the production to determine the pace of the dialogue. The relationship here is between the velocity of surface action and its depth. Depth will be explored later in this chapter through the notion of vertical structure. In the meantime, you might like to try another exercise.

. . . .

AN **EXERCISE**

Pick a line, any line, from anywhere that you think might be rich in Stuff. Shakespeare is an obvious source, but there are plenty of writers to choose from. You might even like to pick some less 'literary texts'. In my own experiments I have found plenty of flip-chart material in fragments of *The Phil Silvers Show*, *Get Carter*, and *Spongebob Square Pants* (but we all have our favourites!). Perform the same activity of analysis that we applied to *Twelfth Night*.

To begin with, check out the context. Then ruminate on your chosen lines of dialogue. Don't disregard any stage directions or indications of the setting. Ask the following questions:

- What narrative information do the lines contain (how do they further the story)?

- Are there discernible themes? If so, what are they?

- Do the themes shift and jostle, twitch and harmonise as the dialogue progresses? See if one line carries the themes of the whole piece. If so, how does it do that? Through the choice of words? The rhythm? By what is not said?

- Are those lines echoed elsewhere in the play? Are they set up previously, paid off later, or both?

  Do this now, or at the next available opportunity. And, having done it once, do it again. And again. And keep on doing it for as long as you value the act of writing.

. . . .

It is said that the six rules of writing are 'Read Read Read Write Write Write'. Some of that is to do with quantity. Gorge yourself on all the Stuff out there and throw your own over as many pages as you can. Get used to writing; just writing. You can get used to standing on one leg if you're prepared to fall over to begin with. Likewise, you will get used to writing, just the simple act of it, if you can get over the occasional production of rubbish. But if you read back over last night's masterpiece and realise it's a crock of less than satisfactory ramblings, don't despair. The fact is, you have moved on. Last night it seemed acceptable. Today it isn't. Your standards have been lifted. Rejoice. The next work will be better. The trick is to not take it personally.

Most writers I know are prone to moments of self-excoriation. I don't have a cure for this, since I indulge in it myself. But I can tell you that it doesn't help and, in any case, what does it matter? Just write. If we were engaged in marble sculpture I'd say be a bit more careful. But the only thing we've got to lose is paper, which can at least be recycled – along with some of the ideas on it. The aim is to get better with practice. Of course, the ultimate aim is to write good things, not just many things. But you can wait a long time for that good thing to come to you. So go in search of it. The same with reading. It's not enough just to plough through books. Reading as a writer involves a deeper penetration of the text. If it works, why does it work? If it's rich, why is it rich? And, importantly, if it doesn't work, why not?

In my occasional rounds as a teacher I sometimes come across the brittle individual who denounces almost everything as rubbish. My question is, why is it rubbish? I am often met by a blank stare. But they have to get past that point. They have to read in depth. They have to see the workings and, if the workings aren't working, they will only learn by seeing why not. Almost invariably, those who decry the works of others without taking that step go on simply to write rubbish themselves.

VERTICAL STRUCTURE

What you might have noticed when carrying out the previous exercise, apart from any material you came up with, is that there is a particular process at work; the simple, natural and quite ordinary journey from apprehension to comprehension. We see or hear something. We understand what it means. Thus we move from a line of dialogue, or action, in context, to the implied realm of theme and meaning. It happens so quickly that it's more of a shift in perspective than a process of thought, like suddenly spotting a fish beneath the surface of shimmering waters. This shift of perspective, or perception, can be represented diagrammatically as a kind of vertical structure, in which a line, or any given moment of text, consists of certain people in a certain place, doing and saying certain things, and the universal themes present within that.

Universal/Theme

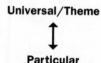

Particular

In the example drawn from *Twelfth Night*, we saw a young lady querying her whereabouts and expressing concern that her brother is dead. From there we delved into questions about mortality, vulnerability and the social order – to name but a few. And while we had the luxury of stopping to ponder, in performance the story moves on, this moment of insight taking place instantaneously. Opportunities to reflect might be offered with passages of soaring oratory, or just a slowing down of action so the audience can digest the material. In more superficial pieces, the whole thing generally rushes on at a pace sufficient to keep us from noticing its vacuity.

So let's apply our simple diagram to *Twelfth Night*.

Universal/Theme
Mortality/Loss/Loneliness

Particular
A shipwrecked girl in a strange land,
alone after the death of her brother

Just as we can apply this process of interpretation to the text of an existing script, so we can apply it to our own experiences, such as the one we considered earlier – that of a young man with his feet on the seat. The particulars of this scenario might be:

- A train journey
- A young man with his feet on the seat
- A sense of disapproval among others present
- The inactivity of those who disapprove

As we've seen, what distinguishes this from the many mundane situations that are lost from memory the moment we've moved on is the discernible presence of Stuff. It is replete with meaning, with themes. The circumstances might be particular, but our shift of perception has detected the universals within it. Beneath the simple outward circumstances of a young man on a train with his feet on the opposite seat is a busy world of thoughts and feelings:

- Irritation at the inconsiderate behaviour
- Apprehension at the underlying sense of menace
- The surliness of a young man challenging the confinement of social norms
- A direct challenge to the people watching (Yeah? You got a problem with that?)
- Despair at the apparent breakdown of civilised society (What is the world coming to? The kids these days!)
- A desire to intervene checked by fear
- A recognition of personal weakness followed by guilt

These enrich the world of mere things with a sense of mind and emotional movement. It is already becoming much more interesting. But note that the thoughts and feelings, seething as they are, still form a part of the outward scene, albeit more subtle than a pair of muddy trainers on a despoiled stretch of cloth. Communicable theme goes deeper than that. At this point the writer might have just huddled back into his book and, maybe, griped about it later to friends. It's just an anecdote. So what made it Stuff?

After jostling around in the realm of thoughts and feelings, the writer suddenly found himself taking another look. He saw those thoughts and feelings. He sensed that they were the product of deeper levels of ideation. Detached from a particular perspective, floating, as it were, beyond the confines of his own identity (the tutting adult), he wondered what the scene might look like to the surly young man. At this point he was witnessing the scene as a writer collecting Stuff. He could turn that moment over in his hands like the wood-botherer contemplating a piece of bark. What did it say? What was implied? Beyond the particularities of the moment, did it speak of universals?

We could represent it like this:

Universal/Theme
Fear, guilt, alienation, anger

Particular
Train journey, young man with his feet on the seats,
the inactivity of disapproving onlookers

The particulars of a young man with his feet on the seats will pass in time. The train, after all, will eventually arrive at its destination. But we all know what it is to find a moment that lingers, hovering on the fringes of consciousness, if not pummelling us to the core.

As writers, we're interested in more than the tangible constituents of a specific instance. We want to know what it means. The instant passes, but meaning is perennial. 'Universal' means that it holds true, if not everywhere and for ever, then at least widely, for a very long time. The longevity of any piece is often related to the profundity of its themes.

Thus the young man finally removed his feet when the train pulled in to the station. But guilt, menace, anger, alienation, etc, go on and on.

There will be other young men with their feet on the seats. There will be young men throwing rocks at the police, scrawling their names on walls, spitting over balconies, or blowing themselves up in the name of some cause. And there will be those who look on with impotent rage. The themes may nuance according to the textures of the moment, but they are always there, if we but look. So we can write about a young man with his feet on the seats and get our meaning across even for those who have never seen a young man with his feet on the seats. A large part of our enjoyment of anecdote rests with its personal nature: 'You'll never guess what happened to me yesterday.' We have to assume, however, that our audience neither knows nor cares much about us as individuals. What they want to know about is themselves. Which is fine. Because we're not just relating anecdotes, we are conjuring Stuff.

....

AN **EXERCISE**

So let's play with this a bit. Turn to your book of jottings, those little moments you scribbled down because they suggested the presence of Stuff. You could even try noting a few more. Or this could be an opportunity to trawl through some of the lesser moments, the petty irritations, the little pauses for thought that made us sigh, giggle, or scratch our heads. What matters here is the process.

Draw the vertical structure diagram:

Keeping it simple, under 'Particular' just write down the situation and its constituent parts. If the cat threw up on the sofa just before your guests arrived, specify cat, sofa, host, guests and vomit. Add your emotional content, for which you probably won't have to dig too deep: perhaps a profound sense of life's injustice, the frustration of your attempts to create a good impression, etc.

Now consider the area of human experience (theme) which this might have revealed. How important is it to make a good impression? How seriously do we take our social identity? How much do you actually like your friends? How much do you trust them? If you want them to see you in a particular way, are they seeing the real you? If not, what's the point of having them around? Can somebody merely familiar with what you are not be called a friend? And so on. I suppose what we're ambling about here is the territory of experience characterised by questions of friendship, but you could equally launch off into an exploration of cat ownership, the need for companionship, your lack of control over the animate world, the paradox of wanting things to go your way, but how dull it is if they do, etc.

So pick your own incident and explore your own themes. But start from something real and, rather than trying to invent anything, simply note what is, quite naturally and without effort on your part, already there.

If you look back at your notebook, what you'll see, then, is the above diagram in notational form. You might not have written up the detail, nor explicated the themes, but they are built into the reason why you jotted it down. Each of those notes is an acknowledgement of Stuff. Stuff is simply a moment with meaning.

....

While some of the Stuff we collect can be hoisted directly on to the page, as in reportage, most of it will require some degree of adaptation. Even true stories need some filtration or selection of Stuff that might otherwise be too rich, messy or vague. Characters and events can be lost, condensed or even invented as narrative coherence and thematic consistency dictate.

But what if your story calls for a situation which you haven't personally experienced? I've never had to defend the family empire and my sister's virtue against the machinations of a local hood. Neither have I arrested anyone, performed heart surgery or stood on battlements calling for revolution. What if your life is as uneventful as mine?

This calls for more than adaptation. This is taking Stuff to another level. It might have seemed a strange exercise to write Big Words above an experience (Vomiting Cat = Nature of Friendship), and it isn't a practice we are likely to undertake very often, at least not consciously. But this is what happens when we write. It happens so instinctively, and instantaneously, that we aren't aware of the process. We are looking at the particular, sensing the universal, and adapting those universals back into particulars. It's a kind of two-way movement which in computer technology is called 'Hyper-Threading' – although, as we've seen, it's not so much movement as a change of perception.

Having already seen this in action with the example of the poor writer who turned to confront the geezer on a bar stool evolving over time into Billy confronting Andy on the streets of Walford, let's take a closer look at how it happens.

Universal/Theme
Who am I? What do I stand for?

$\updownarrow$

Particular
Writer confronts bar thug

When I reflected on the bloke in the bar, what struck me, personally, given my character, circumstances, emotional filters, and the prism through which I perceive the world, was not a clash of 'Geezer versus Literati', nor the pathos of a young artist's lack of finance, but that moment when I needed to stand up, not just for me, but for the art I served. Fanciful, yes; slightly naive, definitely sentimental, and possibly pretentious; but, in that moment, I felt that the struggle of all writers, throughout the world, against all the odds, over all the centuries, had been trivialised and dismissed. And though I could have walked away from a personal slight with no harm to my honour, I could not walk away from that. The sense of who I was, if you like, expanded from one small individual to something greater: a family, a community to which I belonged and owed fealty. Without that expansion I wouldn't have had the nerve to stand up for myself. Poor, thin, frail little writer walks away. Raging personification of the literary arts turns around. He has to. It's a flip of identity, or the shrugging off of a particular, limited identity to reveal something more profound, more universal.

And there it lay, a tiny moment of reckless bravado, festering away in my little Book of Stuff. One day, perhaps, I might have written about a young man trying to get a play on the stage, for which this would have made a moving (or hilarious) scene. But that wasn't how it emerged. Billy wasn't organising a theatrical occasion and Andy wouldn't have descended to ripping up posters. Their story was about deception, betrayal and family intrigue. Still, Andy was definitely the big dude, and Billy the little guy. With a need to write the scene, I could have easily worked up some functional dialogue. Failing that, it would have been simple enough to nick from other episodes in the series, cheerfully recycling its old tropes. But imitation, like photocopying, always renders a weaker iteration of the thing itself. So I reached for Stuff.

There was plenty of dramatic energy in the Billy/Andy moment: power struggles, intimidation, and the attempt to protect one's family. But would that give us a moment beyond two people shouting at each other, or one shouting and the other slinking away? And even if that's all it amounted to in the end, outwardly, could we make it more meaningful, authentic, and real?

When Billy slunk from the malevolent sneer of an ascendant Andy, something of that moment in the pub began to fidget. Going deeper into the scene, there were questions of identity, of drawing strength from a greater sense of oneself. So Andy threw out that line about the Mitchells, and Billy remembered who he was. When he turned, it was with all the reckless ferocity of that playwright in the pub. I had my Stuff. I had the moment. And I could write it.

This may not have been a conscious, in the sense of a monitored, process. It happens too quickly for that. One is simply in search of authenticity. The Stuff provides itself. And it was only in retrospect that I could trace a connection between the scene on the page and an incident 20 years previously. Different writers will approach this in different ways. But many that I've spoken to say that it happens outside of their control. It is a part of the frenzy of writing. You don't always – perhaps you rarely – know where it's coming from, but it works for us, when we need it; which, in the end, is all that matters.

So let's take a brief look at the process itself, which we have called frenzy.

THE POET'S EYE

It seems you have to go slightly nuts to be a writer. Perhaps we start off slightly nuts. I wouldn't like to say. But the act of writing is akin to a kind of madness, of frenzy.

Various writers, artists and philosophers have written about this over the years. Edgar Allan Poe said, 'Men have called me mad; but the question is not yet settled, whether madness is or is not the loftiest intelligence – whether much that is glorious – whether all that is profound – does not spring from disease of thought – from moods of mind exalted at the expense of the general intellect. Those who dream by day are cognizant of many things which escape those who dream only by night.'

Similarly, we have Socrates himself: 'If a man comes to the door of poetry untouched by the madness of the Muses, believing that technique alone will make him a good poet, he and his sane compositions never reach perfection, but are utterly eclipsed by the performances of the inspired madman.'

According to William James, 'When a superior intellect and a psychopathic temperament coalesce... in the same individual, we have the best possible conditions for the kind of effective genius that gets into the biographical dictionaries. Such men do not remain mere critics and understanders with their intellect. Their ideas possess them, they inflict them, for better or worse, upon their companions or their age.'

When Edvard Munch was told that his afflictions could be 'cured' with a period of psychiatric hospitalisation, he retorted, 'I want to keep those sufferings.' Emotional torments, he declared, 'are part of me and my art. They are indistinguishable from me, and it would destroy my art.'

Shakespeare, meanwhile, considered this madness with characteristic precision in *A Midsummer Night's Dream*.

> *The poet's eye, in a fine frenzy rolling,*
> *Doth glance from heaven to earth, from earth to heaven;*
> *And as imagination bodies forth*
> *The forms of things unknown, the poet's pen*
> *Turns them to shapes, and gives to airy nothing*
> *A local habitation and a name.*

It might be useful to unpick this a little.

The poet's eye...

Shakespeare is speaking of a particular way of looking. We have already considered this as a shift of perception from the specifics of circumstance to universal themes. In the previous lines, he describes the apprehension of madmen and lovers. The former are possessed by fear and aversion; the latter by desire. Both are fixed positions, and both account for much of our daily routine. When the writer on the train first noticed the young man, he wished for more courtesy in the world. This was quickly joined by anxiety that intervention might result in a bloody nose. Desire and aversion. They make the world go round.

Even the aspiring dramatist turning back to confront 'Geezer on Stool' was possessed by a desire to do right. These are characters in the scene. They are not the poet's eye, which, as we noted in the transition of the writer on the train from passive combatant to detached witness, disengages with the particulars to observe its deeper levels. The writer on the train wasn't just watching the young man; he was watching himself.

In a fine frenzy rolling...

There is a chuckle in here. Having compared the perceptions of lunacy and love, we move on to the rolling eyeball in the head of a crazed artist. As we've noted, however, this rolling has less to do with an agitated mind than a precise movement in the faculties of observation and interpretation.

In using the term 'fine frenzy', Shakespeare is nodding to the Renaissance philosopher Marsilio Ficino who had much to say on the subject, referencing, in his turn, Plato. This isn't a rampage (although sometimes it's nice to let your characters rant), but more akin to play. My son's analysis of the literary arts as 'being silly', as it turns out, was not incompatible with the classical view. The body sits in a study somewhere in genteel suburbia, while the mind does battle in the Far East, or at the end of the Second World War, or on the streets of Liverpool. It is a kind of crazy, but craziness tempered by its opposite: precision. 'Fine' means 'consummate in quality, delicate, subtle, handsome, excellent, admirable'. So there are two forces at work here: reckless abandon and fine control. It is letting go and holding on. This is dancing, or running, or even skiing, at its most exhilarating – to skim the precipitous edge of chaos; although the most we writers risk is a ruined piece of paper, as distinct from a shattered femur.

This twin energy, of creativity and form, is crucial to the artistic act. If the one is experiment, freewheeling, riffing, or whatever one wishes to call it, the other is control, precision and structure. The two are not antithetical, but complementary. Plato referred to these as the operation of love and law. And he said they were like the two wings of a bird. There is no limit, therefore, to the reaches of your madness, so long as your craft can keep up. If not, you'll end up flapping in awkward circles – that's if you even manage to take off.

Take a look at some of the pieces you've seen (or written) that don't work. In some instances you will find that there is simply too much formula and not enough creativity. It's all slapped together out of prefabricated components. Or it might be too wild, and inchoate, lacking the means to communicate. Remember the wings. Remember the bird. Now look at some of the great works, and marvel.

Doth glance from heaven to earth, from earth to heaven...
The rolling movement is thus a brisk transition from the particular to the universal and back. If the madman's eye is fixed on his demons,

and the lover on the object of adoration, the poet's eye is a more nimble organ. We might appear to be staring open-mouthed but our perceptions are rapidly assimilating the data. Although described as a movement, we have also explored it as a kind of double vision in which the cloud becomes a camel remains a cloud. We see both the particular and the universal at the same time. They have become each other.

Shakespeare's terminology might be Judeo-Christian, but the source, and import, is all Plato. In any case, one would expect Theseus (the character speaking these lines) to be more classical than ecclesiastic. In Platonic terms, then, heaven is the realm of Universals, invisible to the senses but comprehensible through the intellect. We've toyed with a few of these. You can't bottle love or justice, courage or hope – or even the softer concepts of squeamishness, resentment, nostalgia, and that feeling we get when we've hidden something for safekeeping but can't remember where – but we can experience them. We know what they are.

It stands to reason – in Platonic terms, literally – that a primary purpose of drama is to enable us to savour the realm of intangibles. And we can, to some extent, do so without risk. Through *Catch Me If You Can*, *Shattered Glass* and *The Wolf of Wall Street*, we can frolic cheerfully in the world of doing terrible things, emerging unscathed even if the protagonist ends up in gaol. Through *When Harry Met Sally*, *Green Card* and *Love Actually*, we can experience and enjoy the most divine consummation of a passionate romance, even if we wake up, the next day, alone.

And as imagination bodies forth the forms of things unknown...

Bearing in mind that Shakespeare scholars can draw blood over the meaning of a piece, my contention is that this describes the process by which our reflections on a given theme give rise to a particular expression of setting, character and action. The things unknown are unknown to the senses, but they can be represented through images. As dramatists, our imaginations find form not in a disquisition, sermon, moral tract or psychological paper on the nature of jealousy, but in the embodiment of its agonies through a spurned character.

Arguably, the dramatist gets closer in the sense that we evoke the very presence of jealousy itself. The psychiatrist merely finds words to describe it for the purposes of medication.

The poet's pen turns them to shapes and gives to airy nothing a local habitation and a name.

The poet's pen is you sitting at your desk, or on the top deck of a bus, or strolling to the shops, taking note of something that catches your eye. It is the mechanism by which you produce writing. The moment a character springs to mind, you are playing with shapes. Thus 'Courage' becomes a rebel in the Scottish Highlands, and 'Family Loyalty' morphs into the head of a mafia clan trying to keep his youngest son out of the business. When we write, we name. We name the place and the characters. We name the world they live in and their nature. We name their friends and their enemies. When something has name and form, it exists in the tangible world. And the moment something has name and form, it begins to obey the laws of its nature. You can make your universe as fanciful as you wish, but, once made, it has laws by which it operates. And those laws will govern how you tell your story.

FIXED POSITIONS

Vertical structure, then, delineates the relationship between universals and particulars. If vertical structure is more of a process, or movement, than a static object, it nevertheless provides a fixed point to which everything in the story should relate. If something isn't quite working, it might be because the narrative has wandered too far from the purpose of the story. Put another way, it comes from somewhere else. That's why you have to kill your darlings, however lovely, because they're not the result of your frenzy. They've drifted in from a momentary spasm of vanity, myopia, or desire to impress.

As a motif, this structure can be found in many cultures, through different ages, and is, in itself, a kind of universal. Thus Plato wrote of the divided line to articulate the distinction between that which is constant and universal (the realm of being) and that which is transitory and particular (the realm of becoming).

In classical Sanskrit drama, which had its heyday circa 500 BC, the term for this vertical structure was 'stambha' (from which, oddly, we get the English word 'stump'). Traditionally, a stambha – divided into three sections representing earth, sky and heaven – was erected, either literally or figuratively, in the centre of the stage. Whether literal or figurative, its symbolic value remained the same: to assert that what was taking place on the stage was, through particulars, the representation of universals.

It is interesting that Shakespeare also deployed the metaphors of earth and heaven to signify the transient and eternal. But then we are creatures of both matter and mind. Meanwhile, there are spires, minars, minarets, totem poles, may poles, and Christmas trees. Odysseus, like the careful artist mindful of his intent, strapped himself to a mast to avoid distraction. If vertical structure is symbolic of the human being, that composite of ghost and flesh, Christian imagery nails the point, quite literally, home.

The image of vertical structure is to be found in almost every culture on the planet. It carries a meaning that echoes deep within the human psyche. Its meaning is meaning itself. And meaning, its apprehension and comprehension, is at the heart of who we are.

THE MIRROR

Another way of looking at this is to flip the pole horizontally, giving us what Shakespeare called 'a mirror up to nature'. The purpose of the play, he says, is and has always been 'to hold, as 'twere, the mirror up to nature; to show virtue her own feature, scorn her own image, and the very age and body of the time his form and pressure.'

Virtue is all that's good in us; those universals of courage, loyalty, hope, etc. Scorn is all that denies it, resulting in their opposites. Virtue has a feature because it is a real attribute of the human psyche. Scorn is merely an image, an overlay; echoing a view consistent with the Platonic notion that there is good, essentially, in all things. Form and pressure refer to the ideas of the day, in which pressure is an emblem stamped into wax. These ideas might be so pervasive, so firmly rooted in our culture, that we never distance ourselves sufficiently to see them as anything imposed, or outside of ourselves. They might be positive or negative, useful or destructive, but to conform blindly is a form of slavery.

The mirror enables us to recognise our virtues and thereby strengthen them; acknowledge our vices and let them go; and observe the ideas by which our lives are ruled and choose whether or not to follow them. The mirror, in other words, wakes us up to what's going on. In that moment we are restored as free-thinking, volitional human beings.

I remember a production of Harold Pinter's *The Caretaker* during which I caught a sudden, powerful glimpse of all the words and actions that I performed entirely mechanically. I could hear the repetitive drone of thoughts and impulses, like a broken record, governing my life. It was uncomfortable but liberating. Stories can have a potent effect. Sometimes it's the only chance we get to take a long, clear look at ourselves.

THE CIRCLE

When Giotto (1266-1337) was approached by an emissary from the Pope asking for a drawing to demonstrate his skill, he reputedly picked up a pen and drew a perfect circle on the wall. He got the gig. Try it yourself. Grab that pen next to you, a piece of paper, take a breath and draw a circle.

How did you get on? Perfect? Probably not. Presumably Giotto had a lot of practice. So ask yourself how you could have drawn a better circle. Obviously, you could have drawn around a plate. Or you could have practised like Giotto, or been born with an extraordinary talent. Usually, if we need to draw a decent circle, we'll use a compass. There's no mystery about it. We stick something firmly in the centre and use that to determine exactly where the circumference is going to fall. So long as we remain true to that centre, the circle will take its perfect shape. If we sneeze, or someone jogs us, or the point slips in some way, we end up with a wiggle, bulge or indentation.

You can probably see what I'm getting at here. The stick in the ground, our vertical structure, viewed from above, is simply a dot. But that dot governs the direction and shape of everything that takes place. If we read something and ask 'What's the point of this?', we are attempting to establish the centre of the circle. If we ask 'What is this about?', we are asking around what point does this rotate. That point is where your pole stands, your vertical structure, your connection to meaning. If you waver when you're writing, you end up with bumpy bits. If you go off on one, regardless of what the piece is about, you get a misshapen lump instead of a pleasing form. Knowing what your story is about will help you to plot every step of the shape. It governs your decisions. This is more powerful, and useful, than simply checking every line for consistency with your thesis. A strong sense of your central premise will tell you, instantly, when you've strayed. You will feel your hand pulling back to the line.

This is not to dismiss the fun of improvisation, experimentation, and pushing the boat out. But the centre, once revealed and understood, will help you to edit back to coherence. Neither is this a manifesto for neatness over creativity. On the contrary, the stronger your centre, the wilder you can be with the outward form without the whole thing becoming a misshapen lump.

....

AN **EXERCISE**

Here's another exercise you can try. Call a busy friend and speak for as long as you can without actually saying anything. How long will it be before they interrupt you? How long before you can sense their despair and frustration? How long, perhaps, before they ask you if everything is all right? How often can you do this before they block your calls? Speech exists to convey meaning. Story works to elaborate, embellish, enjoy and convey a point. No point, no story.

So next time you feel the urge to write (or say something), note how you dig into the realm of meaning to wrestle out a nugget of sense. Otherwise, as Shakespeare bemoaned, it's just a tale told by an idiot, full of sound and fury signifying nothing.

....

WRITING VERTICALLY

Let's return to the example of the scene from *Eastenders* in which Billy faced off the much more menacing Andy. What gave Billy strength was a sudden sense that he was more than the shambling, self-doubting, timid individual he usually took himself to be. He was, in that moment, a Mitchell. This realignment of his identity with a greater power gave him enormous – even reckless – courage and strength.

I described the process by which I dug into the outer fabric of the simple plot point (the moment when Billy tells Andy that he's going to tell Kat about the infidelity – if you want to know!) to find something that resonated with my own Stuff. In doing so, I was confronting, and attempting to solve, a narrative problem: how to make that change in Billy convincing. There were simple solutions, of course. Billy could have mentioned it to someone just as Andy happened to come round the corner. Earwigging is a favourite cheat for the hard-pressed soap writer. Alternatively, Billy could have 'blurted it out', a perennial and exasperating phrase in many a story document. In this instance, I found a moment of change from my own experience. Exploring that moment of transformation, I was able to find the change in Billy. It felt right, it worked, and everybody was happy.

While a writer in a Hampstead pub and a garage owner in the East End are circumstantially different, the trick was to find the common material, meaning, or Stuff. This is the act of rolling, or glancing, from particular to universal and back. Laid out on a page it might look something like this:

Universal/Theme
Who am I? What do I stand for?

Personal Experience	The Story
· A pub	· Albert Square
· A Writer	· Billy
· A poster for a play	· Billy's sister
· A drunken lout	· Andy
· An act of menace/violence	· An act of menace/violence
· Walking away	· Walking away
· Realignment of identity (I am a Writer)	· Realignment of identity (I am a Mitchell)
· Turning back	· Turning back
· Confrontation	· Confrontation

What we have is a process by which the circumstances of a particular narrative begin to swap material with personal experience, and vice versa. The lout in the pub becomes Andy; the writer turning back in the name of Art is Billy remembering his family. This is Stuff at work. It is a process natural to all writers, more complex to explain than to experience. But, if you do get stuck, the lesson is: go back to your notebook, to your Stuff.

Of course, that bit of Stuff could have been used in different ways, for different stories. The great thing about Stuff is that you can use it again and again. That moment of turning back in the pub could become a young man realising that he needs to avenge the attempted assassination of his father; or a villager in France during the Second World War witnessing an injustice that makes him join the Resistance; or a journalist who refuses to be intimidated by the covert menace of a sinister power. The truth of the scene is not in the accuracy of your portrayal of a French Resistance fighter (though you could always do some research to get the history right); it's about the veracity of its Stuff.

So practise a bit. Just for the fun of it. Here are some things you can do:

- **Take the incident of the young man with his feet on the seat.** Can you relate to that? If not, have you a similar experience that you can draw from? What are the themes at work? What is the territory of human experience that can be explored? Fear? Defiance? Anger? Hesitation? Savour those concepts. Have you ever known fear, defiance, anger or hesitation? Note the circumstances. Go back to the themes. Now emerge again but let the circumstances change. Set it in a different historical period, a different place. Change the gender of the characters. Set it on the Moon, or a space ship, or in a hospital. Pick a particularly volatile period of history – war, riots, slavery – and allow the circumstances to explore any one, or more, or all of those themes.

- **Savour those lines from *Twelfth Night*.** What do you know of loss? What do you know of loneliness? When have you turned to strangers, hoping they might be friends? When have you staggered out of an unexpected disaster? Write about it. But go back, and come out again, changing the material just as we did for the exercise above.

- **Pick a line or moment from any film that feels, in some way, potent.** Michael, in *The Godfather*, fishing a gun from behind the cistern, for instance. Work with it. What's going on? What does it remind you of? What can you see in it that tells you something about yourself? Then follow the steps in the first two exercises here. You might achieve two results from this. The first is greater familiarity with the process, the fine frenzy, by which we write meaningfully. The second is a recognition that a rich piece of work carries its meaning in every detail.

Writing can be hard work. It can be frustrating, worrying and sometimes a bit scary. If you want to conserve your energies, then it's important to direct your effort to where it's needed. Trying to polish a line of dialogue when you don't know the point of the scene is a futile pursuit. Trying to shape a scene when you don't know what the story is about will drive you to despair. But time spent establishing your vertical structure, which is to say finding out what it's about, is never wasted. You'll benefit in two ways. The first is that many of your decisions – about character, plot, dialogue, etc – will be made for you. Secondly, it will provide the energy you need to tell the story. You won't be fabricating dramatic guff, or slotting things into each other in a frantic attempt to generate the illusion of meaning. Just as the child running indoors to tell its mother about the grass snake doesn't have to summon up the enthusiasm to do it, you will find that the story, to a great extent, tells itself. The goal is not to find the energy to write, but to find that energy which makes it impossible not to.

VOICE

Different people, of course, notice different things in any given situation. If I lived in a world where people regularly duffed each other up, it might have been more remarkable if the man at the bar *hadn't* grabbed that poster. So the same moment can yield different Stuff to different people, or different Stuff at different times to the same person. Some moments can yield Stuff we'll revisit through different projects over many years. Some might be so powerful that they will shape, for ever after, the way we think, feel and write. Out of all this, we might find, looking back over a body of work, that there are consistent themes, or variations on themes, or a way of exploring themes, that is characteristically ours. This is a part of what others might call our 'voice'. It probably isn't a good idea to become too self-conscious about it, or attempt to fabricate one. Mozart was bemused when people described his work as 'Mozartian'. He said it must be as characteristic of him as his nose, but not something of which he was especially aware. His focus was only on getting that music out as authentically as possible. Your voice will be dictated by what your instincts tell you works at any given moment of writing. Those who care too much about how they are perceived might be caring about the wrong thing.

We have spent some time exploring rich, layered and philosophically potent literary sources such as *Twelfth Night* and, er, *Eastenders*. But not everything you write needs to be the stuff of someone's PhD (although that depends what the PhD is on). John Wayne once said of his characters, 'There's no nuance. They drive ahead, usually fighting something bigger than a petty little argument with someone.' The principle at work here is depth of field. Your story can be brisk, entertaining and shallow, or slow, ponderous and deep. It is a question of optics, not qualitative judgement. You might have your own preference, both as a viewer and as a writer, which may change over time, or even from day to day depending on your mood. Similarly, different pieces might require different treatments. You might have an idea for a cheeky chap drama, funny, engaging and not too demanding on the grey matter. Or you might have seen the heavens move. What matters is authenticity.

It's usually refreshing to hear someone speak without guile or deception. We appreciate honesty. So does your audience. So be true to your voice; find it if you have to. (*The Rum Diary* is all about Hunter S Thompson finding his voice.) It might not be obvious at first. Sometimes the struggle to write is the struggle to write as someone else. No surprise it's a struggle! At the same time, the industry sets great store by 'voice', even if the processes of production can sometimes homogenise it. The way to find it is by writing, discarding, and writing again. You'll know it when you've got it. And so will your grateful audience. We might subsume ourselves, as writers, into the machinery of production, but the audience hasn't come to hear a machine. They could phone an automated switchboard if they were desperate enough for that. The refinement of a script might entail the elimination of vanities, but don't cut so far that it ceases to live and breathe with all the beauty, vibrancy, and even majesty, of the human heart.

SUBTLETY

If you look at your notebook, what you'll probably see is a whole bunch of quickly jotted vertical structures: incidents that reveal meaning. Often they will be in the form of a local habitation and a name. A child on a train tugs at his mother's arm to point out a horse in a field; but she is too busy with her smart phone to look up. The deflation in his eyes, which tells you of his sudden sense of being alone, might result in a note such as: 'Kid on train, horse in field, looks round, mother too busy.' What you have gathered is a little bit of Stuff. The circumstances may adapt to a particular narrative, as we've seen, but the meaning is immutable.

Sometimes we might be ambling along and suddenly think: 'Justice! Wow. Must write about that some time.' But we are rarely inspired by mere abstracts. Our experience is of tangibles, of particulars, and our language, the language of story, reflects that. Which is why the best kind of story conferences delve into the realm of personal experience, while the worst merely refer to rival programmes. A recent attempt to mimic the success of *Mad Men* took everything about it (the sixties, the moral *faux pas* of the times, the style and fashion, the naivety, the primary colours) while missing the very thing that made it a story: Man Falling. It was a doomed enterprise. But, then, imitation often is.

At the same time, taking a Big Theme, and trying to work that up into story material, can be an exhausting enterprise; both for you and your audience. At best you'll end up with a final act in which somebody stands to deliver your message. When we say that theme is a territory of human experience that can be explored, we could expand the analogy to a series of large rooms each headed with a grandiose word: Love, Truth, Exploitation, etc. Within these, however, are the myriad nuances of ordinary life. When Don Draper invited his colleagues to reveal the personal reasons behind a particular ad campaign to the client, those reasons being an infatuation between the two creatives involved, we spun on a loop of cringing anticipation, along with the characters. There isn't a big word for that. There isn't a mighty concept etched in stone to describe what it is to find a biscuit under the sofa. I can still recall, decades later, a line from an Alan Bennett play in which one of the characters has been berated by her husband for throwing away an important document. 'I didn't throw it away,' she replies, 'It got thrown away.' Sweet, subtle, and, in its way, priceless.

POWER

Theme is what gives drama power, not action, histrionics or explosions. Every detail of the final form, from hair and makeup, costume design, photography and music to SFX, is, of course, given its due measure of care. The same can be said of dialogue and visual motifs. But unless they mean something, unless they are rooted in a sound verticality of structure, they are mere pictures, tunes, and a bit of nifty speech. Many a writer, producer, actor and distributor has looked at their poor reviews thinking, 'But I got all the bits in the right place...'

Cinema comes out of a curious, but perfectly natural, confluence of two distinct media: theatre and spectacle. Theatre is all about meaning. Spectacle, whether circus, variety, *son et lumière*, or peep show, is all about entertainment. Since a good portion of cinema's DNA comes from the end of the pier, there is no point being snobbish about it. Different writers will have different scoops of the gene pool. When you're in a frenzy, you are unlikely to be concerned much about the precise ratio.

The example taken from *Eastenders* deals with a scene written in haste to a looming deadline. At the time I was mainly concerned with getting it down so it felt OK. There was no conscious trawling through the mists of time, or flicking the pages of a notebook. If we worked like this, we'd never meet our deadlines. It would be like a pianist having to tell every finger where to go. The average sonata would take hours. At first we have to be deliberate about our methods. Just as the pianist will begin by forcing every digit to the key. But in time this becomes natural and effortless. The way to achieve that, again, is to write and write. Practise. Write without thinking too much about it. The part of the mind that likes to think it's in charge might feel slightly displaced by an activity of this nature, but displaced it should be, since it doesn't do much, in the end, but get in the way.

ARTISTRY

If all that sounds simple enough, it's possibly because we've left out one of the most important elements. We are not machines. And our writing is not the outpourings of a pianola. What we emphasise, what we choose, the micro-spaces between moments, or notes, and the passion with which we play, has a bearing on the sound we produce. Themes are human life, infinitely complex, infinitely varied. A rich piece of work will have multiple variations on a theme, or different themes that contrast, harmonise and conflict to create an overall experience of something known, even if you can't quite pin it down.

We could try formulating rules but they would end up so complex, and so shot through with exceptions, that you might as well just try things out and see how it feels. Too many themes will feel like a mush. Too few, too carefully defined, will feel preachy and/or cheesy. All you have to guide you is your writer's eye, which is like the perfumer's nose, or the distiller's tongue. It all depends on your sensitivity as an artist, by which I don't mean your emotional tenderness on a Monday morning, but your ability to savour the nuance of a dramatic moment, and fine-tune accordingly.

It helps to read the works of others. Let them soak in. Enjoy them. Learn from them. If something touches you, ask why and how. If it leaves you cold, do the same. This absorption of the literary conflux of which you are a part will develop your writing in ways you will not even be aware of. We are a mere moment on this long journey of literature that reaches back to the first words spoken. You cannot escape this flow, so you may as well join it.

Lastly, hear what your audience is telling you. What do they like about your writing? What don't they like? In what way have they failed to recognise your genius? To what extent have you managed to fool them? Since my early experience of production was in fringe theatre, I was able to benefit from the terrifying privilege of being in the room with my audience. Why aren't they laughing? Why did they laugh just then? When do they cough? Or shuffle? Or look at the programme notes? Almost inevitably, if something didn't quite work, I'd remember the little voice at the time of writing that had muttered, 'Hmm, doesn't quite...' But either it hadn't muttered loudly enough, or I had chosen to ignore it; or I hadn't yet developed the skills to find a better moment. But the voice was there. It's always there. Listen out for it. It will tell you all you need to know.

IDEAS

HANG ON A MINUTE, LADS...

If theme, then, is an experiential phenomenon that we can feel but not necessarily define, what is this mechanism by which we communicate it? We've looked at vertical structure and considered how particulars evoke the presence of themes, just as themes can express themselves through particulars. The means by which theme translates into characters, actions, dialogue, scenery and so forth is Story. And story always starts with an idea.

Ideas are slippery phenomena. We can be strolling along, waiting for a train, or dodging the bullets of crazed gunmen in the back streets of a Columbian drugs town, and there's no idea in sight. Not a sniff of one. It's simply not there. And then it is. We have it. We write it down. 'Hang on a minute, lads,' says Michael Caine in the last scene of *The Italian Job*. 'I've got a great idea.'

Without ideas, we won't have stories. Ideas give us our next project, or future projects. Ideas solve story problems. They flesh out the Stuff of an episode for which we might have been given the outline. If a producer asks to see any ideas you might have and you don't have any, the relationship, and your future, isn't going to move much further.

There is no button to press or switch to pull that turns on the ideas tap. At least nothing sold legally. What we can do, of course, is prepare the ground, by watching, hearing, feeling, reflecting, and keeping a notebook. Nothing, as Shakespeare says, comes of nothing.

An idea may come in any shape; a fragment of conversation, a character insight, an event. It is the earliest, most concentrated form of story. It's the acorn of what you hope will grow into a mighty oak of literature (or at least a decent episode of *Doctors*). Like any seed, it has within it all of its potential. If you study your idea carefully, you will find the beginnings of narrative, character, setting, and even some dialogue. It might not be very obvious at this point. Some of it might not be apparent at all. But a seed is only a seed; it isn't yet the whole thing.

Setting arborial metaphors to one side, the word 'idea' is strongly linked to light. Hence a bright idea, seeing the light, or the light-bulb motif to signify ideation. 'That's brilliant,' we'll say of a particularly good one, or 'I see what you mean'.

If theme is a territory of human experience, then it remains dark until we illuminate it. If the theme is jealousy, for instance, the idea might be a cat pained by the tribal supremacy afforded the family dog. The cat decides to usurp the position of its rival to become Supreme Pet. Thus, jealousy as an abstract – a dark area, if you like – is gradually illuminated as we shine our disgruntled cat around. You'll notice that within this simple idea, we already have a central character, a motive, an antagonist, various ancillary characters and even some obvious moments.

When you're rooting around in the realm of theme, you'll probably stumble upon all sorts of interesting variants, adjuncts and maybe an old stick of rock from that time you went to the seaside. It is up to you to show as much or as little as you like. And you don't have to share everything. If you find, as you poke about, a bit of nostalgia nestling up against ennui, or fortitude sitting next to courage, you can pick and choose, mix and blend as your artistry decides. Remember the wood-botherer. There is artistry also in the gathering. But be prepared to find something you weren't looking for. Dig deep. The first unfolding of the idea might not be the best. Your story might surprise you. Being surprised by your own writing, after all, is one of its greatest pleasures.

The idea, then, is both the starting point and, usually, your slug-line or pitch. It might well provide a listings summary and, who knows, even feature in the publicity. *Rise of the Planet of the Apes* reputedly began with a pitch about an ape on a child's swing. Ideally (pun intended), your pitch will contain everything about the final product in its most essential form, including theme, central character, and story.

But, as we observed elsewhere, neatness alone is not enough. An idea isn't just a piece of truncated narrative. It is a means by which themes are illuminated. It has to say something. The ape on a swing asks immediate questions about the relationship between humans and apes. A good idea should light you up, and light up anyone you're telling it to.

When you test your ideas, on paper or to others, try to feel what they're saying, what they're implying, revealing, suggesting. Do you feel something move in the deeper, darker aspects of your understanding of what it is to be human? Or does it just feel like a device to get people running around for 90 minutes? If the former, then it is likely to make others respond in the same way. If the latter, try to discern what the idea might be suggesting and, if necessary, focus the beam a bit more. It is the richness of depth that makes an idea rock, not the tidiness of its articulation.

WORKING WITH IDEAS

Ideas, of course, can vary in quality. Any working writer knows what it's like to say, 'Hang on a minute, lads... nah, forget it.' Likewise, you might have dismissed something only to find, later, that it contains hidden gems.

When attempting to judge whether an idea is a good one or not, there are a few questions you can ask which might be of help:

1. How did I get this idea? If it arose from a real observation, it most likely has something about it that can be pursued. If, on the other hand, it was triggered by somebody else's observation, or idea, or lazily pulled together out of a song you heard, a story you read, or some other pre-processed material, ask yourself if you've

really seen something unique, distinct and powerful that deserves further exploration.

2. Does it make you want to explore it? Does it generate the tingle we get when we hear a good idea; the tingle that needs to run from one end of your screenplay to the other. That tingle is engagement, entertainment, the promise of something profound, the revelation of something powerful. If you don't thrill when you think about it, be cautious about devoting the next six months of your life to its exposition. Running out of tingle halfway through a script is an especially dismal experience.

3. Does it keep coming back to you? Does it demand to be told? Is it like a child who has spotted a grizzly bear in the back garden while you're heading out to sunbathe? Shouldn't you be taking notice of it?

4. Does it reveal itself as you turn it around in your hands? Do you get glimpses of deeper themes, instant story, a few characters, even some dialogue? For instance, we've already begun to elaborate the jealous cat story, but consider what it gives us pretty much *gratis*. We've got the cat, the dog and the family. We have a world with its own power structure, rewards (being favoured) and hazards (being ignored). Our cat even has character. The dog we can develop later. But I guess we need a moment when the cat sees the dog being favoured. So that's one moment. Then the plotting of revenge. Does the cat have allies? Are there other disgruntled pets he can win over to his cause? What could he promise them if he becomes Supreme Pet? When he puts his plan into action, what are the obstacles? Does he win or lose?

   If an idea yields easily, you can be fairly sure you're on to something. But if it lies inert on the page, reluctantly discharging the odd moment if you kick it hard enough, you might find it more work than it's worth.

5. Can you tell it, simply, to somebody else? Do their eyes glaze over halfway through your twenty-third, 'No, wait, it's not that, it's...' An idea

needs to be simple to do its job. Your themes can be complex and deep. Your story can be multi-faceted and full of twists. But an idea is a beam of light. It needs to get from its source to its destination in one quick move, taking the shortest possible route. If your idea is a meandering labyrinth, then everyone's going to get lost.

6. During the writing, do the characters have to keep stopping to explain what's going on? Dialogue shouldn't perform the function of idea. The moment it becomes explanatory, or didactic, it ceases to tell story and develop character. A similar symptom of weakness is Q&A, when characters start asking each other questions in order to solicit narrative information. There is a reason why the question mark is so awkward to type. It should only be used rarely.

When I first went along to *The Bill* to meet a commissioning editor, I found myself in the reception area with another writer who was there for the same reason. We wished each other luck. After a few minutes my editor came in, introduced herself, and led me away to do my pitch. About a year later I met that writer, by chance, in a London pub. I asked how he'd got on at *The Bill*. He said that, sadly, they hadn't liked his idea. Then he asked me how I'd got on. I said they hadn't liked four of my ideas. Another four they'd already done. The rest (four in number) they'd commissioned. He stared at me with the look of one rapidly recalibrating his professional strategies.

....

AN **EXERCISE**

Take a film or TV show that you've watched recently. Try to write down the idea. Think of it as if you were hoping to pitch it to a producer. Consider it from different angles. Ask how it developed into the final piece. Now think about the themes.

Do this again. And again. When you watch something, ask the same questions. What was that about? How would I pitch it? What did it mean?

If you watched it on DVD or Blu-ray, have a look at the special features. Find out what the director intended (the writer is rarely asked). Better still, if there's a screening somewhere with a Q&A involving any of the key creatives, go along if you can. If the film is of any worth, and the audience reasonably clued up, the creatives will soon be discussing themes. Integral to that will be the shape and form of the idea. If people are asking daft questions about what it was like to work with George Clooney, stand up and ask something useful.

The simple purpose of this practice is to develop a familiarity and dexterity with the mechanism of idea. By understanding it through the works of others, you will be better able to apply it to your own.

....

RAT LADY AND OTHER STORIES

We've looked at the use of a notebook, where a notebook stands, physically or figuratively, for the writer's accumulation of Stuff. We've explored the nature of Stuff and, hopefully, discovered that it's a bit more than the detritus of circumstance. On the contrary, it is redolent with meaning. We then examined how Stuff works and developed something of a schematic that we called vertical structure, indicating the relationship between the particulars of a given moment of drama – that is the words and actions – and the realm of meaning. Finally we took a brief survey of how to employ all this as a writing method.

It might help at this point to offer one or two examples. I'll draw from my own experience, since at least we won't have to guess what the writer was thinking. I mentioned, earlier, different ways of going in search of Stuff, which included pre-arranged research trips. As an occasional writer on *Casualty*, I did plenty of overnight sessions in my local A&E unit. These were always an eye-opener, the hospital in question taking patients from one of London's most affluent neighbourhoods, as well as some of its seediest. Usually I staggered home in the early hours fairly traumatised. Which is always a good

Rats lady hysteria -

CLINIC
psychiatric day

Seaford - claims bothers,   Goes here.
to avoid exams?

W.P.C. cut by burglar -
Offries come in -

cello leg ⬭

- Beaten up by boyfriend - medical details
only -
⊙
Shins / leathers - Ski-Jacket. leathers
                        everywhere -

millie look at it, punched.
always when CD's on Keeley.

if his psychiatric record.
may affect marriage prospects -

"wall" punching - the other guy.

[Sub Stories]
Theft of things - Jeremiah.

thing for a writer. The research consisted of chatting to members of staff, many of whom were keen to tell me their stories. I also shadowed a doctor, just observing whatever was taking place. By around three in the morning, almost as exhausted as everyone else, I had usually been accepted as a member of the team. From time to time I'd retire to the rest room to jot down a few of the things I'd seen. Here, on the left, is a page from that notebook.

The notes, as you can see, are brief. That's because there wasn't time to go into any more detail. But each one seeks to encapsulate a moment of Stuff, of story. I'll take you through a few of these. We'll start at the bottom of the page and work upwards.

THEFT OF THINGS – JEREMIAH

While talking about life as a hard-pressed A&E doctor, one staff member mentioned having his stethoscope stolen about a week previously. He was especially aggrieved because it had been a gift from his parents when he'd graduated. I'd never thought of a doctor's emotional attachment to a stethoscope before but, when you consider it, it makes sense. It's not just an instrument, but a badge of office, an approbation, a confirmation; it is – through all the years of hard slog – what they eventually see themselves wearing around their necks. I'm getting carried away now, but so did he. The point is, it mattered and it was stolen. And that hurt. With a little questioning I found out that theft was a lingering problem. People would come into the unit with some pretended complaint and wait for their opportunity to prowl around nicking valuable medical equipment, for which there is a thriving black market. You can see why I wrote this down. The doctor mentioned someone calling himself 'Jeremiah' who was particularly adept at winning over the trust of the staff with a superb act in humble pathos. So we have here some good material that could pad out an episode. But it isn't yet Stuff. Stuff, as we have seen, is not just a sequence of events.

As often happens, this little bit of semi-Stuff had to wait until it met another bit of semi-Stuff before it could form the basis of story. On a previous occasion I'd met up with a young GP, introduced to me by a mutual friend, who talked about his earlier professional life working on a building site. One day he'd been sitting in a café with his work mates, close to where some medical students were having breakfast. Suddenly, it crossed his mind that he'd like to be just like them. So he went to college, got A-levels, went to university, and achieved his dream. I offered him to *Casualty* as a new character: Mike Barratt. They didn't quite have the nerve to make him a former builder, giving him an office job instead (hence my gorgeous line, lifted directly from the GP, 'I traded in my hard hat for a stethoscope', became the slightly weaker, 'I traded in my clipboard for a stethoscope'). Still, regardless of what he traded in, there is an obvious link between the doctor for whom his stethoscope is the very personal symbol of a life-changing effort and the doctor I spoke to whose instrument was stolen.

At this juncture, there are many ways to tell a particular story; what matters is that the character learns something through what happens. We'll look at the transformational nature of character later, but it's not hard to see that story isn't just things happening to someone, but very much about how those things bring about change. I settled on a young, nice-looking couple who come in with the symptoms of a very rare, very obscure complaint (which actually tagged in another bit of Stuff I'd come across). She's all fluttering eyelids and clearly in awe of the doctor. Mike, feeling flattered, gets rather excited about spotting a little-known disease. When he goes off to get a second opinion, however, they steal his beloved stethoscope. That the scammers stole his beloved stethoscope is not the point. The point is that they exposed his pride. Theft is an event. Pride is a universal theme. I had my story.

WALL PUNCHING

'Wall punching' was just a remark. Someone said they'd hurt their hand punching a wall, at which a nurse muttered to me, 'I'll bet we see the wall later.' And we did. I used the moment, and the dialogue in its entirety, to provide some background colour to a scene about something else. Why? Because it struck me as funny. Comedy has its own rationale. In some ways its meaning lies less in the articulation of a profound human cause, though it will embrace that function, than in the sudden delight that seizes the heart and mind when we experience it. That lightness of play is also what drama is about. It is the sunny side of witnessing, and carries its own sweet sense of freedom.

PSYCHIATRIC REFERRAL/MARRIAGE PROSPECTS

A young Asian woman came in suffering from anxiety. The doctor suggested calling in the psychiatric registrar but this was vetoed by the girl's family since any hint of psychological intervention might damage her marriage prospects. To be honest, I can't remember if I used this. I think somebody else might have stumbled across the same material from their own research. But it would have made a good story.

WILLIE

A man regularly appeared with a penis complaint. He would always time it so that he had a female doctor to examine him. We did use this as part of a doctor's over-arching story but the episode came in long and it was lost in the edit.

FEATHERS

A couple of nurses told me about their attempts to cut off a patient's ski jacket, which resulted in the unit being flooded with feathers. I like it. I haven't yet used it. It needs a bit of work. At the moment, it is merely an anecdote. Again, it could make for some nice colour.

BEATEN UP BY BOYFRIEND

A young lady came in with some very nasty facial injuries but refused to discuss how they had happened. After a while we managed to elicit a hint that she'd been assaulted by her boyfriend. We asked ourselves why she was so anxious to protect the person harming her. This made for a major strand in an episode. The girl was played, brilliantly I have to say, by Julia Sawalha.

CELLO LEG

This refers to a polite elderly couple who came in after the woman had injured her leg on a cello spike. With all the inebriated victims and perpetrators of violent confrontations writhing and moaning in the cubicles around them, it seemed the epitome of a middle-class injury, sublime in every respect, except I couldn't quite think how to use it. At one point it evolved into a story about a young boy who comes in with a hand injury which, after a while, the doctors suspect has been caused by his over-demanding father slamming a piano lid on it after the child once again mangled Debussy. But this never made it, perhaps for obvious reasons, to the screen.

WPC CUT BY BURGLAR

A policewoman was treated for a minor injury, little more than a few bruises, sustained while arresting a burglar. The doctor patched her up fairly quickly, but it was clear that the woman was still badly shaken, fighting back the tears, unable to walk. When her colleagues sauntered in to collect her, we said that she hadn't been seen yet and, moreover, the paperwork had been inexplicably lost so we couldn't advise them where she was. We kept them away until she told us she was ready.

I thought this was a great story but it was turned down. I proposed it the following year, and it was turned down again. I made the policewoman a policeman. It got through. You can see why. In its raw form it suggested female weakness (which hadn't occurred to me). But a man who can't admit that he's had his nerves shaken is a more compelling story. My problem was that I had (and still have) a powerful image in my mind of this young lady, in her uniform, sitting on the edge of the trolley, head down, while a nurse tried to comfort her. Sometimes, you can be fixed by an image when the process, as we've seen, of working with Stuff, is to go from the outward to the universal and back, again and again, until the shape of the action, characters and dialogue most faithfully embodies your themes. Getting locked into fixed particulars at too early a stage makes for a lot of hard work and can, if you're not prepared to let them go, scupper your idea.

SCAFOID (SIC)

At some time in the night, somebody came in with a painful hand. This time it wasn't wall punching. The doctor had it x-rayed and, when the plates came through, sought a second opinion. She suspected that the patient had fractured the scaphoid bone, but this can be very difficult to spot. A colleague said to plaster it anyway. Which we did. This wasn't exactly high drama, but I liked the idea of an injury that you have to assume is there, even if you're not sure. It was a quick leap to create a young student, remiss in his revision, faking an injury to avoid exams. Cute as this is, however, it isn't quite story. One of the strengths, and pleasures, of returning series is that you can use this sort of thing to further the stories of the main characters. The doctor in my telling of it, Beth Ramanee, was facing litigation for negligence. When a nurse questions her decision to plaster the hand she retorts, 'His father's a barrister, his uncle's a judge. If he'd wanted a hysterectomy I'd have done it.' The incident, presented at this key point in her ongoing narrative, showed us that the litigation was beginning to affect her decision-making processes as a doctor. The ethical questions raised by this are huge. The effect on Beth Ramanee was a devastating sense of compromise, a betrayal of the profession to which she had dedicated her life. Simple story. Big themes.

BORN HERE

'Born here' is another instance of a very simple note yielding a huge amount of material. It became, in fact, the major storyline in one particular episode, providing a thematic basis (family and belonging) for all the other narrative strands.

It started with an agitated young man of Afro-Caribbean origins, with a can of lager in one hand and a nasty gash in the other. The doctor poked the wound a bit and asked what had happened. The patient mumbled that he'd cut it on some glass. The doctor asked when. The patient said yesterday. The doctor said he couldn't stitch it. Why not? Because it's been open for too long. There might be debris in it, which could lead to an infection if the cut were stitched. The young man said, well, clean it out then. The doctor said they might not be able to remove all the bacteria. The young man said he'd take a chance. The doctor said it was his clinical decision not to stitch it. The young man asked for a second opinion. The doctor, getting a little irritated by now, said that any of his colleagues would tell him the same thing. The young man said, it's my hand and I want it stitched, so stitch it. The doctor retorted that, professionally, he was unable to comply with that request. The young man then said, 'I don't know why you're talking to me like this, I was born here.' The doctor visibly recoiled. The nurse, who was in attendance, took a step back. Nobody likes to be accused of racism. In fact, even raising the issue could damage a doctor's professional record. The doctor thought for a moment then obviously decided to meet the issue head on. 'What do you mean?' he demanded, 'you were born here?' The young man looked down for a moment and then, in a tremulous voice, said, 'In this hospital, man. I was born here.' I think, in that moment, we all felt like hugging him. This vulnerable young man, so clearly nervous, hurt and afraid, had thought he would find a kind of welcome in the place of his birth. As part of that place we should have accepted him, regardless of the mistakes he'd made, back into the fold of our loving embrace. In that moment I realised how my empathy and compassion had slowly dissipated over the course of the night, in the face of myriad drunken fools with daft injuries and a surly attitude. And I had allowed my instant judgements, my cold opinions, to distance myself from a fellow human being in need.

There is a kind of 'Oohh' when we come across potent Stuff. It doesn't need to be justified. Which is why a good pitch, or proposal, should rely foremost on its nugget of idea. Just tell it. If it needs an explanation before it works, it isn't working. Good Stuff has a punch to it that is unmistakable.

ETHNIC – PSYCHIATRIC REG

The scribble at the top of the page about 'Ethnic Psychiatric Reg' is probably a reference back to the Asian girl story. I must have thought this was the one. It's curious that I never got around to writing it. Maybe it just doesn't interest me that much, even though it's a decent enough *Casualty* story.

RAT LADY HYSTERIA

I almost didn't write this one down. Perhaps the fact that it's in particularly small writing indicates my initial appraisal of its potential. Sad as it was, there wasn't much to go on. A thin, wheezy lady of indeterminate age, somewhere between 23 and 34, sat on the trolley talking gibberish. Her ramblings circled around something about rats attacking her (she even glanced anxiously into the corners of the cubicle). She said she'd put poison down, which she thought she'd breathed in, as a result of which she was feeling faint. You have to bear in mind that the place was awash with delirious people, some drunk, some high, some just plain crazy. So we received her jumbled wittering without much sympathy. By this time, bleeding heart that I am, even I had become numbed to the suffering of others. There was some discussion about getting the psychiatric registrar down, or a social worker. The doctor explained to the patient that she needed to eat properly and breathe deeper. She asked if there was anybody who could help her a bit, such as friends or neighbours, but there wasn't. I scribbled her down as 'rat lady hysteria' and we moved off to the next cubicle.

What surprised me, though, was how the Rat Lady (which is what I called her, I'm afraid) wouldn't leave me alone. Then I realised I was looking at it from the wrong angle. The story wasn't about her. It was about us. It was about people who had been so overexposed to suffering that it no longer touched them. It was about turning away with little interest from someone who, apparently, has nothing useful (not even story) to offer. If we extend that from the tired indifference

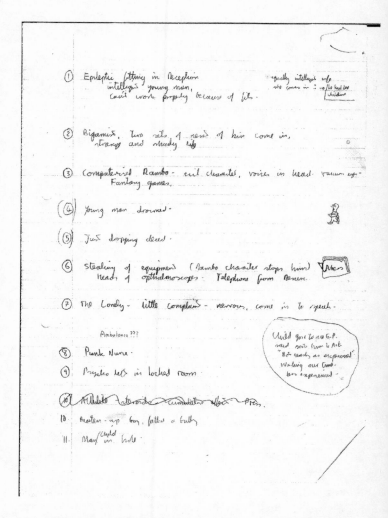

of hard-pressed medical practitioners (and an exhausted scribe) to the world beyond, we see a cold and lonely place. We see people falling through its cracks. We see people, just for a moment, before they disappear from our gaze. That's who this lady was. And I felt pretty bad about it. I felt bad about me. It was something I needed to explore, deal with, learn from. And so I did it in the only way I know how. I turned it into story.

The page of jottings on the left represents the next stage of my ruminations. Over several nights, I'd accumulated a fair load of Stuff. Now I had to sort it into stories I wanted to tell. The bigamist story was already being developed by another writer. 'Just dropping dead' was an apocryphal story given to me by one of the doctors. Apparently a patient was sitting in reception with a broken neck he didn't know about. When his name was called, he turned to look and died on the spot. When I pitched it I discovered that every writer before me had already offered it to the weary editor.

The drowning man did in fact drown in a swimming pool, in an episode called 'Dangerous Games'. And so on. Some were used, some weren't; some became a part of other stories, some of them are still kicking around in my head.

But there she is again, the Rat Lady. Only now she's 'The Lonely', which signifies a move from incident to meaning. It seems we'll be dealing with loneliness and alienation. And what causes that? Well, in part, the indifference of others. Which I knew all about.

She has a little complaint, which is to say no big stunts, no blood. It's an entirely psychological story. She's nervous. And, in the absence of an obvious injury, she's come in to speak. That's how it stands at the moment. It's just a thought; the germ of an idea. Let's take it a step further, with a few more scribbles, which you can see on the next page.

She's Mary now. So she's taking shape: a local habitation and a name. What we see here is the beginnings of some serious thought or, if you like, serious frenzy. I obviously spent a bit of time at this, judging by some serious doodling!

And there's a dead baby. Which is kind of grim. So how did that happen? As we explore Stuff for story, we'll find the need for powerful dynamics such as jeopardy. At the same time we're allowing those intangibles, indifference and remorse, to find form. A moment in which the doctors stop and say, 'You know what? I was such a shmuck in there. I should have felt more sympathy,' is OK so far as it goes, but if we want them to really feel it, we have to deliver real

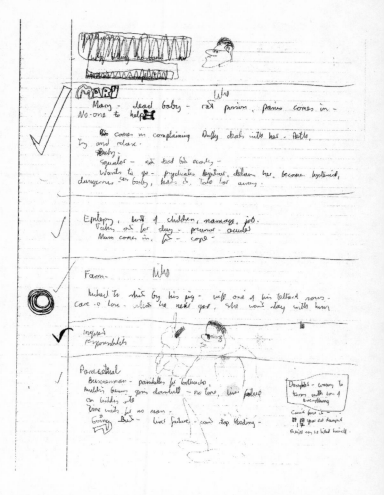

penalty. Likewise, that moment when Mary transforms from irritant on the trolley to an individual human being with a life and needs is given shape in the realisation that a part of that life is her child.

Much of the initial Stuff remains. She comes in, is seen and is advised. I even kept the rats. But my insight is turning into the opposing viewpoints of a nurse and doctor and, along the way, we are finding self-doubt: is there truth to what Mary says or is it merely the ravings of an unhinged mind?

We could have gone in many different directions. An underlying medical problem which the medics miss might lead us to a frantic resuscitation scene, but we've seen a lot of these. Or maybe environmental health officers could visit her flat and run screaming from a rodent infestation. Maybe not. What matters here is the reaction of the team, and their failings. We want to explore the sweeping indifference of the big city. So we'll keep it simple. She faints. That's all. And is brought in.

```
17.  THE LONELY.

     MARY, ill-kempt and tired  is  an unlikely customer at
the up-market maternity shop where she steals a set of baby
clothes.   Accosted  by  the  Sales  Assistant,  MARY  gets
distressed and protests that this  is  for her baby.  Asked
to wait while they  call  the  Police,  MARY becomes faint.
The Manageress calls an ambulance.

     MARY continues to protest about her baby.  In CASUALTY
her fainting is diagnosed  as  under-nourishment.  Her dole
cheque was delayed, she hasn't been eating.

     An ambulance, despatched to  her squalid little 'flat'
finds the baby, filthy, emaciated and dead.

     MARY is just one of  those  people isolated in the big
city, unable to cope, cracking up.
```

So this is frenzy in action. We've gone from the particulars of a woman in A&E to a meditation on loneliness and indifference. From there, we've begun to re-particularise, which is to say that we allow the themes, as they reveal themselves, to take on new shapes, new habitations, new names. Sometimes the story will bear very little outward resemblance to the original experience. Although, in this case, there are many points of direct contact, we do start it in a very different place. It might have worked to open the story with a woman in a cubicle, but the audience deserves a decent introduction to Mary. In any case, there is the danger of long verbal exposition to fill in the gaps, which can be rather tedious. Also, part of the fun of a series like *Casualty* is that you can dip into different locations. The decisions could have been different and no less effective for that. The point is that they were all driven by the desire to tell the story as economically and powerfully as possible, while remaining true to, in the sense of faithfully embodying, the themes.

The upmarket maternity shop brings a lot of the elements of her story together. We can see her incongruity and isolation; we already get the suggestion of a baby. To emphasise her desperation, we could have her attempting to steal. It's not a bad opening, bearing as it does the major themes and ideas of the story. It means we hit the ground running, with the dynamics in place and, above all, we want to know what happens next. The story is telling itself.

Because Mary's story co-exists with a number of others within the same episode, it cannot be taken, thematically, in isolation. In addition to a choice of other 'stories of the week', there are the serial elements to contend with. Sometimes the serial element is just a moment used to knock a long-running narrative on a couple of beats, and the only thing we can do is slot it in somewhere. We cut from our highly complex, densely woven tapestry of deep themes to a conversation about some ex-husband, tricky love triangle, or impending promotion. If possible, however, it is always good practice to find something which embodies, or at least echoes, your central themes. At the same time, the other stories of the week might have to be nudged a little to meet somewhere deep in the realms of meaning.

We've seen how this worked with the broken scaphoid and Beth's litigation difficulties. Interesting as a doctor facing litigation might be, what makes it story is the way it changes her as a medical practitioner. She loses heart. She loses her devotion. She begins to steel herself against emotional engagement. And this is the Beth who finds Mary hunched up in the cubicle. This is not just about Mary. This is about Beth too. In fact, if we're studying the hard indifference of the world and how it creeps into the soul, this is more Beth's story than Mary's. Either way, nobody in that cubicle is just an extra.

Another story beat among the serial elements was that of Kelly, a young nurse who eventually cracks up and commits suicide. My episode had the job of starting off this downwards trajectory. So what could she contribute to Mary and vice versa? If Beth dismisses Mary as a muddled woman with no treatable condition and thus irrelevant to the services provided by A&E, Kelly could disagree, she could harass Beth about it. She could develop a strong suspicion that there is a baby somewhere. She could provoke Beth to call the social services. And when they arrive, in the form of Trish, Kelly could berate Trish for suggesting that, if there is a baby, it might be taken into care. Trish would tear a strip off Kelly for speaking out of turn. Kelly, far too involved with Mary, would find herself in a world with which she can't quite communicate, from which she begins to feel alienated. Mary, Kelly, Beth and even Trish are all tinged by the colours of our theme. They are all essential to the telling of each other's stories. Every beat in any of these stories deepens our understanding of the others. And every strand is working in service to a coherent whole. This, if you can get it right, is what good episodes are made of.

Finally, the story document required us to introduce the burgeoning romance between social worker Trish and charge nurse Charlie Fairhead, with their first encounter. Eyes across a bloody body might have been nice. Happening to sit down at the same table in the canteen, or accidentally touching hands, would also serve. But if all our stories are beginning to tell us something about communication, and the lack thereof, between people who desperately need to say something but can't, the real interest is in Charlie and Trish finding each other attractive but losing the opportunity to take it further, at this stage, because they are unable to say so. At the end of the episode, they encounter each other in the car park as they're heading home. They exchange a few words. Then they pause. This is the moment when one of them could say something to initiate a deeper relationship. But all Charlie can manage is, 'Well, see you around.' And Trish goes. Charlie stands there, wishing he'd said something more. Cue titles. If you think about it, 'Well, see you around' is an incredibly feeble line with which to end an episode full of blood and thunder. But, because it completely exemplifies the themes we've been contemplating, it has the force of a powerful jab to the solar plexus. Better still, we get it without explanation.

And so to the treatment, the delineation of scenes. This is a blueprint for the final script which can, and usually does, change in the writing.

What worked well with the maternity shop is that all the background to the story, and its themes, are there in the visuals. Once we got to the script, this scene was split into two parts. In the first, we just get a view of Mary, and see her being clocked by Mrs Bristow, the manageress. In the second, Mary grabs some clothes, makes a bolt for the door and is caught on the way out. It's in a third scene, when she's waiting for the police, that Mary collapses. The reason we split the scene is because the first carried sufficient information for the measure of the beat. A ragged Mary shuffling suspiciously among racks of expensive maternity ware, the sound of children laughing with their relaxed parents, and a busy manageress just glancing over and narrowing her eyes gives us plenty of dramatic information. It's enough to take in for the moment.

I came across a delightful debate among poets who were asking where to break a line of free verse which isn't governed by a set number of beats. After much discussion somebody suggested: when it's full. Much the same applies to the measure of a scene. Once it has told a story, or completed an arc within a story, you might want to chop it there and go somewhere else for a while. There is no chronological rule that governs the length of a scene. While three pages is quite a long time in television, if the story calls for more, then give it more. Mary's first little moment in the shop lasted a few seconds. But it provided everything we needed to take that first step in the journey.

So we've got our themes, our ideas, characters, moments, a deft interplay of interconnected stories and, most importantly, a compelling desire to write it. The next step is largely a question of structure.

7

14. INT. DAY. CRASH. 09.45.

SUZIE is still critical. MED REG comes in. JULIAN hands
over.

15. INT. DAY. MATERNITY SHOP. 09.45.

MARY is an unlikely customer, she is 29 but looks 39, her
clothes are shabby but she's not quite yet a down and out.
She has let herself go, it doesn't look like she washed this
morning or combed her hair this week. Her movements are tired
but agitated. The Manageress, MRS BRISTOW, keeps a wary eye.
MARY almost recklessly snatches a set of baby clothes, stuffs
them in her bag and goes for the door. MRS BRISTOW blocks
her, retrieves the clothes, MARY protests, they're for her
baby and tries to take them back. MRS BRISTOW tells a Sales
Assistant to call the police, grabs MARY'S arm and forcibly
leads her towards the back of the shop.

16. INT. DAY. INTERVIEW ROOM. 09.50.

GEOFF is giving as much information to DUFFY as he
can. She said she's run away from home, had an arguement,
been living rough for about a week, broke, cold, hungry. He
just felt sorry for her - he's on his own, they hit it off.
DUFFY says what, and you don't even know her second name?
GEOFF says it must look shabby, and admits that it is. What a
terrible way to go if she dies, unknown, away from home, used.

JULIAN comes in. GEOFF says how the hell is he going to
explain this to his wife - now the whole neighbourhood knows.
JULIAN says never mind the bloody neighbourhood, and then,
abruptly JULIAN'S attitude changes. Is GEOFF feeling okay?
He says he's got a touch of flu. JULIAN asks how long he's had
this, (3 weeks), when did he move in? (3 weeks ago). JULIAN
asks DUFFY to get GEOFF a cup of tea. DUFFY looks at JULIAN
as if he's gone mad.

7

STRUCTURE

WHY STRUCTURE?

Why does anything have structure? Look around. The chair you're sitting on has structure. And you're probably grateful for it. A chair without a proper structure isn't a chair we can trust. The window. The room. The walls. The building. The waste bin: it's a container with an aperture. Why? What if it didn't have an aperture? Would it still be a waste bin? And what about your body? Does that have a structure? If it didn't, you wouldn't be much use. You'd be a blob on the floor. You might be charming, sensitive, insightful and fascinating, but all attempts to communicate these attributes would be frustrated by the fact that much of you has soaked into the carpet. The more you look, the more you see structure. It can be elaborate or simple. It might depend on highly refined geometric principles, as with snowflakes, leaves and shells. Or it can be fairly basic, like a table, which requires a minimum of three legs to work (two legs doesn't cut it, somehow, when it comes to tables).

One answer might be so that it can do its job; so that it can function. The job of a chair is to be sat on. If it has a tendency to collapse the moment weight is applied to it, we probably won't sit on it again. There is also a qualitative evaluation, relating to how well any object fulfils its function. A chair that wobbles might be OK to sit on, but it will become irritating after a while. The more its structure conforms to the basic principles by which it is intended to function, the more functional it will be.

A complex thing, such as a human body, consists of many different systems working in harmony. Every organ, muscle and gland operates by virtue of its structure, while the whole arrangement is upheld by a supporting skeleton. It's interesting to note that, while the components of a skeleton need to be rigid, their articulation is arranged to facilitate movement. The stronger the rigidity, the better its articulation. Horses have pretty sturdy structures, not so they can stand still, but so they can gallop.

A skeleton is also a living, responsive thing. Our bones are the factories of blood. They grow and change over time. They can heal themselves, to a degree, when injured. The spine, arguably our most crucial arrangement of bones, is the conduit of much of our nervous system.

Essential as the skeleton is, it isn't necessarily the first thing we remark on about a person. We're unlikely to say, 'Ah, Jim, yes, an excellent skeleton' – although we might admire the bone structure of his face. If there were something awry with the skeleton, we might be drawn to mention it, or politely not. But a properly working skeletal structure is as unobtrusive as it is necessary. In the same way, a good screenplay doesn't display its structure except for the fact that it works. When we come out of a good movie, we usually talk about the moments, characters or themes. The structure just is. Unless there's something wrong with it. A limping plot might be symptomatic of a broken bone. An obvious plot has bones exposed.

If the aim of a good structure is to remain invisible, just as bones should only be of interest to an orthopaedic surgeon, we, as writers, need to start messing around with them. We need to study the anatomy of story in order to understand what structure does and how it works.

NARRATIVE STRUCTURE

Since we take structure for granted in almost every aspect of our lives, it's a puzzle why so many writers find it tricky to master in story. There are some who fear and loathe it. There are even those, leaning on perfectly structured tables, sipping from perfectly structured coffee cups, breathing molecules into lungs where beautifully structured blood vessels are waiting to collect the oxygen, who declare that structure is unnecessary.

Personally, I found it the most difficult thing to get right. At one point I was even that fellow lambasting structure as antipathetic to the creative act; until, that is, I felt the need to communicate my art to more than just a few, equally pretentious friends. As I've said, in my experience, most writers are gifted with a talent or talents for one or more aspects of this art. There are those who can produce reams of effortless dialogue, or excel in catching a mood with some unexpected motif. Others are meticulously brilliant at structure right off the bat. If you fall into the latter camp, this subject holds no terrors. But I have rarely come across anyone who has it all in place, right from the beginning. And what we are not given, as it were, has to be worked for.

The notion that structure and creativity are antithetical is fairly pervasive, especially among the lazy. But, as we've seen, both are necessary. Structure is an aspect of the 'fine' part of the frenzy. It is the care and precision without which the creative expurgation of our inner meaning is just a rant. To go back to the old adage, you need two wings to fly. Those who declaim that creativity must flourish unfettered and those who believe that you just have to get all the right bits into the right order are both wrong. All the right bits, carefully arranged, can be as unsatisfying, in their way, as the dribbling incoherencies of a drug-induced ramble. Structure, as we have seen, is not there to constrain, but to facilitate. Its function is not to enslave creativity but to liberate it. Get the structure right and you have the perfect vehicle for your genius. Get it wrong and your genius might be twiddling its thumbs in a lay-by, waiting for the mechanic to show up.

Structure becomes a constraint when we attempt to learn it as a formula. There are many theories of dramatic structure knocking around, most of which are undeniably useful. You will find advocates of five acts, three acts, 22 steps, journeys into woods and journeys into caves. Meanwhile, the rich terminology of 'inciting incidents' and 'keepers of gates' has a valid part to play in our attempts to understand the shape of story. I would advise you to investigate all of them, if you have time, as a learning process. Once you've got the hang of story, you'll rarely go back to them except as a diagnostic tool to find out why something isn't working: perhaps you've meandered too long before the inciting incident kicks in, or your main character lacks the motivation for a proper hero's journey. Do note, however, that in the industry these terms are rarely used and, in some quarters, are laughed at if they crop up in a story document.

What matters is that you don't lose sight of what you want to say, the themes you wish to explore and the story you want to tell. That it seems to jumble up sometimes, as we turn it into screenplay, is sometimes a part of the process. Writing is as much discovery as execution. It can take a while for story to ripen. That a first draft doesn't yet work doesn't make it wrong. If we can reconnect, in the face of dull characters, leaden dialogue and flat scenes, with the original urge of its Stuff, we might even enjoy the toil of disenjumbling our material into a shape that other people can appreciate (and love).

I won't rehash all the many excellent theories that have helped numerous writers to fulfil their ambitions, since these are readily available elsewhere (I commend anything by Robert McKee, Joseph Campbell, Blake Snyder and my good friend Craig Batty, among others). What I will offer is a few approaches to story that you can add to your reflections. Hopefully you will find them useful. Again, let me say that you shouldn't apply these as formulae. They are a means of unfolding your own sense of story. If your writing says something of interest without conforming to any template, then congratulate yourself. But if you're stuck, or if you want to lay something out before you embark on the writing proper, or if a story is crunching to an intractable knot somewhere towards the end, or if you keep getting to the same place in a story before scrapping it and moving on to something else (thus condemning yourself to a lifetime of unfinished efforts), it's worth considering a little structural theory.

We've already looked at vertical structure. This belongs, in a sense, more to the consideration of theme and idea than narrative form. Still, without it, your narrative form will end up all over the place. It's a bit like a riff from which a jazz musician can improvise. The simpler and clearer that core melodic idea, the more adventurous the musician can get. The moment the music wanders so far from the melody or its variations that it becomes something else... well, then it becomes something else. Your audience will start to fidget. Somebody will turn to the person next to them and say, 'Did we turn the gas off?' As the level of listening noticeably drops, the good musician will hurry back to his theme, returning, if he can save it, the room's attention to the music.

THE ABC OF STORY

This isn't quite narrative structure, but it provides a useful foundation to the development of story shape. It will also help when you're sorting and selecting your material at the outset, or in the rewrite. At some point it will be your trusted friend when you come to pitch the idea in written or verbal form. Think of it as a helpful ghost sitting at the end of your nib (or somewhere in the circuitry of your keyboard), gently pressing you back to the point.

If you have an idea for something, and especially if you've already started to work on it, think of the various bits of material as belonging to one of the following categories:

A   That without which it wouldn't be what it is
B   That which embellishes and enhances
C   That which does no harm

Category A deals with material that is indispensable to your story. What would *The Godfather* be without a mafia family? What would it be without Don Corleone (which is to say a Godfather)? What would it be without Michael? What would *The Sound of Music* be without mountains? Or children? What would *Taxi Driver* be without a taxi? Or *High Noon* without a clock?

Spend a bit of time thinking over your favourite films and asking which elements of story, character, or motif are so essential that without them the story would not be what it is.

This might seem rather obvious, but how many times do we work on a script without really knowing what sits at its core? How many times do we leave out something essential, or elevate to the status of essential something that, in truth, is colour at best, indulgence at worst? I have attended script conferences that go round in circles trying to sort out a story; until somebody realises that one of our integral fixtures is, in fact, an optional extra. Its removal liberates all the other elements to find their proper place. So if your story is refusing to hold its shape, take a long, unsentimental look at its elements and ask if they really are 'A' grade. If not, then reclassify them. If they are 'B' grade, then they will, and must, behave in a different way.

'B' grade material provides our subplots and lesser moments. Often these are optional. The chicken restaurant in *Breaking Bad* could have been a burger restaurant, or we could have gone straight for the laundrette. If you peruse the knock-on effects of choosing a restaurant and the many interesting scenes it created (the boss man being mistaken for a low-paid catering worker, the lovely line 'Enjoy your meal' when Walt declines the opportunity to continue making meths), you will appreciate what a good choice it turned out to be. But the pitch would not have started with 'A couple of crystal meth manufacturers go into a chicken restaurant'. It should be noted that 'B' elements are hard-working components of the drama, in spite of their lesser positions in the hierarchy. Firmly connected to the vertical line, they never waver for a moment. But they allow us to explore theme from a different angle. If, at the last minute, the design department hadn't been able to get a chicken restaurant and had had to make it a burger joint instead, something would have been lost, but the series would not have fallen to pieces.

'C' moments are all those things we add to the story because we want to, because we like them. They are turns of dialogue that particularly tickle us. They are incidents, perhaps drawn from life, that we've always wanted to shove into a script somewhere. They are a little jaunt away from the central premise down an interesting back road to take in the scenery. You can see where I'm going with this. 'C' moments don't, in fact, exist. There is no such thing as an energy-neutral moment in a drama. A moment either contributes to the momentum of the story and the exploration of theme, or it detracts. If a moment, character, line of dialogue, scene or entire subplot doesn't contribute to the whole, then it has to go. Otherwise it will rob your story of its shape, energy and purpose. It will rob your audience of their time and attention. 'C' moments are illegal in the world of story. And the punishment is the sound of seats slapping upwards as members of the audience gradually abandon your film at the premiere (as they do in Venice – they're generally too polite to walk out in the UK).

AN ACT

If the purpose of playing is, according to Shakespeare, to hold a mirror up to nature, it follows that what we see reflected is entirely natural, which is to say integral to our ordinary experience as human beings. The implication is that there is nothing artificial about structure, in spite of the complex terminology and labyrinthine systems which sometimes attempt to explain it. We might hope to find its principles, therefore, within the architecture of common understanding and of our own experience.

The word 'drama' means, according to its etymological derivation, 'an act'. In a sense, then, a single work of drama follows the laws pertaining to a single act. If we can understand the laws of action or, to be more precise, the laws governing the performance of a single act, we will be more than halfway towards a connection with what is more scarily called structure.

Fortunately we don't have to look too far to understand action since we perform it all the time, every day. We are already experts; which might explain why children know a good story when they hear one, or why you don't need an MA in screenwriting to judge a movie. Reading this book is an act. Turning the page is an act. Following this sentence, cognising this word, is an act. Far from being some alien construct, then, narrative structure is as familiar to us as breathing. We can afford, at this moment, but just for a moment, to rub our hands with glee.

So how does an act unfold? Take a moment to study your own understanding of action. Think of an act, any act. It might be some grand pursuit such as joining a profession, studying to that end, writing up your CV or going off to make a cup of tea. Do these different acts, unfolding to various scales, nevertheless have a common shape? As we've just noted, there are acts within acts. Every beat of the heart, every blink of your eye, is an act.

We are back to fish unaware of the waters in which they move. So detach yourself from the overfamiliar. What do we know of action? Obviously it begins at some point, ends at some point, and a whole load of stuff happens in between. Good start. We're almost there. But let's dig a little deeper.

What is needed before any act can begin?

If you like, have a think about this. Go right back to the beginning, to the very foundation of action, to the first, most elemental component of all phenomena. Take some time. I would rather you came up with the answer. It's already there if you take a moment to reflect.

Well, of course, you need time and space. You need a universe. Without a universe, not a lot's going to happen. There would be no one for anything to happen to. There would be nothing.

This might seem a little facetious, but there's an important point here. If you're going to tell a story, you have to create a story world. And precisely what your world consists of will determine what can or cannot happen within in it. It will have laws, content, possibilities and parameters. It will, in that sense, function very much like any world. Just as certain plants can only grow from certain soils, so the constituent elements of your world will be conducive to a particular range of inhabitants. They will dictate a certain kind of speech. The characters will share, to some extent, a common understanding of how things are.

There are many off-the-peg worlds. Even wacky sci-fi worlds can be off-the-peg. This is handy if you're looking for an easy range of predetermined elements. Just bear in mind that, according to our botanical principle, cliché worlds tend to produce cliché characters, cliché moments and cliché dialogue. If you're looking for authenticity and originality, then consider your Stuff. Mary turned up in an upmarket maternity shop because it instantly alienated her; it showed us the world from which she had been excluded (the sort of world our doctors might have been familiar with); and of course it introduced the possibility that she might be a mother.

The stronger your story world, the more liberties you can take with it. But there is a compact between story and audience that what takes place must be natural to, and consistent with, its laws. William Wallace saying 'Stuff this. Let's just use our light sabres' might have won Mel Gibson the battle, but it would have lost him much of the audience.

On the other hand, the arrival of a spaceship in *The Life of Brian* was entirely consistent with a self-referentially filmic world in which the only thing you could expect was the unexpected.

Working to the strictures of a story world can be problematic. And it can be tempting to break its rules for the sake of a narrative movement, or emotional beat. When he was very small, we took our son to football lessons. After brief stints as a reluctant forward, indifferent midfielder and distracted defence, he ended up in goal. It only took a moment for him to solve the problem of balls shooting past him by moving the two posts together. Job done? Perhaps not. What makes the game is what cannot be changed. What makes the challenge is how we adapt to those fixtures. The same applies to your story. Telling it from within the parameters of a consistent world might demand brilliant solutions to tricky problems, but then brilliant is usually better than easy and, in any case, that's half the fun.

Time and place, then, will give you many of the elements you need but there are still decisions to make. In story terms, geography and chronology are merely subsets of story place and story time. Thus, you could set a film in present-day North London with the same streets and shops providing the setting for romantic comedy, geezer movie, heist movie, farce, political thriller, apocalyptic catastrophe, and so on. Each genre brings its own range of elements. If you have two characters, in love since their teens but forced to live separate lives, finally meeting up outside a flower shop only to be blown away by a hitman, you might very well alienate the romantic comedy audience. On the other hand, the same scenario might make for a rather tedious preamble to your crime yarn. Worlds are not just places but textures, tones and emotional content. They even determine the way the characters speak. 'Forsooth, let us prithee robbeth that financial institution yonder,' would sound a bit odd in a heist movie. Likewise, 'What are you looking at, you nob-head?' wouldn't quite square with a Jane Austen adaptation.

Two principles at work here are vertical structure and, if you recall it, the banana. Our banana analogy suggests that all of the elements are aspects of each other. Thus time and place are also theme, idea, story, characters, visual motifs and style. All of these elements are as much a result of your decisions about the story world as your decisions about the story world are drawn from their needs. Vertical structure, meanwhile, dictates that your theme and meaning will determine the shape of the world in which they can be explored.

And, of course, artistry has a part to play in this. Many people admire the film *Insomnia*, both the Norwegian original and the American remake. Personally, I felt that both versions spent too much time and energy lolling about the world. There was so much grey landscape, dripping drain pipes, mist and melancholy that it seemed like we'd forgotten the story. Film buffs might disagree with me over this example, but the point is that you can overdo your world. You can start to indulge in it. It's a bit like enjoying the soil in which you intend to plant a herbaceous border so much that you decide, in the end, not to clutter it with flowers.

At the opposite end of the spectrum is 'white room' drama, in which little attention has been paid to the world in which the characters exist, from which they have emerged and by which they have been shaped. At its extreme, there appears to be nothing in the room, no chairs to sit on, or windows to gaze out of, no decanters to pick up, pour from and set down again. It never rains or shines. All that happens is talk, which gets very dull very quickly. More than that, it is uneconomical, as we shall see when we consider visual motif. The language has to do all the work and ends up working far too hard. The worst instances of this are usually in unmade screenplays; unmade for obvious reasons.

Between these extremes there are shades, and where you want your story to fall on the spectrum is up to you, but here are some points to bear in mind:

- **Everything that happens in your story comes from the story world.** Nothing can happen from outside of it. So choose the world carefully. And, having chosen, get to know it. What are the possibilities? What are the limitations? What is inevitable (winter in Denmark needs woolly jumpers, summer in Los Angeles sunglasses, and busted space stations a good oxygen pack)? Do some research. If it's a particular place that you can visit, go there. Spend some time in it. Breathe it in.

- **Your world is not just a physical place at a point in time.** It is tone, texture and mood. You might have a particular angle that you wish to explore, but check out some others. You never know when some detail might enrich a feel for the place.

- **But don't get seduced by it.** This is a story, not a guided tour. Remember the banana: world that is not story, character and theme is just scenery.

- **You are not starting off with a thinly sketched universe that gets richer as you proceed.** Instead, the world is in place from the beginning and, through your story, you explore it. So you can choose when and how much to reveal at any given time. It might be a while before we realise there are monsters in the cellar, but, when the revelation comes, it has to feel that they were always there.

- **The stronger and more convincing your world, the more fun you can have with it.** You must be able to deliver surprises, twists and unexpected shockers without breaking the spell of belief.

- **Think about the world off-screen.** What's going on outside of what's being shown? Your world is a constantly moving, developing place. Think of its existence before you started the story. Go right back, if you like. How did this world happen? When were the seeds of civil war first sown? When did the tyrant dig his claws in? That alien invasion was probably planned weeks ago: by whom and why? You might not include the information in the script but its implicit presence will give the world authenticity.

- **If your story is flagging, or your characters start to feel weak (or snap under pressure), then take a look at the world.** Is it strong? Does it extend beyond the scene, both spatially and chronologically? Is there stuff going on we never see? Where did that barista serving your main character in Scene 28 come from? Where does she go from here? Does she live nearby or catch a bus? This isn't the neurosis of a director insisting that even the drawers we don't open are full. It is your feel for the world, your themes and ideas woven into every detail. That barista might be slightly distracted, so the already-impatient hero has to ask twice. Or she's feeling a bit tender today and recoils from his gruff instructions. It all adds to the mix, to the story, to the weft and texture of the world.

So let's pursue our original question a little further. What do we need for an action to take place? We've established that we need a world, and hopefully that isn't a debatable point. What next? Have a think. It's fairly obvious.

You need someone to perform it. You need an agent (in the story sense, though the other might be useful too). This brings in the hero/heroine/protagonist/central or main character. Call him or her what you will, their function is to be the agency of the action.

Just as everything that happens within your world must be natural to that world, so everything your hero does and says, or doesn't do and doesn't say, must be natural to his or her nature. Bear in mind, also, that your main character emerges from, and is a part of, the story world. There is much comedy to be had from putting the wrong character into the wrong world. Mr Bean is at his funniest when engaged with some serious and important activity. His boredom during the Opening Ceremony of the 2012 Olympic Games has to be one of the finest moments in comedy history. But you must pay as much attention to a character's incongruity as you would to their propriety. We'll look at character later, but, for now, just consider how your central character belongs (or doesn't) to the world in which he or she will perform an action.

Just as we considered the world outside of the scene, its history, and all the things just round the corner that we may never see, our hero isn't fresh out of the box. Things have happened. Even if we meet him or her at the moment of birth, there is family history to contend with. Were they wanted? Do the parents have issues? Are they poor, rich, kind or cruel? Into what kind of world is he or she born? Again, as with the exploration of the world, your character might be revealed slowly but should arrive fully cooked. The purpose of their first scenes is not to create a character (who is already there) but to establish certain attributes of that character in the perceptions of the audience.

From this we gather that you should know which of your characters is the main one. The act is their act. The spine of the story will be their journey. All of your characters will have journeys, but the line of action comes from only one.

It sometimes happens that the main character remains obdurately passive, as a kind of holding position of attributes, neither too this, nor too that. The other stories start to rotate around them until secondary characters become more interesting and start to hog the stage. But, however interesting they become, the story will struggle with a shapeless blancmange at the centre. This often happens when the central character is too much the writer's view of him or herself; when it's 'my story'. The hero thus becomes the translucent spectacles through which we peer at the world. Either you have to switch to one of the more interesting characters as your hero, or give your hero a proper character. We can be fooled by some much-loved characters who are defined by their passivity, such as Lenny from *Of Mice and Men*, or Chauncey Gardiner from *Being There*, or

Dustin Hoffman's eponymous character in *Rain Man*. But look again and you'll see that, while they are the focus of the story, it is as a MacGuffin, not as the story itself. In these instances, it is usually somebody else, observing them, affected by them, concerned for them, who drives the action forward, whose story it actually is.

There are many great films which don't have one single central character. *Crash, Magnolia, The Big Chill, Peter's Friends, The Breakfast Club* and *St Elmo's Fire*, to name but a lot. An extreme instance of a single movie with multiple narratives is *Paris, je t'aime*, in which the stories have no connection with each other beyond taking place in Paris. But there is a clue in this. Ensemble stories still need a central focus, a vertical structure around which to play. It could be an event or distinct place which brings the stories, and their characters, together. Anything more diverse becomes a sequence of short films either attached end to end or spliced together. It still matters that each story has its central character, in a world, with a journey to undertake.

So let's say we now have our main character, our protagonist. The word protagonist, incidentally, simply means 'the actor of primary importance'. It's interesting that, in the Greek terminology, character and action are one and the same. But this is simply an example of our banana analogy at work. So we shouldn't be too surprised.

We meet our protagonist, then, after they have done and said, or not done and said, all the things that have brought them to this point. But the story will only start when they begin to act. Nice as it is to recline for hours on a chaise longue, watching somebody else do the work, it doesn't make for drama. So what gets us on to our feet? What prises us from the sofa, or the bed? Think about it.

Let's call it an impulse. It's a need, a want, a desire. Something has appeared in the mind; you could call it a thought, but it might not even be as clear as that. Of course, many thoughts and impulses pass through the mind. Many of them, thankfully, we never act on. What passes through our character's mind has much to do with the world and their understanding of it. So let's assume that thoughts and desires are in a constant flux. Shall I kill the king and steal his throne? Meh. Too much trouble. But sooner or later something sticks.

It receives assent. It is granted will. In that moment are summoned the powers of action. Another word for this is 'emotion', which means to move. The power of that assent, will and emotion, should be enough to sustain your character to the grand finale. If it's weak, vague or too whimsical, it is likely to peter out just as you're working yourself up to the climax.

The moment of assent can be obvious, or secreted within multiple layers of material. It could even have happened before your narrative starts. But it must be there, throbbing away, the engine of action, of character. The moment it stops throbbing is the moment your story ends.

Without a motive, action is just reflex. It doesn't make for story because the character performing the act isn't engaged. Likewise, activity without some kind of character commitment is just the noise of particles colliding with all the meaningful significance of Brownian motion. It might make for a good horde of zombies but, somewhere in the middle of them, somebody has to want a better future for themselves (and maybe the people they care about) for it to touch us with the warm finger of meaning. It is not enough just to stagger about eating people.

Quite recently I was taking a seminar with a bunch of young filmmakers. We were talking through stories that they were proposing to write. There was some good in all of their ideas but I was beginning to get fidgety at the constant use of the word 'just'. I would ask: why does the character go abroad? The answer would be: he just feels like leaving home for a while. Why do they get together? They just happen to bump into each other. Why did he kill his neighbour? He just got fed up with the noise at night. The word 'just' is only there to drain our energy and rob the story of its power. Characters are characters because they engage in an action. Dramatic action is motivated by need, desire, impulse and assent. If we study our own experiences, it is often difficult to remember those moments when we didn't particularly want anything all that much, and nothing really happened anyway. They are difficult to remember because the mind has discharged them as valueless. Why inflict this on your audience?

The events we remember always have a need/desire/impulse behind them, either fulfilled or unfulfilled. That's what we're interested in. If you want to understand this crucial stage in the sequence of events that adds up to an act, which is to say a drama, you don't have to look much further than your own daily life.

So where are we? Motive. Our character is now moved to perform an action. It might be spectacular or mundane. Bear in mind that its dramatic strength is determined by the power of thematic content, not by how loudly people shout, or how fast they drive. Sometimes, the tiny things are the most powerful. Rat Lady nearly disappeared under the tumult of far more startling events in the A&E department. But motive has deep roots. And is not to be toyed with lightly. Just as a cat purring on your lap is a sweetly domesticated form of tiger, and a poodle owes something of its nature to wolves, so the mildest of impulses has its origins in a world of much fiercer beings. Sit down for ten minutes, with your eyes closed, and want nothing. Difficult? Of course. Because need, want, motive and emotion are integral to character. They are at the root of our need to survive, to keep warm, to eat, to find a home, to rest, to make love, to procreate. They are powerful because they are powers. Your character fishing under the sofa for a biscuit is a highly domesticated version of an animal leaping on to the back of its prey, risking everything on the accuracy of that lunge, and the strength in those claws. Most of us have moments when the niceties are stripped away and we're faced with a more primeval urge. Those are the interesting times, the ones we write about. Those are what we chuck at our heroes. Bearing in mind, of course, that we don't have to be hanging from a cliff top by our finger-tips to feel worried. It can happen in a thud of post on the door mat.

Need. Response. Impulse. Assent. Tidy words, but it all gets messy in the pulsating psyche of a fully fleshed-out character. Which is exactly as it should be.

What next?

Again, just think about your own experience. After all, we're drawing from life here. The laws of drama are the laws of nature. What happens when you want something and decide to do something about it?

Well, it's there in the question. You do something about it. You make an effort. You want to climb a mountain? Buy some rope. You want money? Go get it. Power? Print leaflets. Grade eight piano? Practise. So far so simple. But what happens when we attempt to achieve almost anything at all? Again, from your own experience, honestly, what happens?

Imagine yourself back in that chaise longue. You feel a need. It's a slightly luxurious need, but a need nevertheless. Let's say you fancy a cup of tea. You click your fingers hoping for one to manifest out of thin air. It doesn't. You sigh. In your world, things don't happen like that. And even if you have serving staff who rush to do your bidding, you still have to click your fingers. Some effort is required. But let's say, in this imaginary world, that you have to get up and make it yourself. You move your legs a little, you take the weight on your arms. It's too much trouble. You give up. The story ends. But let's say you've got a little more gumption than that. Damn it, you will overcome the forces of gravity. You want a cup of tea and neither relativity, space-time curvatures or Newton's laws are going to stop you. Of such material are heroes made. You stand up and get your balance. Ah. The kettle is in the kitchen. You go there. You pour water into it. You wait for it to boil. You assemble all the necessary paraphernalia...

Usually, the making of a cup of tea requires minimal heroic fortitude and the end result is just a cup of tea. Few cups of tea, meanwhile, are life-changing experiences. So we won't have had to dig too deep for some hitherto unrecognised resource in the hidden recesses of our nature. But drama is about character too, and character is revealed through challenge. So let's turn up the heat a little. The kettle doesn't work. The tea bags have been destroyed by mice. There isn't a cup to be found. Now let's see how badly you want that tea. You go in search of a new kettle, but the hardware shop has closed. You drive to the next town, but hit a deer, or a person, or a vampire, on the way.

Not only is the world we live in so configured that we have to do something to achieve something; it seems to be the case that, the moment we make any kind of effort towards any sort of goal, however miserable or exalted, something gets in the way. As we saw, even getting out of a chair demands the overcoming of gravity. And that's just the start.

Much of the arc of an act involves a symbiotic dance between these two elemental powers: effort and opposition. In drama, we harmonise what, in life, can seem haphazard: the perennial determination of the universe to flout our intentions. So we place the obstacles carefully. Usually, we escalate them according to the efforts of which our hero is capable. We'll test him a little at first. And, if he survives that, we'll test him a little more. The idea is to test him, in the end, to breaking point. There is no hard rule, no mathematical equation for when to apply the pressure, how much of it, and what form it should take. Once again, this is a matter of artistry. You provide what your particular story needs at any particular time to fulfil itself.

As we've said often enough, much of what takes place on a daily basis is hardly the Stuff of drama. Our desires are fulfilled, more or less, without too much trouble; or the possibility of their satisfaction is so remote, it's not worth trying. But sometimes we really want something. Sometimes we'll dig deep and make an effort. And we won't be deterred. Not by anything. It might be studying for an exam. It might be swerving the car to avoid collision. It might be training for a marathon, or going on a diet, or giving up smoking. These aren't just activities. These are trials. They test us. And the more valuable the goal, curiously, the more effort they generally require. So have a think about those occasions when you really, really wanted something; when you had to make some sort of superhuman effort; when the challenges were so great you almost gave up; but you kept going. Hopefully you'll have at least one example to ponder! So what happens? Think about it.

The challenges we remember most are usually those that involved the overcoming of limits. These might have been physical, such as 'the wall' experienced by marathon runners, or psychological, such a fear of public speaking. The clincher comes when overcoming the limit seems impossible. The more impossible, the greater the effort required to succeed, the deeper we have to dig.

This infernal dialectic, then, of effort and opposition continues until the point when the character is tested to their utmost. This is when all that is superficial and spurious is burnt away to expose all that is natural and essential. The transformation is not into something or someone else but into ourselves. And that, more than the object of desire, is the purpose of the act. Athletes don't go to all that trouble just to get a shiny thing to hang around their neck. They could buy a shiny thing from the high street or online for a fraction of the cost of hiring a trainer for three years, not to mention pounding the track every morning, rain or shine. They train, I'm told, for that point in the race when they wonder why the hell they bothered, and run anyway.

This moment, when effort and opposition are so closely matched that it could go either way but for the hero reaching in for a handful of their true nature, is known as the crisis.

Drama, remember, is not an event but an act. Somebody wants something and does something about it. Effort and opposition are built into it. Any act sufficiently challenging to be meaningful has a moment of truth built into it. That truth consists of the revelation of a character's real nature. It is also where your themes are most openly exposed.

For this reason, it is not a bad idea, when thinking your story through at an early stage, to pay attention to the crisis. It's where you'll find your characters in their most essential form and your themes at their most powerful. It is the point to which all roads lead. You can tweak the beginning endlessly, but you won't fully know where to start until you know where you're going. Likewise, your plans for the ending could change drastically, depending on the ramifications of the climax. So it's a good thing to get the crisis in place, subject to creative adjustments and spontaneous inspiration, at an early stage of the planning.

In the scene we explored with Billy and Andy, the crisis was, arguably, the moment when Billy turned back and marched up to Andy. This is a moment sometimes called the turning point, quite literally illustrated here. Turning in this sense is of the nature of metanoia, which means a turning around of the mind. It is a sea change in the character. Thus Billy shifts from timid weasel to embodiment of a dynasty. The Billy who embodies the dynasty was always there, waiting to be discovered. Just for a moment the timidity is dissolved and he is free to exercise his natural powers.

Our last question is: when does an action end? You may not have to think about this too hard. Generally, the act is complete when the desired object has been won, or the impulse is expended, or both.

Having wrung your characters out, put them through the mill, pressed them in the mint, given them hell, or whatever it is that your levels of cruelty permit, what remains are the fruits of the action, sweet or bitter. This is the hero walking off into the sunset, or what is sometimes called the 'old men talking' scene. It is also called the denouement, or simply the close. I rather like the idea of 'fruits' because it follows the notion that an action seeded at the outset bears fruit in the conclusion. The two ends of your story are connected by a taut thread, the end being present in the beginning as the beginning is present in the end. It follows that the progression from beginning, via middle, to the end is not a tramline of happenings, but a single, unified act (within which will be many related turns of event). The term 'fruits', like denouement, is also morally and emotionally neutral. What happens simply happens. As the writer, you are an indifferent god. Those that must perish will perish. Those that must survive will survive. The only question you have to ask is: where does the action take them?

Once again, there is artistry and measure to this final stage. The measure, as ever, is quite simply: enough. Once the action is complete, you shouldn't linger too long. There is nothing left to say. And you ought to leave something hanging for the audience to reflect on as they head for home. This doesn't mean unresolved plot points, but a lingering melody they can hum the next day. It is not for you to drain the dregs of the barrel. But that's it, action over, job done, *le fin*, roll credits.

THE FIVE ACTS

I refrained from numbering the steps as we trundled through them in order to avoid converting them into a template, a formula. Along with that comes a kind of rigidity of form or, worse, its application without understanding. We might lapse into 'just get all the bits in the right place' in lieu of a truly visceral sense of action as a universal power. This is the automated approach to structure: maybe a bit more opposition, a bit less crisis, now where was that moment when the main character gives assent to an ideation...? We prod and poke until the living presence of a story that wants to be told gradually declines into a mumbling artefact with all the exuberance of a karaoke routine. Nevertheless, for the sake of clarity, we can look at the steps of action as five acts:

1. **Opening** – the world, the protagonist, the desire, and the assent to that desire
2. **Effort** – to achieve that desire
3. **Opposition** – to the effort
4. **Crisis** – in which opposition and effort are equally matched
5. **Fruits**

This could be called a five-act structure but should not be taken simply as a sequence. It's possible to juggle these acts any way you like. You can open with a hero already in pursuit of a desire. You can shift from effort to opposition and back again until the two are a blur of activity. You can even begin with the fruits and do everything in flashback. The sequence merely describes the fundamental laws of action, which all drama must reflect to be called, by definition, 'drama'.

If you look around you might notice that much of the universe is engaged in action of one sort or another. After a while it might even become obvious that every sentient being is driven by desire. Poke a beetle and see the extent to which it wants to survive. Watch a blackbird on the lawn to see how it needs food. That dog marking a lamppost, the cat delineating its territorial boundaries (over which it is prepared to fight), the sweet-shop owner, the financier climbing out of his fancy car, the fast-food worker glancing at the clock... desire is everywhere and permeates everything, along with the actions we take to fulfil it. Which makes it all the more surprising that so many scripts have 'characters' who aren't moved by desire, propelled by the laws of action, pushing for the acquisition of something for which they feel a need. The reason why scripts which don't fulfil the simple law of action are unsatisfying isn't because they fail to adhere to a particular narrative convention, but because their world doesn't belong to this universe. It isn't natural. We don't recognise it. It tells us nothing.

The key to understanding the structure of action, then, is not to apply formats but to feel it running through every moment of our day, through every thought we think, every emotion we feel. It is to be explored in every being we come across, be it our mother, friend, a train conductor, shop assistant, pet rabbit or random ant. After a while you won't have to fuss over what comes where in your narrative arrangement, because you understand that structure is not a sequence but a dynamic. It gives us the shape of the whole story. But it also informs every scene, every line, every beat in the action. Once this energy is harnessed, it will achieve that most sublime incarnation of a perfect structure: it will be unnoticeable. If we thought about it, we could recognise the skeletal form of a pouncing tiger, evident from the way it moves. But what we really appreciate is the tightening of sinew, the contraction of muscle, the focus of the eyes and ferocity of intent. We're not too much distracted by its bones even if, without them, there would be little more than a rug.

Desire and action are so close to us that, for much of the time, we don't recognise their dominion over our lives. Even when we think about action, it tends to be in terms of a to-do list, or things we're dreading, or looking forward to, or have to do, or can't wait to finish. Our feelings rapidly cloud our perceptions and off we go, never taking a look at the hands of desire and aversion working our strings. Sometimes we tap into the underlying urges that propel us from day to day: survival, procreation, personal development, and so on. When that happens we feel a little less complex, a little more essential. You could even say more human. So we bungee jump, gamble on horses, imbibe potions, or set ourselves challenges to strip away the luxuriance of whim until we feel again what it is to be alive. Or we can watch a movie.

Through the mirror of a play we see, obviously, lots of things happening: people doing things, suffering things, bad karma coming back to bite them, redemptions, retributions, and the rest of it. So much is familiar enough. But this is a special mirror that reflects not just outward movements but inner forces: virtue, viciousness, and the prevailing ideas. In that moment of genuine recognition we are, for the moment, no longer confined by them. We are free beings. This is why Hamlet put the play on. He wanted the king, just for a moment, to see what he was and what he was doing. He aimed to catch his conscience, which is to say, to provoke the dissolution of his identity with the criminal king and a consequent restitution of a man imbued with reason, compassion and understanding. Claudius, stepping free of the weave of desire and aversion, could make his own judgements about his own impulses, his own actions.

Drama serves many functions. It entertains, plays with ideas, gives us a cathartic experience, harmonises the emotions, to name just a few. But it also allows us to see the forces behind our lives. It achieves this by turning us into observers. A room full of people from different backgrounds, with different experiences, having had very different days, entertaining different thoughts and feelings, can share in a singularity of vision that liberates them all. They may be liberated from different things, but the fact of liberation is the same for everyone. No wonder people flock to these places. And it's easier than bungee jumping.

THE ORPHIC PARADIGM

THE POWER OF MYTH

Myths echo through to us from the earliest days of human record. These are the stories told by our forebears for all the reasons we have already discussed. There have been many valuable studies on the mythic content of narrative structure. I would advise you to explore as many of them as you can. Some of them have given invaluable help to prospective writers, helping to nurture potent understandings of the perennial shapes of story. Although the word 'myth' has been oddly derided in recent times, perhaps as part of a general attack on those who take certain myths literally and then attempt to convince others of their misconception, we shouldn't dismiss the medium because of those who abuse it. Myth works to make sense of the world, to guide the human psyche through the labyrinthine complexities of life, to illustrate the deeper movements of ideas, passions and motives, and to express, in figurative form, a perennial truth.

The outward form of myth is often to confer longevity, so that the stories, easily memorable, can be passed on through generations. We'll eat a fruit for its flesh, but, so far as the tree is concerned, the flesh is just a ruse to get us to eat it. The purpose of the plum is its seed. So while we might enjoy the obvious apparel of a myth, the characters, stories, cultural references, and so on, its purpose is to yield, for those who choose to look, a deeper meaning.

According to one scholarly tradition originating in the English Middle Ages, a mythic construct can be interpreted according to four levels.

THE LITERAL

This is the simple, outward appearance of the story. Hands of gods swirl clouds of mist through the inky chasms of a new universe. Brothers betray each other. Trumpets bring down walls. Lions dance to the music of drums. A warrior makes his weary way home over the seas. If many of our oldest myths have religious connotations, it's partly because those ancient philosophers, understanding the power of the medium, had a message to seal in their capsule of narrative; and partly because, for a long time, they held a monopoly on the institutions of learning. But there are classical myths too, and the myths of Bushmen, Maoris, First Nation Americans and others. Wherever people have looked for a way to express the invisibles of cause, the patterns of life, and the inner workings of the cosmos, they have developed stories to do the job. But they are not to be taken literally. This is just the candy coating. Big hand in the sky? Well, maybe. Two brothers squaring up to each other? Perhaps. What the cryptologist, the decoder, the student of myth needs to do is look beyond this level to the wires and pulleys giving it shape and movement. According to some early commentators, the less naturalistic and, in literal terms, implausible the outer story, the more likely it is to hold a hidden truth.

THE ALLEGORICAL

In its basic form, allegory is the crude literary construct of 'this means that'. A dog in the story is not a dog but an embodiment of Appetite, Humility, or Devotion. The man who kicks it is not just a man in a moment of rage, but a figure of Anger, Ingratitude, or Cruelty. In this sense, everything that takes place in the story is representative. When Venus appears on the scene, she is Love. If Satan shows up, he's the figure of Malice, Egoism or Greed. Purely allegorical dramas are most closely associated with mystery plays or productions of a morally elevating nature. They tend to be didactic in some way and, as such, don't quite reach the heights of questioning that belong to the complete play. The danger is a kind of fatuous oversimplicity. This works well enough as coded text, but more depth is generally demanded of the playwright. As we move on, the allegorical level gains fluidity; characters aren't a simple representation of one thing but can carry, at different times, a variety of ideas.

THE MORAL

This can be taken to mean the moral import of the story. For instance, to take care of your neighbours, or be loyal to your friends; or not to cheat, steal or tell lies. At its worst, this is a kind of homily, a wagging finger telling us not to be naughty. But this level has much to offer, concerned as it is with conduct or behaviour. Gregory the Great, apparently, first designated the word to signify rights and wrongs in his analysis of the Book of Job. The point is that a story allows us to consider ideas in action. It is one thing to preach from a pulpit, or a soapbox, another to observe these forces at play, to know them, understand them, and thereby learn about ourselves. We can, of course, take the messages of those whom we consider wise and apply them to our daily life. In some ways, whether we like it or not, the messages we consume will influence how we behave. These might be from a theological text, or the lyrics of a pop song. They might be from a 'self-help' book, a work of philosophy, or the ideas gleaned from a novel or poem. The words go in. They are then experienced in practice. Arguably, the act of engaging with a story is to act out that story through our immediate, imaginative experience. We might watch an act of courage by a Scottish rebel and leave the cinema slightly more courageous. We might live through the consequences of lies as they rebound on a movie character and be a little less deceitful the next day. The moral level is the direct application of meaning on the sensibilities of the viewer. If the literal entertains and the allegorical informs, the moral level can bring about direct and immediate change.

THE ANAGOGIC

This is the real meat of the story. It's where the narrative material reaches into the heart of what cannot be expressed, directly, in words. This is the realm of universals, of theme, which we have already discussed at length. It is the unspoken terrain of the tale; the most coded, encrypted nub of the story. And it has to be so, if it is to bear real meaning, which is to say experience. For acolytes of the Mysteries, Eleusinian and others, the act of decoding was the process of initiation, of making ready to receive. This is achieved through participation. It is important to remember that we invite our audience not to watch, but to engage, to join in. That's why we harness their emotions through action, their empathy through character, and their sensibilities through the transmission of ideas, unexplained but implicit in the story. That is partly why it is essential not to tell, but to present. We have to leave a space for the audience to participate if they are to get to this level, the realm of meaning.

The eagle-eyed will have noticed that this configuration of meaning, from literal to anagogic, is just vertical structure with different labels and, perhaps, a different nuance. The power of any piece depends on how much of the anagogic the writer is in touch with. Whenever you feel something deeply, or have an insistent urge to tell a story, it is very likely that universals are demanding expression. At the same time, when you are exploring a story, it is up to you how far you reflect on its deeper levels. It often happens that a story will take us into territory we hadn't fully considered before, giving us a chance to ponder it as we write. The tousle-haired author staggering about the streets in a state of strange delirium might be engaging precisely with this level. It is the fine frenzy. It is the processing of Stuff.

THE STORY OF ORPHEUS

It is a useful exercise to take any myth and analyse it according to these four steps. But where does myth end and story begin? All stories of any substance are, in their way, mythic. The story of Easter might have given rise to a worldwide religious practice, including school holidays and chocolate eggs, but *The Long Good Friday* is a pretty good exploration of Hubris. So take any story and see if it conforms, in any way, with the levels. I will use one particular myth, that of Orpheus, for the simple reason that it's among the oldest, and most influential, to be found in the Western literary tradition. The story has been revisited many times over the centuries. Shakespeare makes reference to it, as we've seen, both directly and indirectly. The poem *Venus and Adonis*, one of his earliest known works, is a retelling of the story of Orpheus with modifications. It even provided material for a light opera by Offenbach, one tune of which will be instantly familiar as the can-can. My analysis draws largely from its retelling by Ovid, along with other sources. The details vary and you are invited to check them out for yourself. I have chosen one line through its different permutations for the sake of clarity. Here we go.

Orpheus is the son of Calliope, one of the Muses, and Oeagrus, the King of Thrace. He is therefore half-god and half-mortal. He is famous for playing the Apollonian lyre, a stringed musical instrument also known as the 'Orphic lyre', with which he can tame animals, soothe the troubles of an aching heart and even make the stones move. He is married to Eurydice, who is beautiful, intelligent and graceful. And they are very happy together. Unfortunately (that key word in drama), Aristaeus, the god of hunting, develops an untoward passion for Eurydice. When she rebuffs his advances he hides as a snake and bites her. She dies and is sent to the Underworld. Orpheus goes to fetch her, striking a bargain with Hades that she can follow him out, but with one proviso: if he looks back, she will have to remain. He leads her, looks back, and she's gone. He then wanders around miserably, his music so melancholy that nobody can bear to hear it. One day the women of Thrace get so fed up with the effect that he's having (the myth varies a little here but the outcome is consistent) that they descend on him in a frenzy and tear him to pieces. The Muses gather up his dismembered limbs and take him to Olympus where he resides to this day, an immortal.

We could break this down into various structural schematics from 22 steps to three or five acts. In this instance, we'll work with the classic three-act and our own five-act structures.

In three acts:

1. Orpheus and Eurydice are happy together. One day Aristaeus begins to lust after Eurydice. She rebuffs his attentions. Aristaeus is furious and kills her.

2. Orpheus tries, and fails, to rescue her from the Underworld. He becomes deeply depressed, wandering mournfully among the hills.

3. Eventually people get so fed up with him that they tear him to pieces. However, the Muses arrive, collect his scattered body parts and reassemble him as an immortal.

In five acts:

1. **Opening:** Orpheus and Eurydice are very happy together. When Eurydice dies, Orpheus resolves to bring her back from the dead.

2. **Effort:** Orpheus journeys to the Underworld to bargain for Eurydice's release. It is allowed on condition that he doesn't look back.

3. **Opposition:** Not trusting Hades, Orpheus glances back and Eurydice dissolves.

4. **Crisis:** Orpheus is so desolate that the women of Thrace finally rip him to pieces, if only to shut him up.

5. **Fruits:** Orpheus is reconstituted by the Muses and taken to mount Olympus.

It is possible to interpret the story in any number of ways. It is also simple enough to be reconfigured variously to emphasise different themes and story elements. One could say that the primary desire of Orpheus is to be reunited with Eurydice. But this never takes place. Being lifted off to spend eternity in the company of the Muses might seem like cold comfort. If we scratch a little deeper into his impulse, however, we might find that what he really wants is to be whole and complete once more. Losing Eurydice has created an imbalance. It is this imbalance, as we have seen, that demands the commencement of action, of story, of a journey towards restitution. What we have is Orpheus whole, complete and happy except for the loss of Eurydice. This equation of Orpheus minus Eurydice, in which Orpheus could be any protagonist and Eurydice any missing beloved (be it a person, an object or even a feeling – as of freedom in *The Shawshank Redemption*), is the beginning of all story.

As we saw in our exploration of the laws of action, until there is a perceived need, nothing will happen. That need could be looked at as a negative value to be restored. The man who wants a cup of tea is a man whole, happy and complete except for the absence of tea. Until he gets that tea, he cannot be whole, happy and complete. Once he gets the tea, he will be whole, happy and complete again. The quest might be for Eurydice, freedom, gold, or reconciliation, but the journey is towards wholeness, completeness and contentment.

We are using the story of Orpheus not as a template but as a paradigm. After all, his restoration is, essentially, metaphysical. Also, what happens to Eurydice? Moreover, we'd normally want some kind of justice done to the deeply villainous Aristaeus, the excessively pedantic Hades and, for that matter, the women of Thrace. So what does it give us?

Before we proceed, a thought which you might like to reflect on is that all the characters in this story are, in a sense, one character. Which is to say that Orpheus, Eurydice, Aristaeus, Hades, the women of Thrace, and the Muses can be best understood as a singularity. This is the key to its anagogic content.

In story terms, it means that all the characters, and all the narrative beats, are there because Orpheus needs them to be there. Orpheus might have thought that he was whole, happy and complete at the beginning of the story, but in reality this happiness, this perfection, was entirely dependent on the continuing presence of Eurydice, a mortal. That Eurydice would continue for ever is an impossibility. Happiness and eternal contentment are, therefore, incomplete from the start. If Aristaeus hadn't killed Eurydice, Orpheus could not have begun his journey towards a more complete perspective. If he hadn't been dismembered by a bunch of crazed ladies, he could not have been reconstituted. It might all seem a bit cruel, and perhaps it is, but that is how the world works. It is through challenge that an individual grows. The greater the challenge, the more it dismantles, the greater the possibility of change. The crazed women who dismember him are as much his beloved as Eurydice. This is made explicit in Shakespeare's poem, read in the context of the mythic structures from which it derives, in which Venus herself turns into the boar that kills Adonis (for extensive analysis of this see Ted Hughes's remarkable work, *Shakespeare and the Goddess of Complete Being*). And it is Venus who collects him thereafter.

You will have noticed the principle here of rooting character to vertical structure. If the protagonist embodies the exploration of your themes, all the other characters must be related to that. There is no random happenstance, no incidental character, no merely decorative cameo that works irrespective of its relationship to your central premise and your central character. This is the singularity of a play. It is the consistency of story which Shakespeare substituted for the cruder (and arguably misinterpreted) unities of Aristotle.

In a way, we have been treading and retreading the Orphic Paradigm in all of our story examples throughout this book. It's there in the Rat

Lady, the young man with his feet on the seats, Andy and Billy, Viola on the shores of Illyria. Revisiting them through the prism of the paradigm allows us to distinguish several common elements, many of which we have already considered in our exploration of the five-act structure.

THE DREAM

There are two facets to this. One provides that elusive sense of completeness, fragile enough in life and hazardous, of necessity, in the world of story. It may never be attained, but it provides a sense of what is possible if harmony and equilibrium are restored. It haunts the background to a world, however ugly. It may glimmer from time to time, like dappled sunlight, before the zombies lurch round the corner again. It is the aspiration of all characters, even the most evil. It might be called Hope. Without it, there is nothing to aim for, to motivate. It is the balance, harmony and happiness that the central character, however he or she perceives it, will pursue. If attained, the string section is entitled to go into raptures, while the director of photography can saturate the sunset with his richest filters. There is nothing left but that. Although represented in the expression 'And they all lived happily ever after', that happiness which they pursued was there all along, if only as a promise or expectation.

The other facet indicates the underlying, sometimes hidden, fractures of whatever ideal might pertain to the opening. Orpheus had a great life. He was well bred, top of the social order, good-looking, a fantastic musician, with a gorgeous wife. That'll do for most of us. What he doesn't understand is the extent to which his contentment is dependent on the continuation of those attributes. Eurydice, even without the intervention of Aristaeus, can't last for ever. Aside from natural causes, there are hazards in the undergrowth to which her mortality is vulnerable. Orpheus cannot control the world to his liking. He might consider himself happy, but his high-status, well-managed, tickety-boo lifestyle is a dream from which he needs to awake. Orpheus the happy chappy is a fabrication, an illusion. It is illusory because it believes itself to be self-sufficient. It needs to go if the hero is to find real completeness. And that could hurt.

LOSS

We can sometimes go to great lengths to minimise all and any disruption to our happiness. At the beginning of *Sexy Beast*, the satisfaction with which Ray Winstone's character stretches out in the sun will be for many (as it was for him) the apex of human joy. Which is fine. And if we're lucky enough to remain undisturbed in our utopian idyll, all the better for us. It makes for a familiar Facebook update, but not much in the way of story. Only when that peace is unbalanced does story begin: the story of its restoration. How you trigger that loss is up to you. The character might be perfectly content until something unfortunate happens. Or that contentment, as with Orpheus, might be illusory from the start, dependent on the preservation of an intrinsically transient thing. The first approach tends to generate fairly simple narrative yarns. The second can be rather more searching in its exploration of character. It probably doesn't have to be pointed out that the second is more difficult to pull off. But loss there must be. The equation, remember, is Orpheus minus Eurydice. But it could be a chemistry teacher diagnosed with cancer (*Breaking Bad*). It could be a young girl who wishes only to skip around the mountains being consigned to a household run with military precision (*The Sound of Music*). It might be a police officer whose wife is terminally ill, whose best friend has been crippled, and who feels let down by the profession he's served with his life (*Hana-bi*). It might just be a man's efforts to survive with his young son in a dangerous post-apocalypse landscape (*The Road*). This moment in which the imbalance occurs is sometimes called the inciting incident. It is the venomous bite of Aristaeus, the death of Eurydice. From here on, the hero has a job to do.

It might be worth noting that the means by which the loss occurs need to be consistent with the themes. Aristaeus is, after all, an aspect of Orpheus. He bites Eurydice because she has spurned his advances. She does this because of her loyalty to Orpheus. The elements are inextricably connected. So, however you choose to shatter the harmony of your hero, the closer you weave it into your central argument, the hero's character and the various themes you wish to explore, the more powerful your story will be.

THE UNDERWORLD

In strictly narrative terms, one could deduct the journey into Hades and still arrive at the same place. So is it just a subplot? The answer is both yes and no. At the literal level, yes, you could skip it. Although it does add to Orpheus's sense of grief that he's tried everything and failed. It also lets the audience know how much he is prepared to do; it signals his urgency. Thematically, his moment of distrust lets us into a more doubtful Orpheus. The loss becomes rather more than the wicked act of a rival. Orpheus now has some responsibility for her confinement to the Underworld. We know that restoration is not about reuniting with Eurydice, which is impossible, but – hard as it may seem – getting over her. In mythic, anagogic terms, the hero must step into the unknown, make an effort, confront the demons. And, because this is the story of human transformation, the error must be within. Bad things just happening to someone is merely bad luck. They have our sympathies. But it doesn't lead easily to psychological, emotional or spiritual transfiguration. The myth of Orpheus doesn't just have the poor man mourning the loss of his beloved; it makes him culpable. Like all strong writing, it knows how to twist the knife.

The journey into Hades is a journey into the world that remains, under normal circumstances, hidden. One etymological definition of the word 'hades' is 'invisible'. The word 'Underworld' offers another clue: this is the realm beyond the reach of our ordinary senses. It is the substratum. To look at it another way, it is the realm of intangibles that we considered in vertical structure. It is what is actually going on. If the character is to make any progress at all, he or she will need, at some point, to duck beneath the surface of things to explore the machinery lurking there, making everything move. It is Bourne realising that his whole life is being controlled by a sinister force. It is Keanu Reeves, in *The Devil's Advocate*, noticing something amiss at the legal practice where he works. And it is Hamlet, getting a message from the Underworld itself to tell him of something rotten in the state of Denmark.

What turned the young man with his feet on the seats into Stuff, into story material, was a glimpse of the themes behind the circumstances. What made the chap walking out of the pub turn and march back to confront the bully was a sudden sense of greater matter behind the merely personal. What makes so many online blogs impossible to read is that Tiddles the cat might be cute as hell, but we need to see through the cuteness to the hell beneath for any change to occur with regard to our understanding of life, ourselves, or the purpose of kittens in the corporeal world.

THE GOAL WITHIN REACH

That Orpheus nearly got her out provides an important glimpse of what could have been achieved, and what still needs to be achieved. If the object is too far away, too impossible or unlikely, we will eventually give up on it. In your plotting, you may need those moments of 'nearly got it' to keep the desire alive and the action propelled. They reinforce the nature of the action, its purpose, and provide a teasing tweak to the audience's wish to see it through.

DISMEMBERMENT

Cue thunder storms. Cue Dustin Hoffman breathless and sweaty from running. Cue bandages, wounds and limping heroes. One way or another, we have to rip into the poor fellow and pull him apart. This is, perhaps, where our slightly enigmatic statement about singularity becomes a little more obvious. That which dismembers the hero is the agent of change, the emissary of what he or she lacks, creating thereby the possibility of restoration. The villains who challenge the peace-loving, mild-mannered, slightly timid sheriff who just wants an easy life allow him to become more courageous and steadfast. It's painful, but necessary. Worse would be allowing him to languish in the dull comfort of mediocrity. Story, remember, is a cruel world. Call it tough love, but it means that the adversary is the beloved in a different form; just as the Venus who loves Adonis is the boar who gores him. It's gotta be done. What we are not doing is killing the hero, of course, which would end the story. This isn't to say that the hero can't die. The deaths of Lear and Cordelia remain an almost unbearable conclusion to that play, but Lear had transformed long before, stripping his robes and his regal identity on the blasted heath, to find himself sweetly honest, and poignantly content in the arms of his beloved daughter once again. What matters is that the false Orpheus, the deluded Orpheus, is shredded so that something else can emerge. And what needs to emerge is Orpheus himself, so 'himself' – which is to say whole, happy and complete – that nothing will ever be able to threaten that again. At least, until the sequel.

RECONSTITUTION

Billy's idea of himself as a feeble squirt is firmly in place when Andy throws out a parting shot that he isn't worthy of the name 'Mitchell'. Billy stops. The false Orpheus begins to fracture, to fall away. What turns back to face Andy is an embodiment of Mitchellness. We've called it restoration just to nail the concept that this is the real Billy. The false one will float back to take its place soon enough but, just for this moment, we've seen his true colours. It's up to you, the writer, to decide how much damage to inflict on the false identity of your hero. The more you destroy it, the more of the inner fellow you're likely to find. What makes this exciting is not quite knowing if you've gone too far. The audience thrills a little in the moment when they think 'Oops, he's a goner'. In spite of Lear's ultimate tragedy, the king at the end of the play is the true king, whereas Lear the abdicator at the beginning is not. The banishment of Cordelia is Adonis's dismissal of Venus, Orpheus's doubting of Eurydice. They all need to find their heath if Cordelia, Venus and the women of Thrace are to rip them to pieces. But only so that they can be put back together again. Venus picks up the flower into which Adonis has bled. The Muses gather the body parts of Orpheus. Zeus, in a similar myth, retains a small but important bit of Dionysus.

If you apply these steps to any number of stories, you will find their consistent reappearance in different forms. You will also notice how closely they work with our five-act structure. Perhaps more interestingly, you can apply them to your own Stuff to explore why you made a note of anything. Within the molecular structure of any incident worth scribbling down, you will find something of this paradigm at work. It might be that the paradigm has simply wormed its way into our thinking through persistent incorporation into the literary tradition of which we are a part, which would make it merely a convention. Even pointing out that any moment worth noticing has this shape might simply indicate that we have grown, culturally, to understand the world in its terms. Alternatively, the myth might have been framed to articulate a perennial pattern of human experience. This is how it is. This is how we live. The myth digs through the transitory material of particular circumstances to show the underlying, universal form of experience. The mirror might change from day to day, from age to age, but the nature which it reflects is nature itself.

When I was glancing over my notes after a long night in A&E, 'Rat Lady' didn't strike me as much of a yarn. But there was something in her need, as I've said, reaching out to the indifferent world – of which I had inadvertently become a part – that continued to niggle, to erode, to poke at my complacency and prejudice. Eventually, and thankfully, it found the fracture and shattered it. When I saw how the world turns away from people who are considered to be of no use, it was a potent realisation of my own shabby workings. In place of indifference stood compassion. Instead of dismissal, there was engagement. The Orphic Paradigm, as we've seen, is not just a primordial configuration of narrative experience into a literary construct (you might have to read that again), but the means by which we gather Stuff. Our journey into the Underworld, the sacrifice of our preconceptions, and the rediscovery of some hidden truth behind the outward show is the nub of this art. The rest is just arranging words.

STORYBOARD

Less elegant than the laws of action, and far less poetic than the Orphic Paradigm, the simple art of beating out your narrative can nevertheless be a useful practice. In many ways it reflects the ABC approach. You work out the key moments without which the story would not be what it is. And you jot them down. You resist the temptation to go scooting off into detail (although there is no harm in making notes on a separate piece of paper). The trick is to stick to the essentials. One way of doing this is to limit the number of beats, in the first instance, to around six, or perhaps eight.

Once you've made a note of these, you will be able to see your broad story shape from beginning to end. You can now take a long, cool look at what you've got. Taken as a whole, the beats should feel like they're saying something, with a clear character journey working forward from one beat to another. Taken individually, they should have impact and momentum.

Doing this at the outset shows you very clearly what you've got in story terms. This means that weaknesses can't be hidden in the dialogue. You can also see if you've got significant, high-impact moments worth sharing. If not, think again. If, on the other hand, you have a compelling idea bursting with Stuff, throwing characters and scenes into the air like fireworks, you don't want to get lost in the middle of all that. Storyboarding helps you to keep control of the material. The more complex your narrative threads, the more helpful it is to maintain an overview.

Initially, you don't have to be too inventive. Just jot down what you know. What's already there? What are the key scenes which emerge naturally from your idea? The story is about a bank robbery? OK, write down 'robbery' in a box. The hero gets caught. Write down 'gets caught'. Of course, he's only doing the robbery because his wife has been kidnapped. OK, 'wife kidnapped'. You get the idea. Keep it simple. If beats aren't offering themselves, look at the idea again, consider the themes. What are you exploring? What are you trying to say? What grabbed you about this in the first place? Who is your central character and what do they want?

Once you've got your storyboard, fix it to the wall, or nail it to your forehead, and use it to make sure that your story (however far you ramble in the creative exploration) comes back to a coherent shape.

Here is a simple example of 'beating out' a classic story:

JACK AND THE BEANSTALK

Jack goes to market to sell the cow. He exchanges it for beans.	Mother is furious and throws the beans out of the window.	The beans grow into a huge vine.
Jack climbs up and finds a magic place with treasure.	A giant chases him out. Jack climbs back down.	The giant falls and dies. Jack and his mum are rich and live happily ever after.

At some point, you might have wanted to add a little extra motivation to Jack by introducing the girl next door whom he's trying to impress. You've already got some great dialogue for the scene where he meets her on the way to market and tells her that he's finally going to have some money for the bills plus a bit left over to take her to a movie. She points out that the cow isn't as fat as it could be and she doubts he'll get much for it. He retorts, unwisely, and in spite of himself, that... OK, wait a minute. For the purposes of storyboarding, you don't need all that. In any case, it might be better for him to be raising money to help with his sister's exorbitant medical bills after she's diagnosed with severe alopecia. In fact, that scene with the doctor... Again, restrain yourself. Jot down these options in a disposable pad. Right now you're concerned with story essentials. Remember the ABC.

What you are trying to achieve here, apart from coherency, is an engine that will power your writing. Each of the scenes, and the story as a whole, when viewed in this bald grid, should make you want to write them. You can, of course, come back to the storyboard at a later time and change things around, but you shouldn't do this lightly. You are messing with the constitution here, so you need a two-thirds majority to push it through. The storyboard registers fixed positions. If these keep wobbling and shifting, there's a good chance you will never finish your script.

Once the beats are in place, you should find that they instantly suggest sub-beats. In the second beat, above, the mother is furious and throws the beans out of the window. But that begs for the moment when she asks him for the money, and he tries to explain what he's done. Is there another scene, after the beans have been thrown out, when he gazes out of the window through which they've been hurled, feeling wretched? Does he catch a glimpse of the girl next door turning away with a sigh? A good beat will quickly suggest the beats that make it up. Once the board is in place, you can explore it for all its details.

The principle here is Broccoli. Broccoli is a recurring shape that replicates itself in increasing detail. Every floret is the same shape as the whole thing. By storyboarding a few simple beats, you have the broad shape that you can then ripple out into the tiny moments. What storyboarding helps you to achieve is consistency of theme and form, so that, by the time you get to the minutiae, every detail lives and breathes the energy of the whole. The girl asking which country she's in evokes themes of loss, death, and the nature of love.

....

AN **EXERCISE**

Take a few films you like (or don't like) and jot each of them down as a six-beat storyboard.

ANOTHER **EXERCISE**

Take some well-known fairy tales and write them out as I've done for *Jack and the Beanstalk*.

....

Rich, complex stories will demand a rich, complex weave of sequences, scenes and beats. As we've said, it can be easy to get lost in the mix, or caught up in the swirls and eddies of the narrative flow. Surfing can be a lot of fun, so brainstorm, or blue-sky as much as you like. But there comes a time when you have to start making sense of it in order to produce a communicable work. Storyboarding keeps the overview simple, so the details can be as complex as you like.

THE HOT/COLD RATIO

Listen to any decent guitar solo and you'll notice that, often enough, it begins slow and low, works its way into a frenzy of fast and high, and then, perhaps, sinks down the register to ease off. Watch the guitarist and you might see him or her beginning fairly relaxed, fairly methodical, getting more intense, more focused, until they are a blur of fingers, eyes closed, lips pursed, the sweat dropping off their forehead to the fretboard below.

Frenzy has a rhythm. It follows a kind of shamanistic pattern as the oracle releases control and enters into a state of divine madness. In this state, like Orpheus dismembered, something more than the usual is allowed to play.

This ritual is known to us. Perhaps it echoes, like those ancient myths, a genetic memory from the earliest age of art. Or perhaps it is a universal pattern, as we've already suggested, inherent to the structure of any meaningful moment.

If a lead solo follows this shape, so does the whole song as it builds to a crescendo and releases. For that matter, so does sex, or a good meal. Taking a bacchanalian motif, you meet up with your friends, all straight-laced and civilised, exchanging pleasantries and catching up on gossip. After a few drinks you start to get merry, josh, tease, squabble and argue. As the evening progresses, or regresses, you end up climbing lamp-posts, vomiting in shop doorways and attacking random strangers. Well, perhaps not that.

And so with story. The tale of Orpheus begins quite gently as he arrives at the ball, arm in arm with Eurydice, smiling to an admiring crowd. The temperature goes up a notch when Aristaeus tries, and fails, to seduce her. The killing of Eurydice is a moment of startling focus. It eases off a little as Orpheus attempts to cope with loss. But it never returns to the original quiescence. Soon enough, Orpheus heads down to meet Hades, which turns up the adrenalin again. The moment when Orpheus feels compelled to look round has us digging our fingers into the arm rests. And then a steadier pace, for a while, building gradually, until the orgiastic dismemberment of Orpheus, which is our climax. Thereafter, we return to quiescence, albeit deeper than the opening with its latent tensions. Graphically, we can represent this rhythm as follows, with the two axes representing a ratio of intensity (heat) and quiescence (cold) over time.

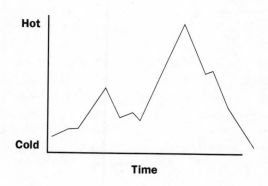

I've added a few ups and downs to indicate that the intensity will build and fall from scene to scene. Obviously, these are not to be taken as a strict template. It would be a mistake to think that every story has to have a particular peak or trough at a particular point of time. This would result in every story looking like every other. It is a part of our service, after all, to surprise. What matters is the general shape. You'll notice that there is an initial rise in the heat levels as the world becomes unbalanced. Then there is the climax. Again, it's all a matter of artistry, but a story shape played monotonously to the same syncopation would look like this:

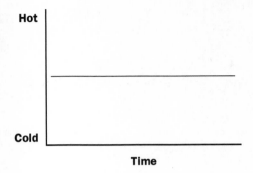

It's a flat line. It's dead. Perhaps a bit weirdly, the more satisfying shape bears a curious resemblance to the ECG pattern of a heartbeat. It would be nice to think that the two are linked in some way. Not only is the universality of story once more confirmed; it suggests another reason why we resonate so well with it. Story is the pulse of every waking moment. Story is the sound of life.

WORKING WITH **STRUCTURE**

MAKING A SCENE

Very few of the actions that we undertake in life are done and dusted as single, self-contained units of activity. Often they are part of a larger act. Equally, a larger act can be said to consist of a series of smaller actions. If I want to mow the lawn, for example, I have to get the lawnmower out of the shed. I have to find the keys to the shed door. I have to ask somebody where they last put them. I have to text whoever it was in my family that might have had them last to ask where the hell they are. I have to find my phone, which was around here somewhere... All of these single actions are simply part of the greater act of getting the grass in my garden neat and tidy. You could apply this analysis to almost anything. Even brushing one's teeth is part of the greater strategy of dental hygiene, which, as it happens, involves not just brushing, but opening the toothpaste, running the tap and so on. This relationship of smaller units of action to a greater act is so natural to us that we hardly notice the process by which we plot it on a daily basis.

The same applies to our organisation of a script. The greater act of the story unfolds in a sequence of smaller acts. For instance, the grouchy, hard-drinking, cynical man's lost lover comes back to haunt him: I guess we need the long-lost-lover-walking-into-the-bar scene. The young man agrees to shoot the gangster who tried to kill his father, along with the corrupt cop who protects him; so let's have the agreement scene, the planning scene, the finding-the-gun scene, the shooting scene. Any of these actions can be played on or off screen. That they are necessary for the logical process of action doesn't mean we have to see them. But they have to happen. As long as you know what has to happen (discovering where the keys to the shed are), you'll know where to place it in the action (before opening the shed door). And for that, of course, you need to know what the whole action amounts to (mowing the lawn), and what it means (why is it always me that has to do it?!).

We have already seen how to go about organising this in our exploration of the storyboard. But you can also divide the five acts into smaller units. There might be more than one effort/opposition sequence, each of which needs an action. Each of those actions might require several scenes to do them justice.

Earlier on I mentioned how, in my first draft of the Rat Lady story, I wrote a single opening scene which began with Mary looking incongruous in an upmarket maternity shop. The manageress notices her but is distracted by a customer. Mary then grabs some clothing and attempts to make off through the door while stuffing the stolen clothes in her bag. At the door, she is apprehended by the manageress and an assistant, and cajoled towards a back room while they decide to call the police. At some point in the drafting process this became two scenes. In the first she is in the shop, moving around, clocked by the manageress. We cut. All of the rest takes place in a second, separate scene. Why did we do that? The only rule is that the split felt better. It slipped more neatly into the rhythm of the show, since we had other stories to conjure with and didn't want the audience to lose track of them at an early point in the episode. Dividing the action also allowed us to pace the introduction and development of her story according to the chronology of the other stories. But in the end, it just seemed like enough to take in for the moment. That's your measure. Your scene can be a long, ten-minute take. Your whole film can be one scene. I saw a Japanese film at the Venice Film Festival (subtitled in Italian) that had just three scenes. Most of the film was a conversation between two people in a kitchen, not a word of which I understood. I can't remember the name of it, I'm afraid. I can only remember that when they went for a walk in the park I almost wept for joy. For the Japanese and Italian speakers the film might have been a masterpiece, so long as the measure was: enough.

But enough of what? Well, in a word: Stuff. We know by now that Stuff is not just something happening. It is a moment that reveals meaning. And it has a shape. All of the structures that we have been looking at, from the laws of action to the Orphic Paradigm, are as applicable to the shape of a scene as they are to the whole story. This is because, as we have observed, they are not so much a framework as a dynamic. The shape of the Orphic Paradigm maps the essential process of destruction and creation which underpins the existence of anything. It is action itself, unfolding according to its most elemental laws. Similarly, the laws of action are, obviously enough, how any volitional movement occurs. Only stones and corpses are completely inert. Anything which fails to pulse with these paradigms is, as we've seen, flatlining; and the best thing you can do for them is organise a decent burial, which is what your trash basket is for, or try breathing life into them, if you have the power.

Every scene, then, has an opening. Its opening (even Scene One) is determined by all that has gone before. The further you get into your story, the more energies you have in play, the richer that beginning will be. Every scene will have a central character, with an impulse, a desire, a loss, an imbalance. And in every scene that character will be trying to achieve a goal. There will be opposition. And this will lead to a crisis. Which takes us on to the next scene. Our hot/cold ratio will determine the rise and fall of intensity. Its rhythm will throb through every scene, every line, every moment. It is the pulse that tells you your script is alive. If it stops, as we've said, then it's either CPR or burial.

You can sketch out a scene according to these schematics, or use the structural models as a diagnostic tool once it's written. But the best way to work with a scene is to get the paradigms under your fingers, as a musician might put it. Feel its buzz. Let that buzz lend its natural shape to the scene. If it starts to gasp, go back a step and try once more, as they say, with feeling. The lead guitarist might be gurning for show, but he is also illustrating an important point about artistic creativity. Connection with the central motif of universal action, via any of the paradigms, is an act of frenzy. You have to let go. You have to do to yourself what you are doing to your central character. Writing is a kind of self-destruction in which all that is vain, false and delusory gets torn to pieces. What remains is what you truly want to say. If all you want to say is what a clever fellow you are, or how much you need this gig, or please could the world acknowledge you as a genius, then that is what your audience will see. And they won't be as impressed as you might have hoped. Go the whole way, humble yourself to the power of story, and you will begin to touch (and be touched by) these simple, potent universals that are as essential to your story as they are to you and your audience. You can fake it, as we have said, but only up to a point. Most likely you'll end up going straight to DVD – that's if it ever gets made.

Most writers (that I know personally) are geniuses in the art of procrastination. They will do anything but sit down to write. This isn't because typing tires their fingers. It isn't because they are idle. It is because there is a natural resistance of the ego to letting go. Ego is by nature an attachment. It is an attachment of your most profound sense of self to some detail of circumstance: a name, a job, a house, an ambition, an idea about who you are and what you want to be. We go to great lengths to strip these vanities from our heroes. We earn the right to do so by stripping them from ourselves. It can be scary. It can be painful. But it's the only way to be creative in the true sense of the word. The alternative is merely to repeat in novel configurations the same old gumbo. Do it if you have to. But make sure you get paid! The more you write, the better you'll get at it. Without meaning to state the obvious, writing is an art form. We may begin with the help of paradigms, rules and various constructs, but these should be discarded as extraneous to the practice once the knowledge becomes intrinsic to the practice itself. You won't need to cross-check with a paradigm to know if a scene is working. It will either work or not. If it doesn't, you will look to the material itself, its dynamic and content, and then you can tweak and nudge, or scrap and reshape it according to what it tells you. Once we can ride the bike, we don't need a diagram across the handlebars advising us when and how far to lean and under what circumstances; the road tells you what to do. The bike tells you what to do. At first, the whole package of rider, bike and road is an ungainly, wobbling thing getting nowhere fast. But, with practice, the rider, bike and road become one. There's a thrill in travelling like that. You don't have to think about it. Of course, there is a cerebral component to writing. You have to plan, you have to analyse and you will probably have to explain. But the most profound part of the activity is intuitive. Just as watching a film doesn't require a process of thought separate from the watching, so the thought, the writing and what is written are a single indistinguishable flow as the words hit the page. You are both creator and witness. In the end, it's impossible to separate the two. Suddenly you're as surprised by a line, a turn, or a character as your audience will be. It's a great joy. And it is, as we've said, why many writers write.

WHERE TO START

What governs all your creative decisions, even in the frenzy of writing, is your Stuff. Theme, character and structure are all aspects of your story material, working together to convey meaning. In Ron Nyswaner's screenplay for the film *Philadelphia*, directed by Jonathan Demme, Andrew Beckett, played by Tom Hanks, is a promising lawyer who fights for justice after he's fired by his bosses for contracting AIDS. The story focuses on his attempts to establish that being gay doesn't make him less of a human being. The narrative kicks off when a boss recognises the symptoms and realises that this aspiring, brilliant young man has contracted the disease. Of course, there is a long backstory, much of it compelling, such as the moment when he realises that he's gay; or when he first goes to a gay men's pick-up place. There's the powerful scene when he is diagnosed. After that he has to come to terms with it. There's the long scene in which he stares forlornly out of the window wrestling with despair. There's another scene when he breaks the news to his family. All of which would make a powerful story about a promising young lawyer who contracts AIDS. But that isn't what it is. It is about justice and humanity. When we meet him, therefore, he has already come to terms with it. We don't even question that his family is on side. However tempting all those other scenes are to a writer, they do not explore the central theme. They would be about something else. So the place to begin is when he is 'found out' by his employers.

There is no harm in writing the whole thing out at an early stage. Sometimes we might not know what our theme is until we've rambled around the many permutations of its narrative. But sooner or later you're going to have to shove that vertical structure in the ground, like a maypole around which all your stories can dance. There is a difference between the 'sprawling' epic which roams over any number of subplots and secondary characters, but absolutely and inviolably knows what it is (*Doctor Zhivago*, *There Will Be Blood*), and a mess (*Heaven's Gate*, *The Hunting Party*).

It is to be hoped that your characters, and the world they emerge from, have a potent backstory. After all, everything that's going to happen is a consequence of it. Orpheus and Eurydice are happily married but I haven't found much of a reference to their wedding, or their courtship, or the moment Orpheus comes away from a gig to notice her smiling face in the wings. But it's there. It has to be there. Similarly, the story as I heard it doesn't fuss around with Aristaeus's previous relationships, or his lonely hours on the ancient Greek equivalent of a games console. If you want the story world to be rich in material, you need the past to be as coherent as the present. I have read many scripts which begin their worlds and characters on page one. No amount of chivvying along the action can ameliorate the gnawing sense of vacuity that seeps from the ulcerous chasm of its opening. So think about the whole sequence of events leading up to the tale you intend to tell and even beyond. What happens next? After the sunset? The next day? The next few years? Then, with your theme in mind, find the right place to start. Err on the side of late. This way you aren't just kicking off a world in the first scene, but joining a flow of events already imbued with purpose and momentum. You hit the story running, with an instant choice of references to past actions. In any case, these days the practice is less 'Are you sitting comfortably?' than 'Hang on to your hats'.

A good exercise, when you're contemplating your story, is to write some of the scenes that are outside of the structure. You can write a crucial piece of backstory. You can write something that occurs off screen. This will serve to enrich both your understanding of what's happening, and, by extension, the mood, texture and depth experienced by your audience.

WORKING WITH MULTIPLE NARRATIVES

Unless you're writing a short film or one-act play, there's a good chance you'll have multiple stories in your script. By stories, I mean distinct, distinguishable narrative threads. These might consist of your main plot together with various subplots that augment and enhance its themes and characters or, as in much series television, a variety of different stories which unfold distinctly through the episode. The question is: how do you manage them?

Even a simple yarn, focusing on a single protagonist, might have several stories working together. Every character, after all, is a character by virtue of their story. So the moment you have more than one character, you also have more than one story. In a singularly focused narrative, all the characters come into being to develop the central thread. Our Orphic Paradigm has shown us that their nature is determined by the needs of the main character. So it's easy enough to see who they should be and what they need to do. They can still move independently of the main strand, however, and the logic of their narrative needs to be as thorough. So it's a good practice to beat out all the stories of all the characters. This will enrich them and, in turn, your central story.

With multiple narratives, as in episodic television, there may be stories and characters which never converge. This provides us with a few extra challenges. The key is to link them thematically. Thus 'Rat Lady' was about communication or the lack of it, which was reflected in Kelly's bafflement and Charlie's caution, to name just two of the stories in that episode. Your vertical structure will apply to everything that happens in the episode, giving even the most tonally disparate stories a sense of belonging.

One of the problems which multiple narrative throws up is that of simple organisation. You've sent one character on a time-specific errand only to find that they're needed elsewhere to serve some other, time-specific narrative development. Much tearing of hair. Much pacing around the room. You might try to sort it out in your head, on index cards, whiteboards or sheets of A4. I would advise against organisational software – which offers to do the job for you – since this process of rumination is a way of getting the story into your soul, as distinct from your hard drive. Painful as it may be to begin with, you want to reach the place where you know and understand the implications and effect of every moment of the script. Wrestling with logic is another way of getting there.

Whether you use index cards, scraps of paper, ideas-clouds, mind-maps or columned grids, either on real paper or your computer, there are a few basic stages that you will most likely go through.

The first thing you need to do is work out which story is your main one. This goes back to ABC and simple storyboarding. In series TV it is often called 'the spine', which is a good metaphor since the whole structure depends upon it. Once you've decided on your main story, set out the beats, which can take the form of bullet points. You should have a fair idea of how it starts, what the main obstacles are, when they happen, what it builds to and, perhaps, how it resolves.

I can remember a story conference a few years ago on an emergency rewrite for a TV series. The existing scripts had crashed and burned and we needed to write the whole series again. We had roughly four weeks per episode from 'What are we going to write about?' to production draft. I busked an idea about a prisoner escaping to get revenge on a former business partner who had, apart from swindling him and framing him for a crime, got the girl. We kicked it around a bit and rather liked the 'rogue in the woods' notion. But the script editor wasn't happy. 'Why now?' he kept saying. The room fell silent. And then I said, 'Because they're getting married.' He leapt to his feet. 'A wedding!' he cried. 'You've got your story.' The point is that we now had the whole shape, including a set-piece location for the climax. It also provided a ticking clock for added jeopardy. No wonder he leapt to his feet. I could go home and write. ('Why now?', by the way, is a good question to ask.)

Once you've got your main beats, you can fill in some of the details. How do we get from 'a' to 'b'? There's no rule about this, but, as we've said, it can save time and enhance focus if we get the main beats down first and fuss about the smaller ones later. If we start off going from small beat to small beat, we can lose the rhythm and end up with a mush in which no moment is more significant than another. You lose the ebb and flow, the crescendo and diminuendo, that fundamental shape essential – as we've seen – to an engaging structure.

Now do the same for your smaller stories. Make sure that each one has important moments and a credible movement from one to another. This is a good time to test the strength of your narrative construct. Are you fudging implausibilities? Are you forcing a story to fit something outside of itself? Do all the stories, to put it simply, work? You can also get a feel for how they'll work thematically and tonally. Be honest. If something tickles you but looks increasingly strained in the script, either find a genuine rationale which makes it worth including or park it for another time.

At this point, I'll sometimes turn to a spreadsheet for help, running the individual stories down vertical columns. Putting a title at the head of each column is a quick way to see how many stories you've got, along with their relative strength and significance. Doing this on a recent serial for TV (*Combat Kids*), it became pretty evident after a while that I had one story too many. I fought for it, struggled with it, and finally took the advice of the executive producer and let it go. I think everyone around me breathed a sigh of relief. It was a great story strand, but I had 90 minutes to play with and there was simply no room.

At the same time, you'll be able to gauge the strength, and dominance, of your main story. As a rough guide, the more beats a story has the more important it is in the script. Just as you will instantly see if a lesser story is eating up more time than it deserves, you can judge whether or not the primary narrative has sufficient material to earn its keep.

As you lay out the stories, in their columns, you might like to leave spaces to indicate the natural time lapse between the various beats. At this point, the measure can be approximate, but it will show up some of those logistical problems that may come to plague you later. Consider the following example:

A. Dead Rabbit	B. Carwash	C. Vegetable Mystery	D. Other Beats
Jack is driving to Celia when he feels a thud under the car. He stops on the side of the road and looks. There is a badly injured rabbit.	Morris is upset about having to do overtime again at the carwash. He calls Celia to say that he'll be late home.	Herbert sees that his allotment has been raided yet again.	King Rabbit confides to his trusted aide that he's concerned about a coup.
			Celia's phobia about aubergines leads her to see a psychiatrist (Audrey).
	Morris scratches William's windshield accidentally but William doesn't notice.	Herbert buys a shotgun.	Nigel takes up swimming.
Jack arrives at the vet's clutching the dying rabbit. He sees Audrey in the waiting room. She stares at him.			
	William accuses Audrey of scratching his windscreen.	Herbert keeps watch overnight but nothing happens.	
Jack sees a 'missing rabbit' notice on a lamppost.	Morris notices that he's missing a rabbit.		

(In case you're wondering, this is for demonstration purposes only!)

Once you've got the stories 'beated out', as they say, you can see the points at which different narrative strands intersect. Now you can start laying them out so there's a chronological consistency across the rows. Before long, you will have a rough outline of your script which you can cut and paste from the spreadsheet to a scriptwriting program as a solid start to your working structure. However, resist, if you can, the temptation to do that for a little longer.

I won't always use a spreadsheet. Sometimes I'll use index cards laid out on the desk. I have also experimented with a whiteboard and a flip chart. Sometimes I'll just riff all the threads on to a single sheet of A4 in tiny writing with flow lines, arrows, annotations and the occasional doodle. Perhaps different ideas require different kinds of planning, or perhaps it depends on the mood. Of course, on occasion, you don't need to do this at all. You already have a powerful feel for how it's going to work, or you just instinctively know that it's going to work, or you're happy to find out how it's going to work as you write it. It really doesn't matter how you arrive at the finished script. But many scripts are unfinished, even if the story begins and ends, because the stories have not been optimally ordered. A sure sign of this is a whole series of scenes that do just one thing each. They are thin, repetitive, things, slogging their guts out to shove the stories along with exposition, explanations, and a frantic need to justify their existence. If your characters keep stopping to tell each other what they already know, you should take a look at the beats.

The beats are not just about clarity of structure but momentum. The next beat should draw from the energy of its predecessor, just as it generates energy for its successor. Different beats from the various stories should bounce off each other, gaining power, building heat. By the time you're hitting your climax, the forward drive should be unstoppable. If the projector were to break down at this moment, you'd want your audience to riot.

Once you've laid your stories out with the intersection points working nicely, and the whole thing making logical sense, take a step back and study the various threads; consider how they work, both individually and collectively. Where are the strengths? Are there any weaknesses? Is there repetition? This is the time to be honest.

The three great questions of editing are:

1. Is anything superfluous?
2. Is anything missing?
3. Is anything in the wrong place?

Looking at the grid above, we might ask whether we need Nigel at all. Wouldn't it be better if Jack had taken up swimming? Nigel doesn't develop much as a character, and Jack certainly needs a bit more oomph. OK, lose Nigel and give his story to Jack. Also, do we need the running-over-the-rabbit moment? If it doesn't provide the intensity or suspense we're looking for at the outset (it might do, but let's say it doesn't), how about opening with the arrival at the vet's? And what if Audrey recognises Jack from swimming lessons? You get the idea. You can also ask questions like: why is he driving to Celia? What's the relationship, if any, between Herbert and Celia? What if Celia were crossing the allotments when Herbert took a shot at her? Hiding in a shed with the deranged Herbert prowling around, Celia suddenly realises she's surrounded by aubergines and has to call Audrey, her psychiatrist, just at the moment when Jack walks into the vet's... And why the hell is Audrey at the vet's, anyway?

You can see how this can both boggle your brain and be a lot of fun. Some writers enjoy this part of the process; others find it tiresome. Either way, it's pretty much unavoidable. Get it right at this stage and you move into the next with ease and confidence. The next stage is when you can't wait to write those scenes. The purpose of everything described here is only to arrive at that point. If you scan your grid and can't see a moment so powerful that your hand reaches for the pen (or keyboard) with all the urgency of a tiger pouncing, or a zebra fleeing, then why not? Look again. Remember your Stuff. What made you want to tell this story? Is it here, in the outline, lurking? Perhaps you've dissipated it over too many threads, or the stories have started to wander off into tangents. Wrestling it back at this point will save a lot of pain later. Once you've thrown some dialogue you're desperate to defend into the mix, it will be even more difficult to pull back to what's essential.

To which I shall just add the caveat that, if you want to write the whole script out from beginning to end before you consider the story, do it. Some people like to work that way, and I have happily done it myself. My first produced stage play began with a little twitch of ink on the page that became a line of dialogue, that revealed a character, that developed into a story. And I never revisited it. The whole thing was there, bang, in one shot. Which is great. But it was a simple story. More than that, it owed much of its style to a kind of postmodernist narrative spasm which made anything more or less forgivable. With *Combat Kids*, I had five major strands to contend with, complex characters, the need for it to make sense to a younger audience, and an anxious producer drumming his fingers on the desk as my deadlines approached. I took the methodical route. But I did so only in order to go wild safely when it came to the writing itself.

At which point I'd like to add another caveat: this is not a formula. I'll say it again: this is not a formula. There is no absolute law that a particular story development has to happen in accordance with a particular sequence at a particular time. By all means work with convention, but never confuse convention with law. 'Tried and trusted' is usually more like tired and crusted. We have a duty to surprise. So don't put a clock down the left-hand side of the grid. It doesn't matter if the moment when your central character conceives a desire is ten seconds or ten minutes into the story. It matters only that it feels right when he or she does.

But let's go back to our grid. You will have noticed the column marked 'Other Beats'. This is more likely to be needed in series TV than a movie but not always. An 'other beat' is really just a single, self-contained narrative moment. In series TV it's usually a beat in a longer-running strand that isn't part of the narrative of the episode; perhaps a set-up for later or something to keep a story in play. Series TV writers often hate these because they disrupt the fluency of their stories. The art is to weave them in so they don't look too much like an 'other beat'. You can achieve this by slotting them into an existing scene, or by giving them some story shape, expanding them to achieve a degree of fulfilment in the episode. Ideally, you'll find a way to link them to your theme, your vertical structure. Kelly's involvement with Mary in the episode of *Casualty* which we looked at is an example of taking an extraneous narrative (Kelly begins her decline towards emotional collapse) and aligning its centre to the main theme of the episode (communication). Thus, the first blow to her sense of self-worth is the rebuffing of her efforts to communicate a concern. The last resort is to stick them wherever you can, hoping they won't look too incongruous.

Careful weaving of the different threads allows you to achieve a convergence of stories in the individual scenes. Thus, Kelly's feisty exchange with Trish brought three stories together: the fate of Mary, the alienation of Kelly, and the loneliness of Trish (who is about to find solace in a romance with Charlie). So, in a way, that's *four* stories thudding away in the line: 'What I choose to do with my patients is frankly none of your business.' Trish's despondency, brought about, in part, by her behaviour towards Kelly, sets her up nicely for an honest moment with Charlie as she confesses her remorse and distress.

This has a powerful effect, since you're getting multiple narrative hits in the one beat. Ten seconds of drama, in other words, can hold ten minutes of story. If you think about it, the converse is ten minutes of drama holding ten seconds of story, which, as we all know, is rather unsatisfying. The late, great comedian and actor Ken Campbell once asked a group of aspiring writers (including myself) what the purpose of drama was. After he'd dismissed our various theories (even those as elegantly coherent as the ones listed earlier in this book) he said the purpose was to make an hour feel like 50 minutes. It got a laugh, but it also got us thinking. How does one achieve that? As we've seen, one way is to distill our narrative, evaporating all the weak and wasted set-ups, the longueurs, the small moments lugging even smaller pieces of story, and the moments that do only one thing. At the same time, look at any beat in any strand and ask how this serves any other beat. Can they be brought together? Do those two conversations have to take place separately? Does that action have to affect only one character? Since you can observe the progress of each thread, operating in isolation, you can easily merge them without losing their singular narrative function.

This isn't to say that your script should be boiled down only to incendiary moments. There should be space to linger, to burn slowly, to reflect. But you should be in control of this. It shouldn't be there simply because the story threads are running one at a time. The more condensed your dramatic material, the more time you have to hang back a bit, to pan slowly or fade gently, to tease the images and the mood.

Check out some existing material to see how the writer used its moments to combine threads. Take a scene and pull the weave apart to see how much is going on. We did as much with Viola's first lines in *Twelfth Night*. Apart from anything else, this will help you to understand exactly what a story thread is and how to work with it. Once you master the art of one thread, adding more becomes easier. But, as a general rule, start with something manageable and work up from there. That applies as much to general technique as it does to the specifics of a particular script.

A little work at the outset can save a script from knotting up, falling apart or feeling too thin for all the polishing it subsequently undergoes. It can even save a script from the bin, which, after all, is never the intended destination. And remember that, even if it does end up in the bin, if you have worked at it intelligently, no effort is wasted. You will have learned. And the next one will come more naturally.

LEITMOTIF – THE USE OF THINGS

THE POET'S WORLD

For those who dare to venture out of their homes from time to time, the world can be a bewildering array of things. Lamp-posts, plastic bags, cars, cats, shopping trolleys, a discarded glove in a puddle, leaves on a tree, birds flying past. Most of these we don't even notice. And even if we do register them in passing, it's usually just to avoid stepping on them.

....

AN **EXERCISE**

If you're at home, perhaps in an office, bedroom, or your sitting room, just have a look round. Some of the things you notice might be transitory, like that old pizza carton. Some will have a bit of history. Most things are there because someone, perhaps you, at some time decided they should be. Pick an item, make a note of when, where and how you acquired it. What were the circumstances? Who else, if anyone, was there? How did you feel at the time? Repeat as necessary.

If you are in a strange place, look at the objects around you. Let's say it's a railway station. Perhaps a woman looks into her handbag. Think about that handbag. And then imagine when, where and how she came to have it. If you're in your car, waiting at traffic lights, consider some of the housing that might be visible to you. What's in the front garden? A kid's bike? What does that tell you? A disabled parking space outside? Same. If you're in a park, sitting down in the sunshine, or crossing it to get to some assignation, check out anything you can see. A sweet wrapper on the ground? Somebody dropped that: when, why? What does that tell you about them? (You will never know for certain, but imagine a character in a scene you're writing finishing a chocolate bar and ask what they might do with the wrapper.) Finally, take a look in your pockets. What's in there? Coins? Fluff? An old receipt?

What you'll notice is that everything has some kind of history. It was conceived for a purpose, if only decorative; it was crafted (by hand or machine); it was acquired (honestly or not) for some reason; and it was either kept for that purpose, or simply forgotten about. In other words, it has significance; it says or does something; it has meaning. This might be very slight, or deeply traumatic, but there will be something about it that carries a smidgeon, at least, of story.

....

Go to any film set and you will see people, sometimes a lot of them, working extremely hard to populate the visual experience with relevant objects while removing anything that has no place. The screen world is a hyper-controlled environment. Everything is there because it needs to be there. It takes time to get this right, to sift every superfluous item out and bring every meaningful one in. Which is why the more intensely controlled the screen world, the more it costs (generally) to create.

I once directed a piece for television in which two uninvited guests are surreptitiously let in through the back gate of a walled garden. While I was setting up for a different scene, the art director came over to say they'd found the gate, and would I like to see it now or was I happy just to move the crew over when we got to it in the schedule? I said I'd have a quick look, just so I'd have it in my head. What they'd found was a wrought-iron gate, open to the air, full of curls and shapes, brimming with photographic possibilities. But the two characters in the scene needed a moment to speak before the gate opens. They couldn't do that if the insider was watching them. I could have had them meeting up just before the gate, exchanging their words before the other person came into view, but I wanted that moment of wondering if the gate would be opened or not, which they could fill with their nervous remarks. So I said we needed a solid gate and went back to the scene at hand. A little while later the art director returned, grinning. They'd found a nice wooden gate in the wall. Great. I nipped over. It was a brand-new gate, recently installed. But the story had an old, disused gate that nobody (bar the insider) knew about. The art department said they'd get the painters on it. An hour later I took another look and was very pleased to see that they'd painted in cracks, warps and lichen. But the ivy over the top had obviously been cut back fairly recently: hardly in keeping with the idea of neglect. I asked for foliage, lots of it, hanging down. They got me foliage. I wanted more. They got me more. Finally I was satisfied. The characters met, had their words, the old gate creaked open. The characters pushed the foliage aside to get in. The moment bore a slightly mythic quality: secret entrances, inside knowledge, initiations. It was a decent moment – and a happy director.

It helped, of course, to have a fat budget, a full art department, and an indulgent producer (not to mention an art director restrained enough not to throttle me). But my attention was on story. That gate told a huge amount of story, instantly, with no dialogue. The insider didn't need to talk about his personal relationship with the previous owner, or how things had changed. He didn't even need to emphasise the rigid security surrounding the occasion and the paranoia of its host. Neither did he have to describe the lucky happenstance of a secret entrance. He needed only to say, 'I know a way,' and the rest came from cracks in the paint, lichen, moss and ivy.

What we're looking at here is the storytelling power of a visual image. I was berated by a director/producer once, on set, for a ten-second – dialogue-free – scene I'd written which included 15 extras. In his director's hat, he shot it. In his producer's hat, he gently chided me the indulgence. Which made me wonder why I'd written it. When it provided a central motif in the title sequence, on our publicity materials and the DVD cover, it became obvious. A few seconds of image gave us the essence of the story. It might have cost the same as five minutes talking, but it delivered more for its brevity and power.

There is often a tussle at some stage in the production between writer's dream and budgetary constraints. At that point it helps to know what the images, the objects and the moments are for. Since writing is rarely a mechanical activity by which you assemble your various things, carefully noting their thematic import, and judiciously including them in the scene according to some rule about how many and how often, you don't always know why they're there. The scene wanted them. The story asked for them. Your imagination – bodying forth the forms of things unknown – did what it's meant to do. It turned those airy nothings into shapes; into an old gate, a platoon of soldiers, kids on bikes, a red balloon.

In a story for the CBBC series *Roman Mysteries*, I had a ship containing exotic animals destined for the gladiatorial games run aground, disgorging its contents into the woods. I gave way on the giraffe and zebra but dug my heels in for a lion. OK, I'd always harboured a little dream that one day I'd write a lion. After fighting me for a day or so, the producer finally sent me a photograph of the lion they'd found, a gorgeous beast who lived in Wales and performed in front of a green screen. Actually, she sent me about 20 pictures. Once convinced, she loved that lion. We all did. What the lion gave us, however, apart from a thrilling moment of tension, and plenty of suspense before and after (in the story, as well as the script conference), was an opportunity for a slave-girl to stand up to it in the defence of the man she loved. She could also calm it down through her words and manner, contrasting her empathetic connection to the natural world with the act of shooting it, which somebody else was about to do. In a virtually wordless scene (most of the dialogue being of the nature of: Grraaarrraough) we were able to show a love so great that a girl was prepared to die for it. And we showed, while we were at it, that there is another way to tame the beast. That lion earned its place in the story, and in the budget.

On another occasion, I had a group of friends chatting round a camp-fire at night. The producer balked at the stresses – and expense – of a night shoot with child actors. In the end I couldn't argue with the inevitable and we shot it in daylight. But people speak differently around a camp-fire at night, and I can hear, in the final scene, strangely displaced nuances of tone, which still bother me.

You win some, you lose some. As an instance of losing it big time, I suggest you watch (if you haven't already) David Mamet's *State and Main* (2000), in particular the scene in which the writer is told to lose the old mill. The writer struggles a bit, gives up, turns away and, as he does so, we see the title of the script he's holding. It reads 'The Old Mill'. Of course, I'd have turned at the door and marched back in to confront the producer in the name of art… or not.

The shamanistic poet, in a fine frenzy, doesn't know what a mundane world is. Everything is significant. Everything speaks. Everything has a kind of narrative animus. This is a sublime state and we're lucky if we can get to it. It's a part of the pleasure of living, for a period of time, in the world of story. It is a part of the pleasure that our audience gets from watching the screen. Nothing happens that isn't laced with Stuff.

Smiley buys a new pair of glasses. Rick pours himself another drink. Travis Bickle hesitates for the tiniest moment before pushing open the door. Walter White drives the least charismatic car on the planet, and Gustavo always adjusts his clothes before walking. Nothing is wasted. Everything means something. This induces a strange kind of rhapsody, equivalent to the frenzy, the hyper-attuned perception of the poet's eye.

As we noted at the outset, this is a key function of drama. We seize the audience's attention, hold it, intensify it, and leave them more awake, more alive to themselves and the world around them, at the end. A key element in this process is the use, both overtly and subliminally, of motif.

As a term, motif embraces all the objects in a scene, including costumes, hairstyles and even makeup. Every year, all around the world, costumiers, coiffeurs and makeup artists step up to collect prizes, be they BAFTAs, Oscars or any number of Silver Cuttlefish and Golden Spatulas. This is not in order to recognise their admirable ability to do someone's buttons up, or comb hair, but to acknowledge their powers of storytelling. The same applies to set design, lighting and music.

Motif, for our purposes here, is everything that makes up the sensory experience of watching a film or television drama. It even includes camera angles. In *Taxi Driver* there are two recurring positions of the camera, used to draw us into the story. One is a slow movement upwards. If you study the first scene of the film (when Bickle applies for a job with the firm), look for those moments when the camera moves. You'll notice their precise concatenation with a change in character. The other is an overhead shot, often looking down at a desk, across which some form of transaction is taking place. We may not realise, consciously, what's happening here, but the shot is emblematic of a key theme in the film: Bickle's search for real communication in a world where everything, even people, exist merely to be bought and sold. That it operates, as a motif, below the radar of our conscious thought processes, confers upon it immense power. It goes right through to our emotional intelligence, festering along with all the other Stuff of the film, to draw us into its meaning. This is what distinguishes motif from symbolism, although there is clearly a symbolic value in motif. The former does its magic in the emotional, intuitive realm. The latter is a label which communicates to the intellect, or at least that same rational faculty which reads the ingredients on a jar of pickle.

Our banana analogy suggested that all of the elements of a piece are simply attributes of each other. Motif, by this equation, is as much story and theme as it is, say, a visual embellishment. This isn't to say that every single object has to carry an esoteric indication. Getting on a tram doesn't necessarily make that tram a potent image of cosmic migration by which the galaxies swirl. But if the hero has to run to catch it, or wait in a queue, or push past people getting on, or fumble in his/her pockets for change, or if he/she looks around nervously, unaccustomed to being so close to strangers... it begins to speak. If it doesn't, then it's just a thing. If there are too many mere things, the story will start to sag under the weight of meaninglessness.

I once had to direct some pick-ups for a BBC drama after the rough cut came in with no discernible shape. This involved writing some additional scenes in an attempt to knit the whole thing together. One of these was of a tense conversation in the front porch of a house. After running it through with the actors I looked round for the camera, which had wandered off to the far end of the drive. When I asked what it was doing there, the director of photography said he wanted to shoot through the rose bush. 'We haven't come here to shoot the flowers,' I snarled; and we moved the crew forward. The first assistant director leaned over to me and whispered, 'Thank God someone's finally stood up to him.' Several expletives have been left out of this account. But the point is that the roses added nothing to the moment. With no discernible purpose, they would have resulted in nothing more than a bewildering mishmash of random images, confusing for everyone.

The film *The Hunting Party*, with a screenplay by Richard Shepard (who also directed) and Scott Anderson, is a brisk enough story with a fine cast. But it doesn't work and was poorly received. One of the problems is that its motifs are entirely haphazard. It begins with a street battle full of gunshots and explosions, while Richard Gere's character tries to locate a cigarette. Perhaps it's there to show us what a cool, slightly wacky, inured-to-danger kind of guy he is. But it never comes back to us, or adds up to anything meaningful. It's a bang to get our attention. It isn't a motif. After that, the whole thing becomes a meandering ramble, never quite digging into any real sense of Stuff as it shifts erratically from comedy to action, to social comment, to love interest, around in circles and back again.

....

AN **EXERCISE**

Watch a few scenes of anything with the sound off. What are you getting from the use of the world? How much story is told through visuals, camera angles, colour tones, facial expression, gesture and costume? If it's any good the answer will be: loads.

....

We have already seen how important it is to set up your story world. Everything, including the central characters, their needs, desires, imbalance and actions, emerges from that world. It cannot be otherwise. In the same way, every physical object is a part of that world. This might seem blindingly obvious but we've seen from, say, *The Hunting Party* how this can go awry. To be a part of that world is to engage with vertical structure. A car doesn't just get someone from here to there. The make and model of car, its condition, whether or not it has anything hanging from the mirror (dice, fluffy bear, crucifix, air freshener...), what music it can play, how fast it drives, is rooted in story, which is rooted in theme. When you think about it, the resident of a twelfth-century Italian village is unlikely to climb into a Cadillac – unless, of course, it's a Python film.

Much is made of Aristotle's unities, at least in certain quarters. Otherwise, they are honoured more in the breach than the observance. My academic friends tell me that his original injunctions come to us in a maligned form, having passed through the gut of certain French intellectuals at one of those recurring periods in history when non-writers make a living telling writers how to write. So perhaps we should either disregard them or take a closer look. Either way, we have seen that, if all our material (story, characters, motif, etc) comes from an item of Stuff, and remains faithful to that origin, a natural unity is inevitable. Story is the singularity of a complete act. Characters are not a compendium of quirks but a core impulse emanating through their attributes (about which more later). Even the scenery owes its place to the consistent laws of a coherent world. At the same time, each of these work together as parts of the whole – a whole that, in the end, becomes far more than the sum of those parts.

That singularity of intent, or story, begins with the opening shot, even with the titles. The first object on screen apprehensible to the senses is an expression of story, character and theme – which is to say, Stuff. Getting a hold of this principle adds enormous power to your storytelling. At the very least it saves the tedious need for explanatory dialogue. So let's look at this a little further.

LEITMOTIF – MELODY AND RHYME

In music, motif is a foundational melodic pattern, which is to say a tune. Leitmotif means the leading melodic pattern, the core phrase (or phrases) around which the entire piece is built. In Indian music, this would be akin to the 'Raga', a precise, often traditional, musical sequence from which the musician improvises. We see the same in jazz. Whatever the genre, a composer or performer will establish the phrase and then explore its possibilities. The stronger the phrase, the more of these there will be and the further they can be taken. There is a beautiful moment in *Amadeus* (directed by Milos Forman, with a screenplay by Peter Shaffer) when Mozart takes a tune from Salieri and dances through some of its variations, turning something quite ordinary into something delightful. The skill is in taking the detour, the off-road, off-piste, option, without getting lost. Returning to the core phrase, from time to time, will re-establish its presence in the ear of the audience.

In drama, a motif is simply a thing with meaning; call it an atom of Stuff. It could be a glass of whiskey, a cheque book, a gun, a piece of chewing tobacco; or a camera angle, a phrase of dialogue, or a piece of costume. It can also be a musical refrain. In the James Bond films, we'll often know when Mr Bond is under extreme pressure, or is about to find his mojo, by the appearance of that familiar riff. It's a good tune, but it isn't lobbed in any old where so we can hum along.

It means something. In the same way, the magnificent compositions of John Williams for the *Star Wars* films toy with different motifs for different characters. Even when the music is more moody than tuneful, and more pervasive than occasional, such as that of Philip Glass in *The Hours*, it is telling us something of value and significance (the relentlessness of Woolf's depression and the heavy burden of time upon the day).

In the same way, as we've seen, visual images, which is to say objects, can be played to evoke a particular, recurring resonance. Mountains, for instance, feature heavily in *The Sound of Music*. In fact, the moment you read that title, there's a good chance an image of mountains popped into your head, quite possibly with Julie Andrews prancing among them. The mountains are redolent of freedom, beauty, simplicity, the majesty of nature. These are all qualities dear to the heart of the lead character, Maria. Whenever they recur, they remind us of those qualities. In story terms, they signify the freedom from which the poor girl is sent to work in a quasi-military household as governess to a bunch of insufferable brats. They are that for which she yearns; the Eurydice from which she has been parted. With children, those qualities of innocent delight and spontaneous freedom might seem to be innate. But not with these kids. At least, not at first. In a crucial scene, Maria takes them on a jaunt. To where? The hills, of course, to rediscover the children they should be – that they essentially are. When the Captain's heart finally melts (releasing the emotional sterility into which his persistent sense of bereavement had enclosed him), he sings of the 'Edelweiss', a flower which flourishes in the upper pastures. As a motif, the edelweiss is, to some extent, Maria. In that moment, she knows he's in love with her. My apologies for the spoiler, but when, at the end, the whole family escapes from the Nazis, it is over the mountains with which we started our story.

Mountains also feature heavily in *The Deer Hunter*, topping and tailing the narrative as with *The Sound of Music*; although when Maria sings 'Do a Deer', her import differs considerably from that of Mike, peering through the crosshairs of a high-powered rifle. In both films, the mountains represent a kind of freedom, though the nuances are very different. For Mike, they are more about his need to find the single-minded intensity of a moment in which he can feel unequivocally alive; similar to Maria but less cheerful.

In *Vertical Limit*, we have more mountains. But this time they are a challenge; they can kill you. In many ways they are more Aristaeus than Eurydice. The same goes for *Touching the Void*, in which mountains, for all the beauty that Maria loved to revel in, are mutely indifferent to the niceties of human welfare.

Many objects bring their own, ready-to-wear signage, or common associations. These might vary between cultures, and from age to age. Cigarettes would have seemed like the height of raffish elegance just a few years ago; now they're more akin to a nervous twitch. Mountains, on the other hand, remain majestic, whether dangerous or inspiring. A glass of whiskey can unite two characters in a moment of bonhomie, or provide the lonely solace of a bitter man, but it remains an intoxicant of sorts.

The gorgeous wheat fields at the beginning of Peter Weir's *Witness* are instantly redolent of the natural good, of providence; a central tenet of the Amish ethos at the heart of the film. This motif recurs many times. The love scene takes place in a barn. The big community moment centres around the construction of a barn. The shoot-out happens in a silo. I'm not sure if the giving of a biscuit to Samuel in the police station is a recurrence but I wouldn't be surprised!

Another leading motif in the film is modes of transport. It is by horse and cart that Rachel and Samuel go to the train station to join the modern world. From the train they marvel at the sight of a hot-air balloon. The train brings them into the big, bad city, epitomised by the rush and bustle of a metropolitan station. It is here that the murder happens. Later on, John Book travels by car from his familiar territory (the big, bad city) to Rachel's Amish community. Rachel and John get it together, romantically, around his car (rather beautifully tuning in to its radio). The bad guys arrive in cars. When Book gives the game away, thumping a young man who taunts the Amish for their archaic appearance, it is after he's ventured into town by horse and cart.

Here wheat is more than landscape, and modes of transport more than means for getting about. Each is replete with metaphorical significance, which Weir exploits to perfection, digging them into our psyche without us even knowing.

Aside from those motifs that arrive pre-soaked with assumed significance, you can take an otherwise commonplace, or at least ordinary, object and imbue it with your own meaning. In *Dance of the Wind*, directed by Rajan Khosa, screenplay by Robin Mukherjee, the lead character, Pallavi, is attempting to find a mysterious old man who appeared in the streets at the time of her mother's death. It is clear to Pallavi that the old man knows something about her mother, some secret that sits at the centre of her life, and her art. The old man was accompanied by a small girl. Later on, Pallavi is in the market place when that young girl, more in mischief than malice, steals an orange from a fruit stall and is apprehended by various affronted traders. Pallavi comes to her rescue but loses sight of her again. As the mysteries deepen and Pallavi's attempts to resolve them have become intense to the point of obsession, she goes back to the market place in the hope of seeing the girl. Time passes. Night falls. No sign of the girl. By now tired and a little ragged, Pallavi stands in front of the display of oranges and takes one. She is mobbed by traders until her husband rescues her. The moment wouldn't work without that earlier instance of the orange. We have imbued oranges with a sign which reads: small girl, connection to old man, resolution of the mystery. It also says: 'Pick up without paying to find out that you have sunk through all the social orders to that of petty thief. You have nothing left. You are without social standing, or respect. You have only the quest.' It also says that the last person to stand by her is her husband, and even he can't take it any more.

Similarly, in an episode of *Eastenders*, it became necessary to sow discord between two of the characters before and during a dinner party. The host's criticism of the hostess's attempts to make a perfect lasagne earlier in the day gave lasagne quasi-mythic import as evening fell and the guests tucked in. The hostess had only to slap a violent dollop of it on her husband's plate to tell us all we needed to know of their relationship at that moment.

Leitmotif works through repetition, allowing one instance to power the next, as they develop a progressive resonance. In that sense, it's akin to a rhyme. One instance of a sound is just a sound. Two instances establish a relationship. This isn't a cerebral reference back to the previous instance but the act of two sounds together, in the ear, combining to form a greater sound.

Thus, mountains in *The Sound of Music* don't just gild the opening scene, but recur with different nuances, building up their collective effect. To begin with, they are just a happy place (Orpheus whole). Once lost, they become an aspiration of the central character (freedom and joy = Eurydice). Later, they provide a moment when the object of desire seems within reach (Orpheus does a deal with Hades). Further still, they become a catalyst for, or signification of, change (dismemberment of the Captain's grief, releasing him to sing 'Edelweiss'). Finally, they are a means of escape to the freedom and happiness lost at the outset (reconstitution). By marking out the key moments of the Orphic Paradigm in this example, we can see that what Maria (Orpheus) gains at the end is what she lost, but transfigured into something greater. She was happy enough at the outset, but alone. She has to find a greater, more complete, less dependent sense of freedom. At the end she's free, happy and complete, among the mountains but with a family. When Mike sees a deer at the end of *The Deer Hunter*, he doesn't shoot it as he does at the beginning. This isn't because he's gone soft, but because he no longer needs to.

Whether the motif works subliminally or becomes an overt metaphor, it operates as a shared code with the audience, an intimate engagement through an established language of signs. This is a very obvious application of the Aristotelian principle of participation, by which the audience is invited to engage with the writer in a shared language, a series of signs for which we hold the keys.

The judicious use of repetition means that, with each recurrence, the motif gains power. This is partly why, as the story builds, one has to do less and less to gain more and more. If, by the crisis, you are still having to stop and explain, then you simply haven't done enough in the early stages to establish that potency. Towards the end of a Chekhov play, the slightest word, look or pause can send your senses reeling. This is not by chance. Those simple, elegant, highly refined references in the last act were carefully, even strenuously, established in the first.

WORKING WITH THINGS

As with all of the elements, the principle of leitmotif is simple enough to explain, but its uses are subtle and the applications infinite. It isn't enough just to drop an object in and flick back to it every so often. The object has to be rooted in the story world. It has to be rooted in theme. It has to be pertinent to the character and the story. And, depending on your artistry, it can bear powerful resonances all of its own. In this way, once you've rooted a motif in theme, you can deploy different motifs as instances of a category of objects. Wheat becomes a barn, becomes a silo, becomes a biscuit (possibly).

In Giuseppe Tornatore's *Cinema Paradiso* (1988), we begin with a lingering shot through a Sicilian window with flower pots, looking out over the sea. Salvatore's mother is attempting to call her son in Rome to break the news that Salvatore's mentor, Alfredo, has died. The homeliness of the mother's house contrasts abruptly with Salvatore's glitzy Roman flat complete with reclining starlet. The boy's done good. He's a hot-shot movie producer but his life, for some reason, has become hollow. When he gets the news, he reflects back on his childhood and youth, his relationship with Alfredo, the discovery of a passion for cinema, and the lost love that has rendered him, Rick-like, bereft of joy (Orphic spotters, gloat).

All of this – which makes up most of the film – builds to the moment when he comes home. After a few shots of him in the taxi heading towards the village where he was born, we watch his mother knitting. When the doorbell rings, she knows immediately that it's him and heads downstairs to the front door. Crucially, we stay with the ball of wool as she drops the knitting needle and hurries off. The wool unravels, unravels, unravels and then stops. We know they've met. Only then do we pan to look through the window and see a taxi moving off, mother and son in an embrace.

Wool doesn't otherwise feature hugely in the film. But it links strongly with the honest simplicity of the mother's life. It is the simplicity which Salvatore has lost and is therefore central to the theme of the film. In its eloquence, it shows us her emotional charge, the displacement activity of furious knitting, her practicality and earthiness, and that her own life is missing something (her son). The unravelling of the ball feels like the unravelling of time as she finds herself once more in the company of Salvatore, whom she hasn't seen for many years. The fact that his arrival makes her completely forget the wool tells us that his presence wipes all other considerations from her mind. Finally, by sticking with the wool rather than going for the big 'hello' moment, the audience is allowed to fill in the gaps, to interpret the signs; to experience the reunion more intensely than if they were actually seeing it. Understatement (less is more) is a powerful tool when used carefully. Get your motifs in place and you can understate with aplomb. Create a thin, hazy world and you'll probably end up with yards of tedious dialogue struggling to get the plot across.

In Takeshi Kitano's *Hana-bi* (1997), Nishi is a disillusioned cop who takes his terminally ill wife, Miyuki, on a kind of bucket-list tour of Japan, having robbed a bank to provide the means to do so. In one scene Nishi and Miyuki visit a temple, where we leave them for a moment as we transfer our attention to a grandfather and his grandson admiring a temple bell. Of course, the little boy wants to ring it. And, of course, the grandfather explains why he cannot. However, as the grandfather and boy move off towards the exit, the bell rings out. The grandfather stops and listens. We see Miyuki smiling as the bell rings again.

Apart from the glorious directorial decision to play Nishi's bell ringing on the grandfather, this scene is evocative for much the same reasons as the knitting moment in *Cinema Paradiso*. Nishi knows that both he and his wife only have a short time to live (they're being pursued by criminals to whom he's heavily in debt). So he decides to make the most of what's left. And he rings the bell. Part of his concern is that all his life he's never rung the bell. The grandfather, meanwhile, who was initially so pleased at his prudent adherence to the rules, suddenly wonders what his life might have been like if he'd ever flouted convention and rung a bell or two. Nishi and Miyuki – just like the little boy who would have rung the bell because he hasn't yet been conditioned to respect, or fear, the conformity of a rigid social order – have become like children again: innocent, free and a little bit naughty. This is the only time that a bell features so heavily in the film and yet it pulls together myriad ideas, themes and motifs to say much with very little. Neither Nishi nor Miyuki says a word. They don't have to. And the scene is all the more eloquent for its lack of verbosity.

Another potent function of motif is to mark change. You can establish constants by which to measure the transformation of character, mood and understanding. In Martin Scorsese's *The Aviator*, written by John Logan, Howard Hughes is crestfallen to see that his hard-won aerial-combat footage looks a bit lame. He realises that there is nothing by which to gauge the speed of the aircraft, so he reshoots the scene against cloud. In the same way, you can use an object, or instances of a type of object, such as mountains, a deer, or a ball of wool, as a fixed point against which to demonstrate the distance travelled. The deer in *The Deer Hunter* is an obvious example. At the beginning, Mike shoots it because that activity forms a part of his sense of moment, of the urgent game of life and death. At the end, he puts the rifle down. He knows all there is to know about life and death. He doesn't need to kill. Maria, at the outset of *The Sound of Music*, is alone. At the end, she is part of a family. By revisiting mountains at this moment, we simply, clearly, elegantly and powerfully reinforce the sense of transformation, which, as we've noted, is a crucial component of the Orphic journey.

IN THE WHITE ROOM

Unless you're writing a white-room drama, which is a very particular and, in some ways, limited genre, your characters will be moving around in a world full of things. And all of those things, as we've seen, are a part of the texture and meaning of that world. Rick runs a bar. So a glass of the hard stuff is bound to crop up now and again – along with a piano. Actually, since we've got a piano, why not have a piece of music that means a lot to Rick in the sense that it takes him back to the loss of Eurydice? Hey, Sam, play it. You can see how, so long as you've set up a world, you don't have to look too far to find things that can be used to further the story. If anything, you should be spoiled for choice. You will also see how, once you've used something, you can use it again to greater effect. (What else can we do with that piano? Hmm. About those papers we need to hide...)

Salvatore's mother could have been pacing up and down looking anxious (a touch melodramatic, don't you think?). Or she could have been staring miserably into space (boring). She could have been gazing out of the window (a bit of a set-up). Or we could have followed Salvatore to the door (robbing her of character). Or maybe she could have been standing in a room with her daughter, saying how much she missed her son and how she believed he would turn up eventually (urgh!).

A simple rule is to look at the world, and all its things, before writing dialogue. If you can say it without words, do so. And, once the dialogue starts, never forget that the world is still there. Unless it's crucial to the scene, don't just let the characters talk and talk until the room subsides into the whiteness of a non-place. He's angry? Slam that glass on the table. She's distressed? Hit him with the puppy. But allow that communion of character and world to be a constant, interactive, mutually developing process. After a while, Josey Wales only has to spit to have us ducking behind the saloon-bar counter.

Recurrence, then, is a storyteller's best friend. It might be a pattern of speech, as in the reference to 'papers' in Harold Pinter's *The Caretaker*. It could be a particular camera angle, or lens filter, as in *Taxi Driver*, when Scorsese uses an overhead shot at strategic points to emphasise the theme of communication as transaction. And, of course, it can be an object, such as a ring in *The Godfather*. At the beginning of the story, a supplicant submits to the authority of Don Corleone by kissing his ring. The film concludes with acolytes kissing the ring of Michael Corleone who has, over the course of the story, evolved into the new Godfather. No further explanation is required as to its significance. And we can observe, by the simple use of this single image, just how far we've come.

Although many of the objects we've looked at are essentially inanimate (mountains, wool, chewing tobacco), this is not to say that they are inert. Even as fixed points against which to measure change, our emotional reading of them can change radically. That ring at the beginning of *The Godfather* is impressive; at the end it is disturbing to the point of horrific. In this sense, motifs contribute to the general dynamic of your story. One way to bring them alive is to use contrast.

The temple bell is confronted by a very old man and a very young boy. Salvatore's mother should be a content lady sitting in her armchair, but the clacking of those needles tells us otherwise. In the opening scene of *Dance of the Wind*, a young girl in school uniform steps hesitantly from a sunlit day into the shadowed hollow of an ancient tomb. The very large and the very small; the very old and the very young; the very strong and the very frail: all give us an instant sense of the Orphic loss of equilibrium that we feel, instinctively and unconsciously, needs to be restored. Rick is in a bar that ought to be a festive place of relaxation and merriment. He is anything but. Rachel and Samuel are Amish folk in a very modern, technological world. John Book (ironically named), by contrast, is a hard-bitten cop who suddenly finds himself propelled, seemingly, backwards in time by about 300 years. Things that just sit smugly doing the basic essentials of their narrative job don't add much to the texture, tone, pace or meaning. In that sense, the Orphic Paradigm of imbalance, loss, dismemberment and transfiguration applies as much to things as it does to characters.

The actual paper document that is a script is a sparse beast when you look at it. It speaks of words and actions, with a bit of scene description here and there. What it doesn't have is explanatory notes. So you won't be writing down why you introduced that temple bell; or at least you shouldn't have to. After all, the director and art department will have their own talents and skills to bring to the creative process. If they get what you mean, they'll fill in the details. That tumbler in the hero's hand might be cut crystal or cheap plastic; the design department will choose according to the world, your themes, the character and the story. The stronger these elements, the less head-scratching in the production office, the more the various creatives will enjoy providing their input, and the better your film will be.

If you see someone pushing a car, there are two possible scenarios at work. One is that there is something wrong with the car. The other is that the person pushing it has spectacularly failed to appreciate how vehicles are meant to be used. The same applies to writing a script, which is a powerful vehicle by which you convey your story, ideas, passions and creativity. It isn't meant to be shoved, grudgingly, along. If you do find yourself pushing it, then recognise that there is something wrong with it (unless you think that's how people write). Go back to the themes and ideas, beat out the narrative form. But also look to see that you are making full use of the story world with its myriad things, each of which contains potential resonance. Is this white-room drama? If so, no wonder it's hard work. Use your imagination, see the room, the street, the clothes, the objects and start to build them into the telling of your tale. It's amazing how much horsepower this gives you. Once it's going, you need only the lightest touch on the pedal to get where you need to go.

....

EXERCISES

- Take an object, perhaps from your observations earlier, and make a list of associations, both personal and universal. Don't try to think things up but see what the mind offers.
- Write a short piece in which that object is desired by a character.
- Write a short piece in which a character fears that same object.
- Write a short piece from the point of view of the object. Consider the relationship between you (the object) and your owner.
- Write a moment of crisis in the life of that object – from the object's point of view.
- Use an object twice in a short written piece in which it is viewed very differently from the two points of beginning and end.

....

CHARACTER

DEFINITION OF CHARACTER

You might have noticed that we're all a bit different. One person will lean over a keyboard in quite a different way to the person at the next desk. People chew differently, walk differently, dress differently and, of course, speak differently. One person might hanker after solitude, another after popularity. One person might eat too much, another too little.

At the same time, there are many points of similarity. Most people enjoy subsuming the perennial ache of separation into the comfort of an aggregated identity, be it a church choir or criminal gang. Thus we tend to hang around with 'like-minded souls' who dress like us, drink like us and read the same sorts of books, if any.

We are the same, then, but different. Which concludes our brief survey of the complexities of character.

In drama, we need to stylise our characters to some extent. They can be hyper-stylised, perhaps for comedic effect, or they can be more naturalistic. And they can, like most of us, behave differently at different times. Usually, our own character is tempered by a generalised adaptation to the environment. People who adapt less flexibly are sometimes referred to as 'a bit of a character' or 'quite a character', which is to say they retain obvious and sometimes extravagant idiosyncrasies through a greater variety of situations. By contrast, those who adapt too freely can become a bit dull. They are too varied, too pliable. These don't make for good dramatic characters, unless we're taking them on a journey in which they become less shapeless, partly because they're not terribly interesting to observe, and partly because our observations don't tell us very much; they're difficult to read. It isn't enough that something is going on inside of them, we have to see what that is.

We have two things to consider, then. The first is what character consists of. The second is how we make that known to an audience.

Literally, the word 'character' means a mark, etching or engraving. It is a word that comes from the Greek *kharakter*, an engraved mark, from *kharax*, a pointed stake. The etymological base is *gher*, to scrape or scratch.

It is no coincidence that we refer to the letters of the alphabet as characters. For the purposes of story, character is thus a kind of mark in the psyche, or the soul. The study of where and how the mark operates is beyond the scope of this study, but that it does is fairly undeniable.

Before we go on, just take a moment to ponder your own understanding of character. Study the character closest to you. Which is to say, you. Ask the following questions:

- Do you have a sense of consistent character that you think is probably recognisable to the people you know?

- Where does it dwell and of what is it formed? (See you back here in about twenty years!)

- Do you ever act 'out of character'? If so, what does that mean?

- How is your character maintained on a daily basis? Do you have any familiar statements that circulate in your head? Are there things that you tell yourself about yourself – and are they true?

- Is there a usual pattern of thoughts that you have before you go to sleep? Is there a usual sort of thought that you have when you wake up? What is it? What is its effect?

- How does your character govern your actions and influence your speech?

- Do you know people who fail properly to appreciate your character? Why do they get it so wrong?

Character is not to be confused with personality. Although much is made of personality in the ordinary social environment, and we are often judged by our personality, or wish we had a better one, or use certain attractive facets of the one we have to compensate for its more unsightly attributes, we are not our personality. Persona means a mask. The word comes from classical theatre and refers to the mask through (*per*) which the actor spoke (*sonus* – sound). It gives us the iconic symbol of theatrical endeavour, the comic and the tragic; and, more recently, the logo for BAFTA and the shape of the awards themselves. Personality, then, is a fabrication of sorts and can be changed on a daily, or moment-by-moment, basis; although changing it too often is likely to confuse our friends. It adjusts naturally to circumstances. It evolves over time. But, clearly, it isn't random except in the deranged. Personality is an expression of character. We use personality to make our character known. If it's easy enough to adjust personality, it is rather more difficult to change our character.

At the centre of any story is what we have called vertical structure. This signifies the relationship between all that happens and all that it means, between the particulars of the moment and the underlying causes, between the specific and the universal. Characters are not lobbed into your story to shove the narrative along. Neither is story there just to give your characters something to do. Story and character are one and the same, unified in the vertical structure. Your characters are as much an expression of meaning as any statement they happen to make. Once we understand this, we can easily weigh the characters for their purpose and effect, establishing their vitality in, and necessity to, the narrative.

This is, of course, our banana analogy in action. Character is narrative, is theme, is idea, is everything else about your story. It would be hard to think of *The Sound of Music* without Maria; or *The Godfather* without Don Corleone; *Serpico* without Serpico; *Breaking Bad* without Walter White; and so on. And once we start to explore these central figures according to the key precept of the Orphic Paradigm whereby all the other characters are attributes of the central protagonist, we quickly get Captain von Trapp, Michael, Corrupt Cops, Jessie Pinkman, et al.

Don't spend too long on this, but try pitching an idea without mentioning a character. Even if you manage it, that commission might be a long time coming. A story about slavery? You've got slaves and slave owners. A story about political corruption? Well, cue corrupt politician. A story about geological rock formations that don't change for millions of years? Good luck with that one.

A vertical structure specific to character might look something like this:

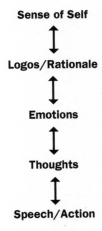

Sense of Self

Logos/Rationale

Emotions

Thoughts

Speech/Action

We can't see an emotion, or even a thought, at least not with the eye. But we can detect the presence of thoughts and emotions by how people behave. And, according to Descartes, if they're in the least bit sentient, we can be fairly sure there's somebody home.

Note that there is a natural exchange between these levels and that the levels themselves, in practice, blur into each other. A spoken word is also a thought. A thought is nearly a spoken word. Thoughts are always influenced by emotion. What we think can change the way we feel. And vice versa. And it all begins, and works, through a sense of 'I', of self.

Let's begin at the bottom and work our way upwards.

SPEECH AND ACTION

There's a lot more about this in our chapter on dialogue. For now, think of speech and action as everything a character says and does. It also includes what a character doesn't say, or doesn't do, since the suppression of speech and the denial of action involve a movement in mind.

Since, as we've already said, your story world doesn't spring from nothing in the first scene, there will be a history of things said and done, or not said and done. Characters may respond to each other according to this history. A king marches into court and everyone bows, averts their eyes and looks suitably humbled (or deviously conspiratorial). A man with a reputation for violence walks into a suddenly silent saloon. A local wimp turns the corner to be sneered at by some local toughs. When Jack Nicholson breaks the door down with an axe in *The Shining*, the other characters are already convinced this is probably not a good thing. Similarly, everything that a character has already done and said, up to this point, will feed back into their own sense of who and what they are. The speech and action of your script begins, therefore, at a point in time during a long sequence of speech and action, stretching right back to the character's birth and beyond. Even if they are unknown to the indigenous population of your story world when they arrive, out of the desert perhaps, what they say and do is an interaction between the circumstances of the moment (as they perceive it) and the circumstances of their past (as they understand it).

The physical text of a script consists of a few simple elements. You have scene headings and perhaps some description of the setting (grubby street, sunlit field). There might be an event (boulder rolls down hill, snow storm, space ship arrives). There are also parentheticals (small stage directions to indicate how the speech is to be played, such as 'whispers', or 'smiles', or even 'beat' or 'pause' to indicate a moment of thought). There will be what the characters say and do. But that's it. That's your lot.

According to another schematic we looked at, the levels of interpretation, this would be the literal. It's what actually happens. It is absolutely necessary, of course, since things do have to happen (exempting one or two extreme art-house movies forever etched into my sense of regret). But writing which consists merely of things happening for no particular reason, with characters who speak and act without thought or emotion, is superficial to say the least. What begins to give it dimension are the deeper levels of character that we infer from the simple description of outward matter: their impulses, emotions, and the means by which these first take shape in the mind, which is to say, thought.

THOUGHT

Even the smallest character can be given something akin to human life. In *Falling Down* (1993), directed by Joel Schumacher, with a screenplay by Ebbe Roe Smith, William marches into a fast-food restaurant and complains about the quality of the burgers which bear little resemblance to the succulent items displayed in pictures above the counter. The cashier could have been nothing more than a cringing uniform. Instead, she rather enjoys William's challenge to the establishment. This in turn connects with the idea that William is standing up not just for himself but for all those too timid to complain. It links right through to the central theme.

I once wrote an episode of *The Bill* that included a simple scene in which our main character, a police officer, receives some information from, as it were, 'the street'. It was easy enough to think of a flower seller with a pavement stall. He's earthy, hears what's going on, and we get a nice outdoor shoot on a sunny day. As the flower seller is talking, reluctantly, to our hero, a man comes to the stall and picks up a bunch of flowers. The seller charges him three quid. As he continues the dialogue, an elderly woman comes along and picks up an identical bunch. He charges her one fifty. The effect was to turn an extra with a small speaking role into a character that we could cast decently. It isn't what characters do and say that matters but why. Which brings us, again, to the realm of thought.

There are different levels of thought: the general noise that floats through the mind, remembered tunes, recurring niggles, odd bits of nonsense, and profound explorations at the fringes of understanding. Likewise, the thoughts occupying the mind of your character at any given time can be the most recent permutation of a long-standing existentialist question, or the desire for a cupcake. While intelligent thought in a character is often associated with intelligent stories, it is perfectly possible to write profound stories with only simple thoughts in the heads of your characters. At the same time, simplicity of thought doesn't always equate with simplicity of character. An uneducated, illiterate character who has never read Proust can nevertheless entertain matters of profound importance. If you do want to be known for profound writing, just bear in mind that it isn't mandatory to afflict your characters with intellectual verbosity.

EMOTION

We are concerned here not with the emotional tone of the story, but the emotional activity of the character. The two might be very different. A character might be feeling despondent in a scene that is, for the audience, hilarious. Similarly, a character might find funny what the audience does not. There is more on this in the chapter on style and resonance, and it is all obvious enough. However, I did once work with an editorial team who confused the emotions of the character with the desired emotional response of the audience. In spite of my resistance we eventually had most of the characters ranting and railing, or weeping copiously, which rather left the audience cold. Part of our error was to separate the emotions of the characters from the story. I'm afraid it's the banana analogy again: gratuitous histrionics do not a moving moment make. In any case, the emotions we look for in our characters are those which make them act. They can weep and snivel for a bit, but too much of it is just red eyes and snotty noses. We begin, as an audience, to disengage.

As with thought, there might be a momentary spasm of emotion in response to a specific stimulus. These might be familiar to the character, or to those around them, appearing once or twice a day, or several times a week: a sense of doubt, or reckless daring, or self-pity. Others are less mutable, colouring the perception over a longer period, even a lifetime. Getting a glimpse of the emotions that operate at this level is always fascinating, just as it's a pleasure when somebody, anybody, is honest with us (well, sometimes). We can see the strings that tug thoughts and propel action. This is an important aspect of that insight into the nature of motivation which drama serves to provide.

Emotions can be categorised by type. The simplest division is between negative and positive feelings. Trying to define these any further is a philosophical labyrinth, but we can observe a broad difference in the iconic masks of classical theatre, and the two dramatic strands of the comedic and tragic (happy/sad, tears/ laughter). Splitting the human heart into four might give us the humours (melancholic, phlegmatic, sanguine and choleric). There have been many other attempts to catalogue the emotional flora. Recently fashionable was the Animal Grid, with Lions, Dogs, Horses, Hyenas, etc. There are nine-point schematics, diamonds, Primal Elements (Earth, Air, Fire and Water), rainbows, and quite possibly a periodic table yet to be devised. If we sat down to list individually identifiable feelings – the ones we can catch – such as Anger, Jealousy, Despair, Hope, Awe, Disgust and Fear, we'd be there a long time. To make this even more complex, emotions can also be mixed, as we probably know from experience.

To create characters from this level, by feeling their feelings, is to produce richer, more powerful creatures to populate your story world. But, in a sense, they are still types. If we square this analysis up to the levels of interpretation again, we might slip thought and emotion into the realm of allegory, in which any object is representational of an idea. Thus a phlegmatic character represents those people who are calm, or sluggish, depending how you judge them. The Silver Back Geezer is an instance of the dominant male. Stock characters from commedia dell'arte, with its long and glorious tradition, bring a simplistic, sometimes delightful, obviousness to the players and the play. This is fine, so far as it goes. But it's not the end of our journey into character.

At this point you might be sitting with your head in your hands. Or perhaps you're sighing with relief. You might even be dancing around the room in a euphoric trance. Because you will have realised that writing takes the whole being. At this point we are committing our own emotional ground to the act of creation. This is a conscious, not a mechanical, act. Up to this point, perhaps, you can cut and paste archetypes, but they can only be scrapbook characters glued to the page. They won't emerge from, be intrinsic to, and reveal the deeper, vital textures of your story world. If you want to avail yourself of the infinite variety of nuance that feelings can merge into and move through, then you have to find the core of the character. If you want your character to be unique, then you need to slip past types, schematics and formulae to join him or her at the root.

LOGOS

This is where the nub of character lurks. This is what we mean by the word 'character'. It's the mark, the engraving, the rationale, the word deep within that character's nature. It is what governs their nature.

In any given character, this might be tricky to define. In some ways, it is pre-lingual. So you'll never quite find the word to nail it. But you can indicate it. You can reveal it. In practice, we're quite used to this activity. If we find ourselves, say, at some kind of business convention, we might have the benefit of name badges. So Heidi or Norman comes up to you and you can see, instantly, that they are Heidi or Norman. I've never been to a convention yet at which the name badges identified the core character attributes, such as anxious, depressed, nervous, untrustworthy or ruthless. We work that out for ourselves through a complex series of clues. We rely on observation rather than information. And, by and large, we're pretty good at it. We have to be to survive the social jungle. We read those exact same instruments of communication, deliberate or inadvertent, deployed by the dramatist to indicate the character. We have what a character says or doesn't say; what they do or don't do. We can use peripheral data, perhaps from how other people respond to them (if everyone ducks behind a table when they come into a room, there's a chance you'll do the same). And somehow – although we don't always get it right – we begin to fathom what makes someone tick. We're also good at hiding ourselves, however, so we're sometimes taken in by the artful. And we can often be disappointed to find out how wrong we were. At the same time, we can be delighted by some hitherto undetected quality. Reading this area of the human architecture is what we're usually up to when we're not on our own. What we're doing, whenever we engage with this kind of sign reading, or behaviour decoding, is looking for the logos, the indelible mark etched, uniquely, into every individual heart.

There are fictional characters who seem more real than real, or at least as real as anyone we've ever met. If the former, it might be that we rarely meet a character, even among our friends, even including ourselves, whom we've seen so deeply. Scarlett O'Hara, Atticus Finch, Travis Bickle, Michael Corleone, Salvatore and Alfredo are good examples. There are many more. Writing characters like these doesn't take more words, or any kind of explanation. It requires only depth of connection. Connecting deeply with anything, seeing past the outward detail to the inner reality, is always a powerful experience. When it is experienced, people want to talk about it, share it. Painters will paint it. And writers, of course, will write it. The power of that insight is what powers the writing. Scarlett O'Hara wasn't put together in a laboratory. She isn't the sum of carefully assembled parts. In a weird way, she lives and breathes as you and I do. That's because she has that most elusive, yet most crucial, attribute of anyone. Shakespeare called it the glassy essence. It's what everybody refers to as 'I'.

SENSE OF SELF

How do we breathe life into our characters so that they're not just bricks in a wall of narrative, nor ciphers for bits of story, nor types or archetypes, nor fabricated composites of technical hokum? We inhabit them. It's as simple as that. Great characters, as we've seen, require personal investment. You can't just piece them together like a heads/body/legs game, picking personality flaws off the shelf and sticking them on to a 'super objective', with crazy hair or facial ticks to make them look interesting. It starts with your collection of Stuff. Story and character, as previously noted, are inseparable attributes of each other, as colour and shape belong to a banana. So, when you're gathering your observations, you're collecting character as much as story. But you aren't simply a geologist picking rocks off the beach, or a botanist painting flowers.

Watching the young man with his feet on the seats could have led to a strident letter to the local newspaper bemoaning the lack of respect among the youth of today. Or it could have formed the beginning of some anthropological study. What gave it dramatic possibilities was the moment when the observer saw the world through the young man's eyes. Suddenly, the guarded, wary literary type across the aisle was seen as an object of resentment, revulsion, contempt. Who does he think he is? Let him say something. Go on, you smug git with your little notebook, say something. In that moment the writer was the young man looking back. The thoughts and feelings, the sense of circumstance, anger and pain, bodying forth according to the laws of imagination, came not through guesswork or analysis but empathy.

If we are stiffly composing a letter of complaint, or completely wrapped up in our own anxieties, or just absorbed by whatever else we might be thinking of at the time, we won't connect with that young man. After all, the young man is sending out a barrage of subtle indicators that connection would be unwise. And that is probably how it is for most people, for much of the time. We draw our collars up and look away. But the Stuff gatherer takes another step. That identification with our own concerns, opinions and preoccupations is momentarily released. The writer lets go of the idea of being a writer and, for a time, is able to see the world as an angry young man looking for trouble. He or she is giving up any attachment to the personal particulars in search of some universal point of connection. It's the fine frenzy. This breakdown of ego is not only key to the creative act, but what story is all about.

While driving through some beautiful West Country lanes one morning, I happened to spot a family having a picnic. It was a classic scene, with mum and dad, a couple of kids, boiled eggs, tea in a flask, and probably a wasp or two, this being England. Then I noticed that between me, in my car zipping by, and them, on their blanket spread over the grass, was a mesh fence topped with barbed wire. A few yards later on I passed the guard post and realised that this was an army base. They were an army family. I didn't know why they were having a picnic; it could have been to celebrate something or to say farewell. But that juxtaposition of a sublimely normal family moment with the metallic apparatus of a military machine was a powerful imbalance. We have already looked at the story energy generated by the position of opposites, or by the tilting of the world through some shift in the centre of gravity. Well, this was just such an instance. But what made me want to tell the story, and perhaps what made me able to tell it, was the question: I wonder what I looked like to them, driving past? And, as that question unfolded (What would they have thought of me? Did they envy me, or disregard me? How far did that barbed wire wrap around their lives, enclosing them into that world, keeping the outside out? How different did that make them feel, if at all?), so I began to see the world through their eyes. By the time I reached my destination a couple of hours later, I knew I had my story. It took a little more research (actually, a lot more research) before I felt able to tell their story, but the seeds had been sown and, more importantly, the Stuff was in place.

That scene which the director/producer chided me over, which became an iconic symbol of the show, was of children on bicycles moving past a marching platoon. It was simply an iteration of that inciting vision, the innocent family moment and the apparatus of warfare. That same imbalance, juxtaposition and question (namely: how does that work?) was there at the point of ideation right through to final execution. It was, in fact, the vertical structure.

All of which only confirms the notion that a little frenzy is mandatory for the gathering of Stuff where Stuff is the substance of character. Billy's moment of transformation worked because it came from personal experience. In the act of writing, I *was* Billy. So when Billy said, 'I know what I am,' he really did know who he was. These were not made-up lines on a piece of paper but the very real life of a very real character.

Billy had circumstances to contend with, doubts and fears in his mind, troubles in his heart, and an idea of his family affiliations that pervaded his every waking day, whether he recognised it or not. All of this was powered by his sense of self. In order to write him, it was necessary to engage at that level, to see myself in his shoes, to know the world that he knew, feel what he felt. And only then could I say what he needed to say in the way that he needed to say it. Good actors will breathe life into their characters in exactly this way. But it helps them to have a start in the writing.

The vertical structure of character may be stable in its relationship between the centre of your story and all of the outward ramifications, but the movement between its two ends is constant, and flows both ways. Whatever the character faces, does and says knocks back into the realm of thought and emotion. What happens there ricochets out again to the tangible world. This describes any normal moment, mundane or otherwise, during which a person is sentient. If someone says something to us, we hear it, comprehend it, react inwardly and issue an outward response, even if the outward response is to not respond. What makes this process story is when the movement intensifies over time, gradually demanding deeper and deeper levels of engagement.

Words and actions are, by nature, transitory. Thoughts can linger for longer, and emotions can hang around for a whole lifetime, but even these are modified according to the flux of circumstance; especially when we start lobbing narrative grenades at them. Eventually we dig down to the logos, where the deepest changes occur. The only attribute of a character which doesn't change is the sense of self. I might be angry, sad, happy, miserable, jealous, courageous or pitying from one moment to the next. I can change my job, my town, my spouse. I can reinvent my ideologies, aspirations and expectations. But what changes is only that to which the sense of 'I' is affixed. The 'I' remains in place and is, in itself, unqualified; we might evolve in many ways over time, but there is that which remains the same in our dotage as it was in our infancy. It's the deepest level of awareness, of existence. It's what remains when everything else may have been taken from us, the unquenchable (so long as we live) sense of being at the root of all we do, say and think we are.

We might remark at this point that a profound sense of being is a rare occurrence. If we're lucky, it'll happen once a year on holiday or at special occasions like weddings and funerals (so long as the latter isn't our own). Usually, it is covered up by what Shakespeare calls the 'muddy vesture of decay', which is to say transient considerations. The sense of 'I' might be latent behind it all, but can soon become identified with an aggregated composite of our various identifications (name, house, job, car, ambitions, financial circumstances, dress-sense, etc). After a while, the word 'I' doesn't refer to our essential existence but this unwieldy conglomeration of attributes. In a way, this is a false logos. It is ego where 'I am' is instantly followed by a suffix (clever, stupid, tired, angry, rich, poor, and so on). This is Billy thinking himself a bit of a wimp. It is the writer on the train thinking he's a writer on a train. As we get older, so the vesture gets muddier, more dense, more opaque, until it can all but smother any sense of our true nature. The removal of this falsity is key to the Orphic myth. It is therefore key, arguably, to all that is character, and to the ultimate purpose of story itself.

ORPHEUS – THE ORIGINAL

Orpheus needs to be ripped to pieces, otherwise he can never find what he's looking for. To find what he's looking for, he needs to become what he is. Eurydice isn't the goal. The goal is true and everlasting love. King Lear didn't need to find Cordelia. He needed to discover humility. The false logos needs to be removed so that the true can be revealed.

Logos itself sits at the interface of the changing outward form and unchanging inner sense of 'I'. In that sense it shares the attributes of both. The more it identifies with the unchanging, the more open and unfettered it is. The more it identifies with the transient and outward, the smaller and more possessive it becomes – as it tries to grasp and hang on to that which is, by nature, ephemeral. The completely universal being (rather rare, I should think) hasn't a selfish bone in his or her body. The completely identified being is insane. Usually, we're a bit of both, shifting from grim arrogance (the image of scorn) to benign translucency (the feature of virtue). In ordinary life, we can modify our behaviour as we go along, tripping along in a state of tolerable compromise. But the classical view, expressed through the instrument of drama, isn't concerned with a few smart tweaks of character in the light of counselling, so that a person becomes more caring or honest. Its purpose is the complete destruction of the false, so that a person loses what they are not to become what they are. It's a different approach, but far more dramatic. It provides us not just with a means of improvement, but a moment of truth.

The dismemberment of Orpheus, then, is the eradication of a false identity. His reconstitution in divine form is the restitution of his true nature. The plot might lead to the hero getting the girl, or the guy, or putting right an injustice, throwing off the shackles of slavery, or repairing that dysfunctional relationship with their father, but the real change has already happened. The rest is merely a signifier, a MacGuffin.

This change, or reconstitution, is what the crisis is all about. By the time we get to Act Four (in our five-act structure) we have hammered the false logos to the point where it begins to crack. That is also the moment when it most wants to stay; it is, after all, invested with a sense of self. All the energies of self-preservation kick in when it's under threat. So the challenge has to increase until the false ego is clutching desperately to the last tendril of its usurpation. This is Claudius in *Hamlet* wrestling with the possibility of admitting his crime. It is any athlete reaching the wall. It is the breaking point. As dramatists, we push it just that little bit further. We send in the drunken women of Thrace to do their thing.

That moment of dismemberment is a point of sacrifice. What is lost is the character's acquired nature. What is revealed is the true. Darth Vader didn't just decide, on balance, that the universe would be a better place if he were more loving. He fractured, gave up and dissolved away to reveal Anakin Skywalker, the Jedi knight. It wasn't a change but the return. Jack Harper in *Oblivion* doesn't simply remember his past, he ceases to be Jack Harper the technician whose memory was wiped for security purposes. Carver in *Seraphim Falls*, having pursued his adversary in the name of revenge, inexorably, for years, doesn't change his mind (after all that!). He lets go of his hatred and thus the false Carver in whose thrall he had ridden for much of his life.

In early forms of theatre, the link between drama and sacrificial ritual was perhaps more obvious than it is today. Classical Greek theatre was profoundly associated with healing (literally 'making whole'), one of its prime amphitheatres being part of a hospital. Ancient Indian drama has its roots in the Rig Veda, the art of sacrifice. So look for the moment when the main character, or any character, bleeds on the altar of whatever idea provides the constant, unmoving point of the drama, which is to say your theme. Sometimes he or she will literally bleed. Sometimes he or she might bleed tears. But there must be that slicing of the jugular, the twitch of the limbs and the death, one way or another, of the false self.

If sacrifice runs through story and the journey of our characters, it also has a part to play in the gathering of Stuff. It is the means by which story is discovered. That letting go of the individual perspective which we examined during our study of the writer on the train is an act of sacrifice. Once the writer surrenders his personal identifications, he is no longer the affronted man watching the kid with his feet on the seat. He is no longer the man driving past the picnic, nor the writer in a pub turning back to get his nose bloodied in the name of art. In order to write Andy facing up to Billy, I had to become Andy. I've never scrunched up somebody's poster. I have never knowingly denigrated the literary arts. But I have, on occasion, been a shmuck, felt powerful, felt a bit superior, thrown my weight around. Writing Andy meant finding that attribute, that scorn, within myself. I had to become the bully on the bar stool, as well as the young writer with hurt feelings.

The writer, then, flits freely between identities. At one moment he has his feet on the seats, is pouring from a flask of tea trying not to think about the mobilisation papers that came yesterday, is staring down some smug little oik who puts on plays. You cannot do this from the fixed position of a locked identity. It is from this mobility that characters are born. The actor, in turn, will find that character, and give it his or her own breath of life. All this is done so that the audience, too, can face the false – and give it up.

THE MIRROR

Logos is just a word (which happens to mean 'word') to indicate something at the root of every individual being. It partakes of consciousness, which powers it, along with the various shifting identities reflected within it. Those identities can be a tool by which we interact with the world, or a burden that robs us of joy. There are many ways to examine this area of experience, and numerous theories and models to illustrate it. We are following here simply an extrapolation from the Western literary tradition with its origins in classical Greek theatre. From our vertical character structure, it seems that logos precedes thought by a long way. It would be a mistake, therefore, to think that we can locate it in the realm of thought. If we think we have, the chances are we've just arrived at another, fairly superficial, construct. It even precedes our emotions. So you can't actually feel it. But it's there. It's the meta-data, or epi-data, of everything we feel and think. And although it thus escapes any analysis by those processes, it is nevertheless evident by the way those processes perform; we know it's there by its effect.

That which reflects both the constant and the transient can be likened to a mirror. It is lit by awareness, a sense of self, but populated by nature, which is to say virtues, flaws and prevailing ideas. According to Shakespeare, as we have seen, the purpose of playing is to hold up exactly that instrument. The power of drama lies in its reflection of our own psyche and the laws of human nature. What we are looking at in drama, through both its construct and content, is ourselves. Which means we'll enjoy a drama we can relate to. It also means we'll know, instinctively, if a drama does or does not conform to the architecture of our own means of experience.

Much of the time we can't see ourselves. We simply act and react according to impulses, possibly modified by social norms and behaviour training, over which we have no jurisdiction. Theatre provides that glimpse within. Like Claudius, we get the chance to observe all that makes us tick, and that which lies beyond the clockwork. And, like Claudius, we can sometimes find that uncomfortable. But it's a price worth paying. In fact, we like the drama to hurt us a bit. Like a good exercise session, like an exam, like anything which challenges us to go beyond our usual zone, drama needs to rip us apart before it can put us back together. The journey of the audience and the journey of the character are one and the same.

CHARACTER AS STORY

In our exploration of story we remarked that if you're going to have an action you need someone to perform it. The lawn, as pointed out to me last weekend, doesn't mow itself. Hence the invention of an agent, or character, with a desire. But we could equally say that in order to test our character we need to give him or her a task, such as mowing the lawn. Character isn't there simply to serve story. And story isn't there to serve character. The two are so closely woven that, in the end, they are indistinguishable.

This is important to bear in mind at any stage of the writing, but if neglected at the outset, the early thinking, we can end up with forced story to provoke a character development, or flat characters moving a piece of narrative from 'a' to 'b'. Allowing them to develop together can mean being prepared to revisit our early ideas. Fixed character traits, or immovable story points, can begin to clash. The trick is to become enamoured of neither until the whole piece finds coherence and consistency.

So don't try to get the structure right before working on the characters, or vice versa. If you're writing for existing characters and existing locations, you may not have this luxury. That's why writing for returning series can be more challenging than writing an original piece. I wrote an episode of *Eastenders* taking advantage of the various locations (the pub, the square, the nail bar and the laundrette) only to be told that, for scheduling reasons, I could only have the interiors of one house for the entire story. But the world is not just the outward physicality. It's also a mood, statement, and a theme. I had no choice but to use the claustrophobic intensity of the single set to heighten the claustrophobia of the story. In retrospect I wouldn't have done it any other way!

But OK, let's assume we have access to a lawn in our script. We get the character to mow it in order to challenge him. That challenge allows us to pursue the Orphic journey of transformation. Simply mowing the lawn might not bring that about, unless we slice the power cable, or our fingers, or accidentally reveal the decomposing remains of the previous owner's wife. Sometimes we need to turn up the heat a little. Positioning opposition against your character's efforts is to create a point of friction, of conflict. Just remember that mere conflict is not drama. It's just people shouting or fighting. The point is the extent to which it brings about transformation. So guard the bank they're about to heist with armed police. Make that man oblivious to the charms of the woman who loves him. Steal the family pet. Crash the car. It's not the bang that matters, but the bucks we get out of it. To borrow again from the analogy of the alchemist, you need lead, you need a crucible, you might need some charms and incantations, but what gets the whole thing going, in the end, is heat.

WORKING WITH CHARACTER

That the vertical structure of character reflects our original structure showing the relationship between universal themes and circumstantial particulars is no accident. The top of the pole, as it were, indicates the realm of most permanence. The sense of self is an unchanging constant in the character. In many ways, that is what the story enables us to reveal. The logos is a little more fixed and we need to give it a good pummelling to bring about change. Emotions ebb and flow throughout the story while thoughts vary from a rigid concept to a fleeting spasm. In our image of the circle, the 'I' is the unmoving point around which the wheel turns. The further out we are on the radius, the faster we move.

With that in mind, it follows that we write character from the centre outwards. We inhabit their sense of self with our own, we sense the logos, feel the emotion, think the thoughts and write down what they say or do, or don't say and don't do. As with all the elements, the more strongly rooted the vertical structure, the more fun we can have with the peripheries. But it also follows that a strong inner sense of the character naturally powers their outward manner. Thus, Woody Allen's stuttering characters are forever struggling to find the words to express a convoluted thought. Many of Clint Eastwood's Western characters would as soon spit as speak. Alan Bennett's characters often talk with a lazy drawl, one eye on their thoughts, another on their words, and a third, if there is a third, wondering if it's time for tea.

A common question to writers of returning series is, how do you maintain consistency of character when you're just picking up from a long-running narrative? Obviously one has access to their story documents (all the things they've said and done in the past, their origins, some profile and the terrible things that have happened to them), and an indication of what they're like by what they're up to now. But the key is to find their sound. Once you've caught their voice, you can write them. Dot Cotton speaks in a very different manner to Sam Mitchell, Billy, Andy, or, for that matter, Lois Lane. In that voice is everything you need to know about the character.

....

AN **EXERCISE**

When you get a chance, try listening not just to the words of someone speaking to you, but the sound of their voice. You'll find it hugely instructive and it can tell you more than the meaning, or impression, that they are attempting to convey. If you like, you can try listening to your own voice. Which might be equally instructive. What you'll get from this is an understanding of the relationship between outward and inward sound. The way we speak is governed by how we think. How we think is governed, to a large extent, by how we feel. And how we feel, as we've seen, is rather dependent on who we think we are at any given moment.

....

You may not need to write up a character profile when working quietly on your original screenplay, but most proposal documents will give an indication of the main characters. A common error is to describe the outward attributes in lieu of the inner voice, or logos. Sometimes this is in order to appear inventive, or simply to transcribe as faithfully as possible the image in your head. I read one character profile which described in precise detail the shape of the character's mouth – and this didn't even have anything to do with the plot. Well, don't. Aside from the difficulties of casting an exact set of physical attributes, these pale into insignificance beside the authenticity of a character's inner life. A useful technique is to show that through story. Of course there is a need for some factual details, such as age and sex. But the character, as we have seen, is formed by their exchange of words and actions with the world around them. So write that.

The following is an example of a fairly weak attempt to create a character. It tells us too much while giving us very little:

Mabel is an attractive lady in her twenties. She has red hair and freckles. She's quite tall, about 5'10", and a bit more when she's wearing heels, which she likes to do on special occasions. She can easily be annoyed by people whom she thinks are idiots. She loves her pet cat (Fluffy, a black and white female with a pink nose) and enjoys paragliding at the weekend. She is also a dangerous spy who travels around the world assassinating drug barons. Her preferred drink is rum, which she never takes chilled. Her favourite colour is maroon. She is a cross between Gazelle and Aardvark. Her Archetype is Machine. Her Number is 8.

We might find her interesting or not, but, personally speaking, this doesn't really do it for me. She doesn't stand out, or up, and I can't find the energies that I would need to tell her story. And that's partly because she hasn't got one. So create her story. The term 'backstory' implies not just a sequence of dates and places but the events which have shaped that character. What makes them interesting now are the remaining imbalances generated by, or left over from, the past. What's bugging them? What do they fear? What do they want? If they think they're whole, happy and complete, to what tenuous set of circumstances are they attached?

A useful word in any character profile is 'but'. Its effect is to turn the character from an assemblage of attributes into a fully fledged Orphic hero. 'But' is the antithesis of static since it establishes a binary that needs resolution. Mabel likes rum but sometimes she's too drunk to find the bottle. Mabel's favourite colour is maroon, but every time she wears it something bad happens. Mabel loved her cat but accidentally ran it over when she came home in a hurry.

Here's an example from the profile of a lead character in a theoretical adaptation of E Nesbit's *The Enchanted Castle*:

Kathleen, Gerald's sister, is 12 years old. She comes from a loving but busy family. When she's with her parents they're great. But her father spends much of his time working and her mother travelling and Kathleen sees more of her boarding school than she does either of them. This has made her a little insecure and rather shy. She's pretty and presentable, well mannered but a bit dreamy. Lonely sometimes, she fills the gaps in her life with fables and fairy tales. Her big regret is that life is never quite so magical as the books would have us believe. Where are the handsome princes, the romantic quests, the enchanted castles? Sometimes, on a bright spring morning, the world does seem like a magical place and enchantment just a gossamer veil away. But this summer, she's fairly sure, is going to be the least magical ever. Her parents are abroad together and she's been condemned to stay with her brother at his dreary school. While she welcomes Gerald's company, living under the bleak rule of grown-ups all summer long is as bad as it gets. To her surprise and delight, however, the magic begins on her first day. As it progresses, she finds herself faced with the chance she's always dreamed of: to live forever in a magical place.

But forever is a long time and what about Kathleen's other life, her real life with its ordinary human troubles and simple human joys? What she needs to learn is that there really is magic in everyday things, in the love of her family, in the twinkle of her own soul. In the end, she has to choose.

You can see that imbalance right at the start. This is Orpheus minus Eurydice. What Kathleen lacks is the attention of her parents and a sense of magic. As we move on, we are setting up story as much as we're describing Kathleen; which is just as it should be.

Here's another one from the same theoretical treatment:

Jimmy, 11, the son of a soldier, is angry at being stuck in school yet again over the holidays. While he accepts that his father is hardly ever at home, it annoys him that his mother has gone to India for the summer without even considering lugging Jimmy along. Sometimes he feels as if he's just an excess piece of family baggage nobody really wants around. An only child, he has successfully transferred a consequent sense of isolation even to the crowded bustle of a boarding school. He thinks for himself and doesn't yet appreciate how useful a quality that is. All he can see for the moment is how much trouble it lands him in. He questions his teachers and gets a roasting. He cheeks his prefects and gets detention. He challenges his fellow pupils and sometimes has to defend himself with his fists. Physically, he's quite slight, but he's also wiry, brave and stronger than he realises. Unfortunately, perhaps, he's grown tired of childhood a little too early, longing to grow up so he can be big, strong, in charge of his own life and free from the endless bosses, be they prefects, teachers or the likes of Gerald, who tell him what to do. He wants to play with Gerald, mainly because there's nobody else around, but he doesn't quite have the strength to stand up to him. So he plays on Gerald's terms since the only thing worse than playing with someone who irritates you is playing on your own.

During the course of the story, and through the unlikely intervention of Gerald, Jimmy finally discovers what real friendship is all about. It startles him. It isn't to do with allegiances, ganging up or pacts. It's do with trust, openness and the ability to listen not just to your would-be friends but, most importantly, to yourself.

Again, we kick straight off with the minus factor. He feels unwanted. And this makes him aggressive. There is tension with the other characters. And, just to nail it, we take a moment to open him up, or break him down, Orpheus-like, to his true nature. This is important because it's the theme of the whole piece. Nesbit was exploring the idea that the world itself is magical if you can see it that way, and that to search for magic outside of it is a hazardous pursuit. We might also notice that this is Kathleen's theme, in a world of absent parents, dull boarding schools and kids alone together over the holidays.

Every writer will find their own way to describe a character. But (that word again) until the imbalance is introduced, and there is some indication of how the character will seek to redress it, there is no story. And no story, as we understand by now, means no character.

ALPHABET SOUP

The word character is also used, as we've noted, for the letters of the alphabet. It should not surprise us to find some correlation between this idea and characters in a story.

Since letters in the alphabet retain their shape, albeit with variations of font, they are generally recognisable for what they are. A is A and M is M. If this were a fluid, subjective rule, it would be difficult to string letters together to make up sentences. Similarly, the characters in your story need to be clearly identifiable. So make sure the mark, engraving, logos – or whatever we wish to call it – is clear, deeply written and constant.

This might seem obvious, but it is often the case that characters bleed into each other, losing their identifiable shape. Or they are too shapeless to begin with. They become indistinct, fuzzy, and difficult to use. Even when you focus them, you might find that different characters share too many of the same characteristics. The distinction between letters matters. It is not just what they are but what they are not. We can't confuse a P with a Z – although the analogy does break down a bit with the curiosities of English spelling. If two characters are too similar, either look for differences to emphasise, or think about conflating them. If one character has too many characteristics, think about splitting it up.

That your logos is deeply engraved doesn't mean your character walks around with his arms pinned to his sides. In a moving, emotionally fraught situation, he can be moved and fraught. In a tense, edgy situation, he can be tense and edgy. We've seen that the more peripheral we are to the centre of the character, the more changeable their responses become. But there must be that, in their centre, which is identifiably them. Even when we break into their logos, we should be able to recognise the revealed nature. It can be a challenge to make that convincing. A big change needs to be handled with care. When Darth Vader finally gives way, we shouldn't doubt that Anakin Skywalker was always there.

I have, on occasion, created – or contributed to the conception of – new characters for returning series. One of them was a paramedic called Dixie in the series *Casualty*. She was accompanied by a colleague and friend called Cyd. We spent a lot of time and effort crafting Dixie with the result that audience awareness of her was off the scale after one episode. She also lasted many years in the show.

Her sidekick Cyd received less attention and, in retrospect, was defined only according to her relationship with Dixie. Although played by a fine actress, Cyd fared less well, remaining under the audience radar for most of her short life in the series. We hadn't defined her well enough, nor given her a powerful logos, nor distinguished her narrative from Dixie's.

Sometimes we'll start a story with a powerful sense of the main character. It might be through character that your Stuff took shape. Even if the story starts with a shard of narrative, such as a bank robbery, it will soon begin to ooze characters: a robber, the robbed, the confidante, the traitor, etc. Either way, we sometimes need to do some writing to learn more about our characters, who they are, their voice, manner, impulses and how they fit with all the other characters in the story. This could take a couple of drafts, or even more. In the process of writing they might suddenly surprise us, or disappoint us. We might find them richer than we'd initially conceived, or superfluous. This process of discovery is perfectly acceptable and the way that many writers like to work. But once the script is finished, the discovery is done. The characters are in place and should arrive, as it were, fully cooked. They don't begin bland and take on detail as we discover more about them (unless that's a part of the story). They arrive seething with a sense of being that we can unfold, strategically, as the audience gets to know them.

In *Oblivion*, both Jack and Victoria begin their story bland to the point of hilarity. Except we know this is a sci-fi movie with a twist, plus neither Tom Cruise nor Andrea Riseborough is under any obligation to perform badly written scripts. By the end, we understand what was present at the beginning, and exactly why they were as they were.

When *NYPD Blue* first hit the screens, back in 1993, it caused a stir in British returning series. When *ER* was released the following year, its BBC equivalent, *Casualty*, nearly had a meltdown with executives running around clutching their heads crying, 'It's all over, we're doomed.' Part of the perceived threat was down to the fast editing, grittier storylines, energetic pace, and bigger budget – meaning better production values. But while neither the BBC nor ITV could equal the kind of budget needed for this level of television drama, it costs nothing to write deeper characters and have them arrive, at the top of every episode, the top of every scene, fully formed. So don't introduce your characters as a blank sheet upon which you will eventually get round to drawing something. The cops in *NYPD Blue* and the medics in *ER* strolled into their first scenes bristling with backstory, hang-ups, ambitions, desires, fears and needs. After you've finished your first draft, then, if not before, look at the first appearance of any character and ask if they are all there. They don't have to be fully revealed at this point, but is everything in place, lurking, potent, edgy and powerful, waiting for its moment? Your characters need to be real, rich, complete, and compelling from the off.

Aside from writing the script, there are many ways to find out more about your characters. Some writers, as we've said, like to crack on with the script itself, enjoying the process of discovery – and not resenting in the least any need to go back and rewrite. Others like to put the work in early, minimising the number of drafts. Rule number one is: do whatever suits you. Rule number two is: every project is different and might need to be approached in a different way.

One approach, which you might like to try, is to lift off the brackets that begin and end your script and consider the whole story of the character. You can go back as far (great-grandparents? great-grandchildren?), or into as much detail as you like. It might be a little time-consuming to get over-obsessed about this, so keep it simple. Where do they come from? What have they done? What's been done to them? How have they changed over time, and why? What have they lost, or gained? Pick a few instances. In this way you can build up an understanding of the character that doesn't resort to adjectives. If you start to enjoy this exploration, write a few key scenes from their history. Write a few non-key scenes. Take them for a walk in the park on a sunny day with a close friend during which nothing much happens. What do they talk about, if anything? Kill their hamster. How do they react?

With this in place, now choose where to start your story. You can make instant decisions, narrowing the timeframe down, but, as you get closer in, five minutes here or there could make a big difference. The question is: why now? Why start here? And why end here? The answer will relate to theme, to vertical structure. *Philadelphia* didn't start with the diagnosis, remember, because this wasn't a story about a young man finding out he has AIDS. This was about a young man with AIDS standing up to the ignorance of the people around him.

You might find the following questions helpful for digging into your characters:

- What would have happened if this hadn't? In other words, remove the major event of your story and consider how your protagonist would have merrily carried on with his or her uninterrupted life. Eurydice survived the snake bite. What happened next?

- What will your hero do after the end credits have rolled?

- How have the characters been influenced by each other? What would they have done if they'd never met?

- Change an important detail of your central character's history (their parents decided to move, or not move, to a different city or country). What would they have done? What would they have been like?

Invent some questions of your own.

TRIANGULATION

Much is made of character consistency, but equally useful is inconsistency. We've said that the more strongly rooted your character, the more adaptable they can be. Likewise, the more complex their inner life, their nature, anxieties, needs, emotions and thought processes, the more shades of themselves they can reveal in any given situation. This provides us with a powerful technique for revealing character. It is certainly more effective than having other characters talk about them (which should be avoided as much as possible).

Just as mobile phones can be pinpointed by their relative proximity to three antennae, so you can triangulate a character by observing their responses to different situations. Thus, for instance, they can be cheerful with a friend, obsequious to a superior and pompous to a subordinate. The differences in their behaviour allow us to locate their centre, their logos, without the need to describe or explain. So give your character a variety of circumstances with which to respond. Walter White (*Breaking Bad*) is a different man with his boss, his pupils, his wife, his brother-in-law and his partner in crime. But at the heart of this is the same Walter White. We use this technique all the time to read the people around us. And, if we're honest about it, what we think is our consistent behaviour pattern, our uniquely identifiable and immutable way of doing things, changes from moment to moment depending on the circumstances.

There is artistry in this, since it demands a very deep understanding, or feel for, our character. Don Draper in *Mad Men* shifts seamlessly from super-cool ad guru, to sleazy lothario, to gibbering wreck, in the space of minutes. A part of his character is the fracture between who he was and what he came to be; but what saves this from a feeling of supremely wayward writing is depth of character. By the time we get to the later seasons, we know enough about him not to be surprised (mostly).

If your character doesn't encounter a sufficient variety of situations to force a change in manner, then take a little time to invent some off-screen moments. Have them crash the car, bump into a pregnant lady, or lose a pair of glasses. Try them out until you have a powerful sense of their centre.

If a character is rooted deeply enough, we will recognise something of ourselves in everything they say and do. We will be compelled to follow their journey. Hannibal Lecter isn't a character with whom we might expect to feel much sympathy or resonance, but his hunger, desire and survival instincts, base and amoral as they are in application, can be found somewhere in all of us. This doesn't mean that we are all potential serial killers; we have other attributes to block any such impulse, if the impulse occurred at all. But we

MoVEd.

37.

                    JED (CONT'D)
        And ... that's gonna save the
        universe ... how?

Christie shows Jed a diagram of an elaborate device which
incorporates a vegetable steamer.

                    XAN
               (Indicates a place on the
                truck)
        That'll go here.

Jed goes over to Xan.

                    JED
        So this ... this geezer. Your arch
        enemy. He's ... I guess he's
        pretty evil, is he?

                    XAN
        Evil, I wouldn't say pretty.

                    JED
        Ookay.
               (Glances at Christie)
        So ... so what does he look like?

                    ZARA
        Like anything he wants to. A post
        box, a tree.

                    XAN
        Always count the trees.

Zara looks round, worried.

                    JED
        A dustbin, maybe? A tea spoon?

                    XAN
        I wouldn't be surprised if he's
        disguised as a human being. There
        are advantages in taking the form
        of the indigenous species.

                    JED
        Like you did?

                    XAN
        This is how we look.

                    CHRISTIE
        And the bucket was for him was it?

                    XAN
        The bucket was for you.

Christie looks at Jed.

know what it is to need, to want, and, sometimes, to cut corners (if
not throats) to achieve our goals. So he isn't completely alien to us.
There are villains for whom we feel no empathy. We're just waiting
to see them defeated or, like Darth Vader and Richard II, revealed.
Our hero, however, if he or she is to be more than just the person

behind the wheel in a car chase, needs to have layers of thought, feelings and the defining logos. It doesn't matter if we like or dislike them. The point is that we can identify with something of their nature. We will all identify with their journey of transformation, the simple, primal process of covering and discovering one's nature. Sympathy is irrelevant if the writing is powerful enough, if their journey is ours.

Once you have strong characters, the challenge may not be getting them to do and say things but to stop them. They have a life of their own. During a quick script meeting following a read through, a producer picked out a line of dialogue from one of the characters, Jed, who was being characteristically facetious, playful and slightly gross. See the figure on the previous page. They wondered if he wouldn't say more. He would. I scribbled in a few more lines. In the end, one of the other characters had to stop him with an interruption. The point is that Jed had his own voice by this time and my job was to honour it.

Which brings us neatly to the next subject in our deliberations: dialogue.

DIALOGUE

MEANING

The word 'dialogue' means, literally, the expression (dia-) of logos (-logue). It is the means by which our characters make themselves known. We all use it, all the time. Even alone, we often keep up a constant stream of interior speech to remind ourselves of who we are, or think we are, and that we're alive. At the most superficial level, dialogue provides the words that the characters say. But, as we've seen, these words are, or should be, indicators of a deeper meaning that originates, pre-language, in the core of a character's being.

· The word is sometimes used to mean simply 'exchanged words between two people', where 'di' is understood as 'two' and 'logue' as 'speech'. As such, it is distinct from monologue in which 'mono' means 'one'. But this isn't quite correct and begs a few questions like: what do you call speech between several people (multilogue?), or the pauses between words? In practice, people tend to speak when others are present, just as the presence of others solicits or provokes speech. So 'two or more people exchanging words' isn't a bad definition. It's just incorrect.

Logos means meaning. All words are expressions of meaning. Meaning is thus the root, and purpose, of all words. If we don't know what a word means, we look it up. If it doesn't mean anything, we are unlikely to use it. The meaning of any word lies, arguably, in the realm of experience. We can hear the word food, we can have the meaning explained, but at some point we'll only get it when we eat something. This experience is not a word but, obviously enough, an experience which the word signifies. All words, therefore, derive from a pre-lingual level of understanding. Logos at its most profound is exactly that, and everything a character does, and says, or doesn't do, or doesn't say, or chooses, or decides, or regrets even silently, comes from that level, from logos. By this understanding, dialogue isn't just the use of verbally expressed words but any means by which a character finds self-expression: gestures, a way of breathing, clothes, a car, and so on. Once again, a component of dramatic material reveals itself to have a permeable membrane. And, once again, we are compelled to think, albeit reluctantly, of bananas.

One advantage of understanding dialogue more broadly is that its purely verbal aspect can be used more effectively, which is to say, usually, less. Thus a character doesn't need to get on his mobile and say, 'Hi, it's Jake here, just stepping out of my fancy car, which I'm really proud of; in fact, it makes me feel vaguely superior to everyone else.' He can just step out of his fancy car, glance back at it, and smile smugly as he walks away. A character doesn't have to say, 'I hear what you're saying but I'm not quite sure how to respond, hang on a sec; oh, OK, I've just thought of an answer which goes...' You can just insert 'Beat' or 'Slight Pause' or even 'Hesitates' in parentheses.

The look back at the car, the smile, the beat or pause, are all expressions of the character's sense of self, their thoughts, emotions, hang-ups and expectations. If you include these in the script, either explicitly in the stage directions, or implicitly, you take the pressure off the words, which don't have to work so hard. It means that, when you do use words, it is to reveal, not explain. Which is to say that how they are used, and what they don't say, gives us as much insight into the character as the words that issue from their mouths. It's an end to expositional dialogue, which is not dialogue at all – at least by our definition – since it comes more from the intent of the writer than the logos of the character.

In early drafts (and on bad days), words can sometimes thud on to the page, weighed down by lumpen import, yielding nothing more than stale information. Characters explain what they intend to do, or have done, or are doing. They tell each other their feelings. To the same eye that flicks through instruction manuals, this might seem to be of value. At least we've been told what the characters are thinking and what they intend to do. But to the poet's eye this is nothing. It has no poetic meaning. It offers no story, no character, no theme. When the man shouts 'Harry, answer that' in the first scene of *Taxi Driver* (it is, in fact, the very first line of the film), this isn't so that the audience will know that the name of the man who answers the phone is Harry, or that there's an important call coming in that we need to signal. It tells us who is in charge, how he runs things, the pressure he's under and that people listen to him. It lays the groundwork for the power dance that follows. It also reduces people to function, and communication to transaction, which is a central theme of the story. As information/exposition, this line could easily be cut. We never even find out who was at the other end of the phone. As character, story, idea and theme, it is perfect. The line sings. And if you remove it, the Q&A with Travis that follows would be subtly diminished; just the bland soliciting of biographical information for the edification of the audience. With the line in, deeper ideas are set in motion which play out right to the end of the film.

In a script conference, once, an executive pointed to a line in which a mother corrects her son's grammar. The boy said 'Christie gave it me', and the mother says 'to me'. The executive asked if we could lose it. I couldn't see what it was doing there. Perhaps it was just one of those twitches of the dialogue-writing pen that occasionally drops in a superfluity. I crossed it out. Later on, as we turned the pages, the mother went to her son's school with a complaint. I suddenly realised that the earlier line indicated that she took his education seriously. Without it, the energy of her arrival at the school was manifestly lessened. We put the line back.

Where speech is used to convey information, as in that first scene of *Taxi Driver* in which a Q&A between Bickle and the personnel officer might seem to offer little more than Bickle's CV, the information is skilfully wrapped into Bickle's vain attempts to communicate on a personal level, until the personnel officer actually tries to respond at that level but is too late. The scene ends with a transaction. The words don't just fly across the room spitting information; they are embodied in a richer, deeper movement of story, character and theme.

If your meaning exists at a pre-lingual level, which is to say there is no one word, nor even a collection of words, that will ever quite pin it down, it follows that you can't express it directly through speech. Instead, you indicate it through signs and allow your audience to become involved with the process of decoding. Not only will this help to prevent them from feeling unnecessary (and thus bored), it will draw them into that pre-linguistic state of comprehension where they can relish your themes and meanings more fully. A character who says, 'I'm really unhappy right now,' does not automatically induce an empathetic feeling in the audience. To evoke the required emotion you have to solicit their participation. This is how you keep them intrigued and enthralled. To put it another way, your character notes don't show directly on the screen. You're not allowed explanatory captions, and it is cheating to have other characters deliver them:

Jake: Ah, yes, Lucy. Well, she puts on a show of being a bit of a socialite, but deep down she's very insecure, probably because her father left home when she was only eight years old and she's had a string of unsuccessful and disappointing relationships.

Marlene: Wow. I hadn't realised that. Tell me about Annabel.

OK, in the postmodern era, we can have great fun with the no-no's, but a) you limit your audience, and b) you are still dependent on the conventions you subvert. If your intention is to write engaging, believable characters, and they're not turning out that way in your script, you need to find out what's going on. With that in mind, consider the following:

Carter: I haven't seen you for over two years and I've lost touch with your life and the family and in fact who I used to be. And I am experiencing a mild sense of regret about it. In fact, to my surprise, I simply don't belong here any more. So what have I become? Who am I now? Have I exchanged something valuable for something tawdry? When I left home all those years ago I thought it was the other way round.

Niece: I used to know you but now I don't. In fact, there's something about you that I don't trust or for that matter like.

Carter: What a pity.

Had *Get Carter* been written in this style, it would not only have been a very long film, it would have yielded few, if any, of the iconic lines that continue to entertain at social occasions. One could argue that it's functional enough; it fills in the backstory and sets up some narrative for the future. But it fatally betrays the laconic nature of the central character, who would have a hard time recovering from this. It also damages the gritty, naturalistic tone with an artificial way of speaking you're unlikely to hear anywhere in this universe. Finally, it leaves nothing for the audience to engage with. We are being told. We are not discovering. Instead, try this:

Carter: So how's school?

Niece: I left school two years ago.

Carter: (Beat) What are you doing now?

Niece: I work at Woolworths.

Carter: (Beat) That must be very interesting for you.

SHE SAYS NOTHING. AN AWKWARD PAUSE.

This is a transcription from the film itself, so I've added the beats. The beat indicates a moment of thought. It is as expressive as anything said in words. In some ways, it's more powerful because it registers a change in idea and feeling. Carter is re-evaluating the situation in the light of a new insight. We know that. And it feels very real. The bathos of the last line is all the more powerful for its understatement. It stands as a wonderful example of underwriting. Take a moment to compare the two approaches and ask what the effect of either is. As an exercise, you might like to take a few more examples of dialogue from different films and write out everything indicated by the text. Write it as bad dialogue. It can be fun to do. That which lurks behind the words is known as 'subtext'. It is what actors act. Those lines on the surface are just a door to its depth of meaning.

If a beat, which is to say an act of not speaking, is part of dialogue, then so is a pause, three dots, a hyphen, a look, a gesture, and a turn of the head. Since everything the character wears, the car he or she drives, the house he or she lives in, and so on, have come about through decisions made, and words thought or spoken, these too are attributes of dialogue. Once dialogue is considered beyond the subset of the spoken word, we can see that it has few limits in terms of its relationship to every other element in drama. We didn't list it in our early elaboration of the elements because it is the expression of those elements, their fruition. It follows that, in order to write dialogue, in the sense of putting it down on the page, all the other elements need to be in place first.

DIALOGUE AND THE ELEMENTS

New writers often try to fill the page with as many words as possible in order to make the writing seem rich and full. What we've seen, however, is that most of the writing consists of invisible text. It is represented in its final expression as words on a page, but these merely indicate the presence of character, story, theme, and so on. Reading a screenplay, for that reason, is an art in itself. A good cure for overwriting is to read lots of screenplays. But let the eye honestly see what's on the page and the mind ask what it means, what it's doing. If possible, read first and watch the film later. Then reverse the process with another film. Learn how the invisible world makes it on to the screen through that strangely austere artefact that is the honed-down screenplay. Words on the page are the last thing that happens.

DIALOGUE AS CHARACTER

We are creatures of speech. Some of that speech emerges from our mouths in audible form – what we call 'talk'. Some of it we might hold back. Some of it we'll wish we had. Sometimes we have so much to say that we can only say nothing. Or we cannot find the words, because we don't have the vocabulary, or because our brains are in a spin. Sometimes we'll want to say one thing and it comes out as something else. Sometimes, we'll make do with a hand gesture, a head gesture, or a twitch of an eyebrow. That we're not talking doesn't mean there isn't speech. It just means we're not expressing it verbally. In fact, when we're not speaking outwardly to somebody else, there's a good chance we're speaking inwardly to ourselves. Speech is a constant process. It not only expresses, but creates. The words we say can change what other people think. More importantly, perhaps, the words we say and thoughts we think can change what we say and think. To speak, at whatever level, outwardly or inwardly, is a creative or destructive act. Even a murmuring drone that hardly makes it into the realm of meaning has the effect of blotting out silence.

Words, when they meet the air, might have been sent for any variety of purposes. They might be cooing noises made to a baby, hardly words at all in the conventional sense, but a way of expressing love, or care, or to solicit a response. They might be prosaically functional, for instance the request for a train ticket. But even this could be coloured by intonation; an expression of haste, nervousness, subservience, superiority or distraction. They might be familiar sentences, the ones that haunt us every morning and accompany us to sleep at night: our own personal catch phrases. They'll catch a view of the world that, in turn, catches us in its perspective. Occasionally they burst out of us uncontrollably in response to some provocation. At the root of our speech are thoughts, some of which we are not even aware of, though we live by their consequences. Powering those thoughts are feelings. Behind those are attitudes and ideas, the precepts by which we function. And those ideas, generally, are formed and honed under the supervision of logos, the central sound of every individual. It's a powerful phenomenon, spoken or unspoken. And, as dramatists, we can have a lot of fun with it.

Our schematic of character, as you might have noticed, can also map the trajectory of speech through an individual.

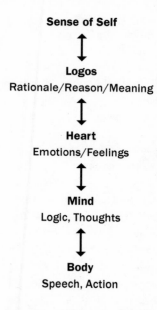

Sense of Self

↕

Logos
Rationale/Reason/Meaning

↕

Heart
Emotions/Feelings

↕

Mind
Logic, Thoughts

↕

Body
Speech, Action

Without a sense of self, the characters have nothing to refer to by the words 'I', 'me' or 'my'. They have nothing to defend, or develop; there is no jeopardy. There is nothing to add to or subtract from their world. If they're lucky, they could get the role of crash-test dummy.

The logos is, if you like, the central sound of a character, the rationale. Once we get this sound, we've got the voice. Once we've got the voice, the character is at liberty to speak. While this powers much of what they say and do, speech that emerges directly, and undistorted, from this area is the most powerful of all, usually reserved for the climax of the story.

Formulation without emotion is useful for instruction manuals but does little to colour our world with interest and vitality (unless you are trying to work the lawn mower). You could call this area the heart. It's where we find courage, trust, a form of love, greed, fear, etc. As with thought, it forms patterns as certain emotional textures become prevalent. This amounts to the basic nature of an individual. It also provides a character with the power to do. This area can be warm and fluid, or cold and rigid. Emotions can be responsive or reactive. They can be open or closed. Speech and action that comes from this level is sometimes called 'heartfelt'.

If the impulse to act comes from the emotional level, then the mode of action, the plan, is conceived in the realm of mind, which is to say of thought, conceptualisation, apprehension and, to some extent, comprehension. This includes logic, basic decision making, choice, the weighing up of information, and the specifics of language itself, with its grammatical structure, stored conventions, dialect and vocabulary. Speech and action that originate here (devoid of emotional charge) are mechanical, dead, articulated through habit.

Under the governance of emotions, the mind can be a cool, clear place in which higher levels of reasoning may be reflected, or a maelstrom of activity in which a thought is lucky to survive, never mind make it to the outside world. The state of mind of your character is integral to the state of the story at any given time. But state of mind there must be, if your characters are to be recognisably alive.

Finally, without expression our characters reveal nothing of themselves. In dramatic terms, they are not characters at all. Character is by nature, like a letter of the alphabet, a manifest entity. Even the failure to respond to some kind of stimuli (short of being in a coma) is dialogue, in that it expresses muteness, numbness or insensitivity. It's quite difficult to write a character that doesn't express anything. The audience cannot see and hear the thought itself, nor the emotion, nor the logos. But they see and hear their expression through words and actions.

Every word and every action therefore ricochets back through thought and emotion to the logos, where they connect to the logos of the story world, its themes and ideas, and everything else taking place within it, including the other characters, their words and actions, along with the various motifs and their significance. Every word and every action is therefore the result of a long process that happens instantaneously. This is Stuff at work.

There should come a point, reading the script, when we don't have to refer to the character names. Who they are will be evident by what they say and how they say it, by their voice. When this is happening, you know they're working. If it isn't, then try to inhabit them, walk them around, speak the lines, hear them, shrug the way they shrug, squint the way they squint, pick some fluff off your sleeve, stare out of a window without seeing anything, flick a stray hair from your forehead: act it out. You can also try some of the exercises we mentioned earlier. If necessary, write scenes that are implied but not essential to the story. Invent moments for them. How do they buy a newspaper? How do they recalibrate the Ergotronic Modificators on the Zetathon? What do they eat for breakfast?

Some writers will note every repetition of a word:

John: I know, I know. I know. Look, OK, look this just isn't working for me.

Depending on how naturalistic you wish your dialogue to be, you can register a change of thought:

Susan: (Pause) I'd like to just talk about – well, I guess I have to talk about the cat.

You can build in small movements of thought:

Sam: Is there any chance we could... I don't know, you said... you said earlier that... that we couldn't. But... well, I was hoping – [to buy some lemonade]

Bill: (Cutting in) Not that again.

You can, as above, interrupt speech. It helps the actor to know what they would have said, had they not been interrupted, while giving the other character a little flexibility with the timing.

What's evident from this kind of dialogue is that we're not just writing words on a page. We are writing thoughts, emotions, the central logos of a character, and imbuing them with a sense of self (in the context of other characters, similarly elaborated, and the situation in which they find themselves). With those in place, their words emerge suffused with the resonance of those levels. This is the definition of dialogue. 'Two or more people exchanging words' doesn't come close.

We might have made extensive notes in our preparations for the script, along with detailed character profiles and marginal scrawls. We could even write in helpful hints to the actors, or use the special features to let the audience into the arcane secrets of our world. But, in terms of dialogue, all that we can put on the screen are words and actions. Through these means, supported by motif, and sometimes music, we convey character, story, ideas and theme. Fortunately, we're used to this in everyday life. In fact, we're masters of it. People do and say things to us all the time, as we ourselves do and say things. Some of that will be of an explanatory nature ('I'm really sorry I forgot your birthday'). Mostly, we allow others to read us through the signs that we give, either deliberately or involuntarily. If we are all experts at this kind of communication (or at least try to be), some are also good at hiding, or mis-directing. Seeing through the charade of misinformation can be, sometimes, half the fun.

Good dialogue reveals more than it says. And we should never, or at least rarely, rely on a character to tell us about themselves. For one thing, they make unreliable witnesses. For another, this kind of speech is very dull. There will be occasions, perhaps, when it is unavoidable (and sometimes it could work). But we should feel ourselves duty bound, unless there's a very good reason otherwise, to bend every sinew of our keyboard, or pen, to avoid it.

In so far as we have created a schematic for character and dialogue, it should be regarded as a dynamic rather than a construct. Sat navs carry highly simplified formulations of a journey; they don't account for every twitch of the wheel, every bend and curve, the hay wagon slowing you down, the sunlight in the trees to your left, the fancy car sitting on your bum, or the fancy car in which your bum is sitting, nor the mood and feeling, energy and pace of every street or lane. It might note the presence of a bridge but cannot tell you of the swans twirling in the river below (at least not the budget versions I'm used to). We might also want to take detours, slow down to enjoy the moment, speed up for a little thrill, nervously or impatiently overtake. The writing will always be a more detailed, richly experienced artefact than any schematic which attempts to explain how it might be done. And while schematics have a part to play in our first journeys, it is my experience that, if you always rely on the sat nav, you will never quite know the road. There comes a time when you have to get an oft-repeated journey (like a screenplay) out of the dashboard and into your senses. You might get lost a few times to begin with, but you'll arrive with a better sense of the territory across which you travel.

We have argued that a word spoken is thought, emotion, and logos revealed. But thoughts can bounce around before they emerge, tossed by feelings, battered by other thoughts. At the centre of it all is the mystery of a man, or woman, their nature, which might be changing, and their rationale or logos, which might be cracking under pressure. When a word or action finally makes it to the page, it will have taken a perilous journey through meteor storms and asteroid showers of contradiction, belief, feelings, unknown fears, known fears, unknown desires and all the rest of it. Even in the area of mind where words are formed, another thought surfaces before the words can join up to make sentences. Sometimes the power of an emotion forces those words loudly into the ether. Sometimes they are killed at birth. And when the words are spoken, or the action performed, the world reflects it back, often instantaneously, with intended or unintended consequences. There is little time (until the old men talk) to sit down for a breather. As indifferent gods, or heartless bosses, we don't give tea breaks. The world is too active, dynamic and, yes, threatening for that.

If alchemy, as we said earlier, is all about transformation (lead to gold, mundane to meaningful), then, as we've also seen, the crucible needs heat. Heat is kinetic energy; it moves. So does a piece of drama. That's why you can make a change in Scene Five and observe its effect on Scene Sixty-eight. That's why a character can walk into a room and walk straight out, or march to the centre, or draw a gun, or sob, or speak. That room, and the character who walks into it, are living, vibrant, shifting things, bouncing off and colliding with each other to the mutual transfiguration of each. You can't get this by tweaking static objects. It isn't static. And, if it is, light a fire under its proverbial.

John Sullivan, the writer of *Citizen Smith* and *Only Fools and Horses*, among other comedic masterpieces, told of how he'd suddenly catch himself at the cheese counter of his local supermarket, muttering, snarling and sometimes ranting to himself. He felt sure that fellow shoppers thought him possessed; as indeed he was, in the Platonic/Shakespearean sense, by his characters. When they came to him, wherever he was, he couldn't help trying them out, sounding them, getting a feel for them. If you simply write what they say and do, you aren't writing character. Thinking their thoughts gets a little closer, and feeling what they feel closer still. To really nail that character you have to connect with their essential nature. You have to see the world through their eyes. You have to sense their own sense of self and allow that to return outwards via the few, sparse signs of expression by which that might be known. At the cheese counter, or at your desk, you have to, as we have already said, go a little mad. Once that's in place, your characters will speak in the only way they can, react in the only way that they can. And that, my friends, is what character, and dialogue, is all about.

DIALOGUE AS STORY

Characters will, on occasion, be forced by narrative necessity to tell us how the story is going, perhaps to recap on what's happened, to explain its more obscure connections, or justify its least plausible ones. The cast of one recurring BBC series recently rebelled against what they called 'whiteboard acting', which required one of them to stand up in front of all the others to explain what was going on. But dialogue, as we know by now, is also story; the energy and dynamic of the dramatic act, and of transformation.

If we apply our five-act structure, we'll see that every line follows this dynamic. Dialogue originates from a world, a context. It is of that world, shaped by it, formed from it, indistinguishable, in the end, from its material. It requires a character to speak or act it. The speech or action is conceived in desire – the need to express something. The character decides that it's worth saying or doing and applies their will to achieve it. Their effort is met with opposition. Further effort is made. There will be a climax and perhaps a resolution.

The opening scene of *Taxi Driver*, as we've noted, is full of simple narrative information. Bickle can't sleep at night. He's an army veteran with an honourable discharge. He'll work Jewish holidays. What rescues this from whiteboard acting is that every line – in addition to the nuts and bolts of narrative which it happens to carry – is story.

> **Personnel Officer:** Alright, let me see your chauffeur's licence. How's your driving record?
>
> **Bickle:** It's clean. It's real clean, like my conscience.
>
> **Personnel Officer:** You gonna break my chops? Trouble with guys like you breaking my chops... if you're gonna break my chops, you can take it on the arches. Understand?
>
> **Bickle:** Sorry, sir. I didn't mean that.
>
> **Personnel Officer:** Physical?

Bickle doesn't just want a job to pay his bills. He wants to join a world. More than that, he wants to communicate in a real way, as distinct from the soulless rituals of self-serving transaction. So when he detects a little rapport in the conversation, he acknowledges it with a joke. It's an act of familiarity, an articulation of trust.

The personnel officer, on the other hand, is entirely rooted in the world of transactions. All he wants is to make sure that Bickle isn't going to do him over, that he'll work hard and, so far as possible, can be relied upon as a diligent employee who does what he's told. In his experience (Harry, answer that!), most workers need to be cajoled if you're going to get anything out of them. So they have to know who's boss. And they have to be a little bit afraid of him. So when Bickle offers the hand of complicity, Personnel Officer slaps it down. Hard.

Bickle instantly withdraws. His smile goes, his face falls, his eyes cloud over. The exchanges after that are a series of single phrase questions and single phrase answers, until the personnel officer learns that Bickle was in the Marines. Now he changes. He leans back in the chair, loses his intimidating demeanour, and reaches out as one veteran, one human being, to another. But it's too late. Bickle is in his shell, isolated, lonely, and to some extent bitter. That first scene, and its story dynamic, is a microcosm of the whole film. But, as we have seen, this is hardly surprising in a great piece of work.

One could also apply the Orphic Paradigm to this scene. Bickle needs company. He tries to get it. He is ripped to pieces. He reconstitutes himself, but into a dangerous, dark and introverted configuration that will require further shredding later. If you study the complete film, which is recommended, observe how this movement of loss/need, search, hope, dismemberment and reconstitution informs every story move, every beat, every scene and, since this really is a very fine piece of writing, practically every line. The whole thing throbs with that energy. And perhaps that is what gives it such an enduring – even timeless – quality.

WRITING NOTHING

Paul Schrader is rightly lauded for his writing of *Taxi Driver* but it would be a mistake to think that he only wrote the words. Equally important are the silences. It is in the spaces between words that much of the story lives.

A key to this is to write not just the person speaking but the person listening. A character does not cease to exist when they cease to talk. There will be change as they listen and, depending on how they listen, and how they change, this may affect whoever is doing the talking. You should be able to look at the gap between two lines allotted to a character and chart the movement, the changes, the story. Look at how Bickle changes from 'It's clean. It's real clean, like my conscience' to

'Sorry, sir. I didn't mean that.' That's a huge shift in attitude, thought and emotion. Likewise, look at the spaces between the personnel officer's lines and you will see a similar movement. Writing the words and writing the spaces are both integral to the process of writing dialogue.

We've observed that, to the eye, a script is a sparse creature. Most of the page seems to consist of nothing. There is a temptation, sometimes, to fill that space in order to demonstrate effort. Writing, we might argue, is the act of putting words on to a piece of paper (if we're not putting words down, then what the hell are we doing?) But this is not the case. Much of the art of writing is an observation of silence.

What happens in that moment, say, when the character learns of some dreaded news? Don't just look at the person delivering the news and then turn to the character to see what he or she does. Chances are they'll erupt in a stream of hysterical expostulation. Instead, see both. Watch the delivery of that news and, at the same time, keep an eye on the character receiving it. When they do speak, it may only be to mark the change. That rush of grief might have brought tears to their eyes but is already being contended with by the time they respond: muted, parked, repressed. And if you find that your dialogue is a little too much ping pong, in which he speaks then she speaks then he speaks and so on, hit the delete key and find as many opportunities as possible to chart the movement between the lines. This allows the audience to participate, to interpret and decode those movements, which, as we have seen, gets us a pat on the back from Aristotle.

Once you get the hang of writing nothing, you'll enjoy it. Your scenes will quickly reduce to a manageable length. Those ten-page discussions will evaporate instantly. You will gain pace and rhythm. You will start scenes earlier, end scenes later, and revel in the narrative power of the cut. The gap between scenes will develop its own life. In Scene 12 the hero is smug until he sees what's happened to his car. He stares, his face falls. Cut. In Scene 13 he is sitting, distraught, in his lawyer's office. The lawyer is handing him a tissue with which to wipe his eyes. A few lines. Cut.

In musical notation, silence has its own symbol. That's because silence is a value. I once asked a sound engineer, a man who spends every working day in the realm of sound – mostly in live performance – about his work. He told me that he used to get stressed out trying to follow each instrument, checking the volume, the tone, getting the balance right, noticing its effect on the other instruments, twiddling that knob, or fader, and checking again. He would emerge from the concert exhausted. Until he realised, in a sudden epiphany, that beneath all that sound was silence. So he tuned into that, letting it rest, letting it flow, watching it shift and change as the various sounds, with their distinct textures and energies, came and went. It became easy. He started to enjoy it again. And he is now much in demand for his expertise, mixing for many of the world's most revered musicians.

We said earlier that reading scripts is an art in itself. The skill is to connect with those spaces between the written words; to visualise, hear and feel the movements of a story that are more implied, or indicated, than explained. This is why we should never seek feedback from the unskilled. They will only judge it by the obvious.

The power of any drama, as we've seen, lurks in its deeper themes. The moment we drag that theme, kicking and screaming, into the cold, hard realm of words, it is already dying. Its natural medium is subtlety. If we cannot haul it out without damage, then we can at least indicate it. We can make its presence known. What we'll find is that our audience will engage with it not as a mental construct, but in accord with their own subtlety. Nobody goes to the cinema in search of the obvious. They don't need to. The obvious is whacking them over the head all day long. They want to seek out the causes of things, the roots of experience. That's why overwritten material is such a chore to read, or see. It is why vacuous material leaves us unsatisfied. And it is why Big Words issuing through the mouths of your hapless characters are no more meaningful, in the end, than a picture of popcorn is food.

DIALOGUE AND MOTIF

Think of words as a resource. The scarcer they are, the more they're desirable; the more we have, the less valuable they become. You listen when Josey Wales speaks because he speaks so little. His big speech, when it finally comes, addressed to the Native American chief, is a masterpiece of cinema. When the personnel officer says, 'Physical?', he is speaking volumes about ascendancy, challenge and the social order.

One way of reducing the word count, or using words to their greatest effect – which amounts to the same thing – is to employ the tangible. A character could say, 'You know what? I'm feeling really angry right now.' Or he could slam his hand on the table. Even when characters do speak, let them interact with all the powerful motifs by which they are surrounded. Instead of 'How are you feeling?' try 'Do you need a drink?' In the same way, use the world to disrupt the dialogue. If you want to avoid a series of exchanged monologues, have people come in, telephones ring, glasses spill. One of the joys of writing dialogue in hospital corridors is the noise and bustle that constantly interrupts and distorts the dialogue. Add desperation to that character's need to speak. Just as in story, the tougher you make the circumstances, and the harder the character has to work, the more of themselves they reveal.

In an episode of *Eastenders*, I had a character, Den, attempting to convey his reluctance to have guests round for dinner. His wife, by contrast, is enthusiastic about the evening.

He saunters in while she's putting on makeup and demands to know if she's 'seen the paper'. She says, 'What?' He clarifies by telling her, 'It's a big white thing with words on it, tells you what's going on.' By having Chrissie putting on makeup, we establish at the top of the scene that she is making an effort. His manner, coupled with the tactical non sequitur, tells her, and us, in no uncertain terms that he is not. She tells him their guests will be arriving in half an hour, to which he replies that it doesn't take half an hour to read the paper. She then asks if he's going to shave, and expresses anxiety that he'll still be in the bathroom when they arrive. Finally, she points out a freshly ironed shirt, looks at him and says, 'And not those trousers.'

The point is that they communicate their thoughts, feelings and attitudes largely by referencing the objects around them. They speak of newspapers, shaving, the bathroom, shirts and trousers. This greatly enriches the speech, intensifies a sense of the world, draws the audience in through oblique messages, and just feels a bit more natural.

You could think of this as 'third-point dialogue'. The characters don't address, directly, the subject, or explain their thoughts and feelings. Instead they find a third point, such as trousers, to talk about. The sample of dialogue we looked at from *Taxi Driver* begins with a chauffeur's licence and a driving record. Even when the personnel officer lets rip, he uses images: 'breaking my chops' and the 'arches'. He doesn't say: 'I become intensely irritated by individuals applying for work when they have no intention of taking me and my company seriously. Those who feel that it is appropriate to jest when I am asking, seriously, for important information will not be welcome here. If you think that this describes you, please leave immediately.'

Third-point dialogue has the other, supreme, virtue of economy. We have all, I'm sure, seen films that stretch an hour of material into 90 minutes. It feels like a meagre return for the time we've spent on it. What we should aim for is two hours of material distilled into 90 minutes (but why stop at two hours?). The feeling should be of a massive yield for our investment. We should leave the cinema enriched, not impoverished. Every line, therefore, should be worth at least two lines; every beat, two beats. So boil them down. Trim out the excess. Refer to third points. Use the world; it is a powerful, and infinitely eloquent, thing to have at your disposal.

....

AN **EXERCISE**

Write a scene in which the characters employ cringeworthy dialogue. Have them explain what they're thinking, what they want, what they're afraid of, and what they expect from the other person.

Now set it in a bar and, as much as possible, exchange conceptual words for objects.

Do the same with the characters having breakfast. Swap exposition for cereal, toast, mushrooms, etc.

Give them a strenuous activity. They're on a raft navigating a turbulent river. Get the same points across but break it up, disrupt it, while using references to objects.

Repeat the exercise with a few scenarios of your own.

DIALOGUE AS THEME

We've already discussed how ineffectual it is to explicate your theme. The trembling-lip moment in which a character talks about Justice, Truth, Courage, Teamwork, etc, might have earned its place in the climax – and can sometimes be quite moving – but handle it with care. Ideally, it will summarise ideas that have already become apparent, rather than hector the audience with your world view.

Den and Chrissie's conversation about shirts and trousers occurred in a storyline that had much to do with appearance and truth. Both characters were concerned with conveying a particular impression of their family life to the impending guests. That theme was implicit in Chrissie's act of putting on makeup. It rippled through their discussion about ironed shirts and suitable clothing, never spoken but always there. Similarly, the first scene in *Taxi Driver* begins with a demand for papers and ends with an exchange of documents: true communication is subverted to the world of monetary exchange. The whole film is contained in the passing of papers across a desk; simple, efficient and very powerful.

DIALOGUE AS TONE, TEXTURE AND STYLE

Dialogue is as much subject to the meta-textures of style and tone as anything else in the script. Just as the editing can be languid and dreamy, or sharp and brisk, so dialogue can be lyrical, naturalistic, comedic, ponderous, menacing or beautiful – though perhaps not all at the same time. Sometimes the best dialogue is the least elegant. There is a moment in *Lost in La Mancha* when Terry Gilliam batters the hell out of Don Quixote's costume to make it more ragged. Brittle, broken, halting speech can be more eloquent than nicely turned couplets.

The rule is: if it works, it works. A list of do's and don'ts would not only be unpublishably long but so full of exceptions and variations that it would also be, in the end, meaningless. So how do you know what to write? Well, you are a writer, so get on with it! Set it down. You'll know if it works. If it doesn't, somebody will soon tell you.

WORDS

We have already said much about words. A last point to note might be that every word has three prime values: a sound, a meaning and an emotional power. 'Chauffeur's licence' and 'driving record' aren't exactly the sexiest words ever to frolic over the sheets of an empty page, although they share the same rhythm. They are meant to be flat, bureaucratic and functional. They are artefacts from the official, soulless world in which people use each other for their own ends, and in which other human beings are simply a means to that end. Which is why Bickle's response is so inappropriate. It breaks the spell of mundanity with something human, quirky, cheeky. 'Physical?' is like a slap in the face.

But even flattened words have a sound, a natural musicality which resonates with the musicality of the whole piece. We noticed, in *Twelfth Night*, how Shakespeare uses sound and rhythm, as much as the bald meaning of words, to convey character, texture and mood. An early effort of mine consisted of a stage play written in verse. I crafted every word for its sonic impact only to find that the effect was of a three-course meal consisting entirely of chocolate. My BBC mentor remarked that he liked the story but didn't enjoy getting 'slapped in the face' by the language. So there is artistry in this too. The tension of music should ebb and flow, trip and tickle, as you pull it in here, and let it go there. Even the most prosaic script, as we saw with *Taxi Driver*, is not oblivious to the sound of words, nor their collective effect.

Words on a page have their own way of striking the mind. Words spoken have another. Although written words do sound in the mind, they have far less sonic resonance, obviously, than words heard by the ears. So it's a good practice to speak the speech. Hear what it sounds like. Is it good to say? Is it even possible to say? I was once berated by an actor for writing 'he fell four feet on to floorboards' – and made a subsequent vow always to speak the lines myself before handing them over. Try saying it now. It made perfect clinical sense. But no human could ever deliver it.

Hearing the words will give you a sense of their rhythm, how they work in the mouth, whether they sound sharp or rounded, fluid or staccato. You will also get a better sense of measure, of phrases that are too long, lines that occupy more time than they deliver in meaning. You will get to understand breath and how it determines, to a great extent, the flow of speech.

WORKING WITH DIALOGUE

Just as our study of structure is best conducted through the understanding of action, and character through the observation of our own, so we can get a good idea of the power of dialogue by seeing how it works through the mechanics of our own speech. A good place to start is by listening to what we say. How are words formed? What lies behind those words? How do we formulate ideas in the realm of mind, in the area of emotion? What is going in in that pre-linguistic place where our impulses, reasonings and choices are made? We may not be able to discern the subterranean rumble of sound that accompanies our every move, and governs our various decisions, both profound and mundane, but we can identify its nature, its character and its logos through its effect. Which, of course, is how we come to understand characters in a story.

Try doing some ordinary task, such as making a cup of tea, going for a walk, or brushing your teeth while listening to what you're saying to yourself. Are you already formulating your next action? Are you ruminating on the last? Are there patterns, familiar constructs and repetitive thoughts that operate, for the most part, unseen? Bear in mind that what we say to ourselves shapes how we comprehend the world. To what extent is our inner speech an attempt to navigate reality or create one that we can understand? A good time to observe this is during moments of stress, when we're under the kind of pressure we like to inflict on our characters. What do we draw on to help us cope? Is it useful? At what point do we crumple, or leap forward to confront the enemy? How do we choose? Are there patterns, or familiar noises, that repeat only because they always have? What is their effect?

When we attempt to express ourselves, we are engaging in dialogue. As we've seen, even the car we drive, or the clothes we wear, are a form of dialogue. At the very least, they're a legacy of earlier speech, with ourselves or others. But it can be quite difficult, sometimes, to get our point across. It's especially tricky if we're hoping to deceive. It's even trickier if we habitually deceive ourselves. But we learn early and, for the most part, get fairly good at it. As a dramatist, we need to master the signs by which logos is expressed, linguistically and otherwise. Study the clues we give to others, and that others give to us. Use this as part of your acquisition of Stuff. A moment of insight, through some indication of gesture or language, into the heart of another person can spark off a veritable frenzy of Stuff-gathering.

As writers, we are joining a confluence of literary activity that reaches back over millennia. Whether we like it or not, everything we write reflects something of the journey and efforts of those who have gone before. We should celebrate that. We should engage with the power it gives us. But we should never allow it to be our only resource.

There is a cute moment in *Iron Man 3* when a kid asks if he can join Tony Stark on a ride and is refused. The kid then evokes the haunting image of his earlier abandonment by his father, indicating that, by rejecting him now, Tony will have to accept responsibility for all the pain of the kid's childhood trauma. It's a typical 'Hollywood' moment, a trope we have seen again and again. Just for a second we are dipped into a bucket of cheese (putting it politely) before Tony Stark accuses the kid of laying a guilt trip on him. The kid acknowledges the trick. We are saved from the agonies of cliché.

It's an agony because it lacks freshness; it feels borrowed, if not stolen. More than that, it lacks authenticity. By all means engage with your heritage, just as the above example owes its cheerfulness to the Hollywood template, but always keep it, as they say, real. That reality is all around you. It is your greatest resource, the visceral origin of all good Stuff.

Since a strong character will tell you what they want to say and how, if the dialogue isn't coming, look to that character. Is there even character? How deep does it go? A few ticks and mannerisms? A feeble coagulate of whimsical thoughts? Is there feeling? Is there will? Is there that inner drive, their essential sound? Is there a sense of self? If not, then explore the story. Does it have tension, energy, heat? If not, check out the structure. Structure should move. If it's lying in a snivelling heap, maybe it's got a few bones missing. Make sure it's all working. That pulse, that energy of the Orphic Paradigm, does it drive the story? Does it drive the scene, the line? If not, then look at theme. What are you trying to say? What is this about? If you can't see what it's about, then ask where it came from? Did it come from real, potent, beware-of-imitations Stuff? Or somewhere else?

Just tweaking the line may not address more fundamental issues. Since a script can evolve over several drafts, you might even welcome a line that refuses to work if it's indicating a deeper weakness. It might even show you where to look for the weaknesses in your characters, story and theme.

After the initial splurge of the first draft, this is the territory of rewriting; and is where a lot of writers give up. What matters is that you stick with the journey. Pretty soon, solutions emerge out of the fog. Treat them as welcome guests. Perhaps they'll tell you where the others are hiding!

STYLE AND RESONANCE

You might have come across one of those lists that do the rounds from time to time: The 100 Greatest Movies Ever, Ten Films To See Before You Die; 20 Romantic Greats. If you've ever been tempted to go through them, you will probably have recognised many of the films named. You might agree with the list-maker or disagree. Sometimes you'll recall a particular movie and, just for a moment, relish it again. Try this now. Write down your ten favourite films, and ponder each of them for a few seconds.

In a very short time we can bring something of the film to our recollection. But what? We can't zip through a super-fast replaying of the narrative. A few key scenes might come to mind but these are excerpts, not the whole thing. Often what we do is savour its taste, as we might a fine food. We connect with its emotional essence.

Think about those times when you recommended a film to others, or when a film was recommended to you. Was the voice flat and the gestures limp? Or did you widen your eyes to suggest an action movie, cringe at that terrifying horror, speak softly of the moving romance, and even chuckle about the comedy? As much as we might be commending the dialogue, characterisation and rare insight into the complexities of existence, we are also conveying its flavour.

The analogy of flavour as the emotional resonance of any dramatic work has a venerable origin dating back thousands of years to the ancient Indian theatrical tradition. In classical Sanskrit drama the word is 'rasa', which means taste. Like many words from that highly complex and richly developed culture, the word has resonances of its own. Along with flavour and spice, which you might expect, rasa suggests the material essence of anything by which, interestingly, it may be experienced.

This might seem an exotic concept but we're quite used to things being in good taste, or works of art being tasteful, or an individual dressing tastefully or not. To have good taste is to have a heightened, or at least competent, aesthetic awareness. The opposite of good taste, again interestingly, is both bad taste and tasteless.

A plate of food will provide a variety of experiences such as colour, shape, arrangement and texture. But what we most savour, once we tuck in, is the taste. If we extend the idea of rasa to encompass the experience of anything, we might notice that our emotional evaluation of a person, object or situation is, along with all the other criteria by which we judge, a governing factor in how we react. Taste, in this sense, is our fine sense of the qualities of anything. Perhaps the expression that something feels right, or wrong, is the application of rasa.

This pervasive sense of taste applies as much to the crafting of a thing as it does to our experience of it. A chef will dip the spoon to test the flavour and add accordingly. Any act of design will involve the testing of its merits against the sense of taste. How does it feel? What does it do for us? How does it resonate? Good designers have a refined sense of rasa. Even an object that fulfils its functional requirements might repel us for poor taste in its form.

The same applies, obviously, to a work of drama. We've seen how we retain the memory of a film or play through our connection with its rasa. Like the chef, and the designer, the writer will have dipped the spoon from time to time to test the flavour. In many ways, rasa can guide the writing: does it need a little more action, or a little less? Has it become over-wordy? Once we have a taste for that essential, subtly sensual experience of the piece, its rasa will provide an instant indication of the wayward scene, or the superfluous line.

Rasa is akin to the attitude, or swagger, of the piece. An angry writer will make for an angry story. A romantic writer will find the tenderness of the characters. A brutal, gritty mood will generate a sharp, earthy work. We might write in different styles at different times, but to get it right for whatever's on our desk at any given time, it is necessary to feel the mood, or experience its taste.

We've all been part of an audience in thrall to a story: laughing, cringing, chuckling, weeping, gasping or holding our breath in the company of others. If none of this happens, we feel cheated. The movie has no flavour. Like food that tastes of nothing, it is inedible. And we sit there thinking of other things. While it might be possible to generate a synthetic kind of taste, chucking in the tearful moment as we might a dollop of ketchup on to an otherwise dreary plate, authentic rasa sits at the heart of all the creative decisions in the act of writing. You don't necessarily spill tears on to the page, but you are aware of the resonance, the gait, the lilt, of what you're writing. The cerebral, structural aspect of writing has a part to play, just as we can appreciate, or not, the engineering of a suspension bridge. But that isn't enough. The drama you're writing has to be felt in your bones. It has to occupy your emotional landscape, as well as your mind. This is why you need Stuff. Stuff is material that moved you. And this is why cobbling together pre-fabricated units of narrative cliché from other people's work, or because you think it's what the market is looking for, leads inexorably to blandness. And blandness, or tastelessness, as we've seen, is not a virtue.

In the era of Classical Sanskrit theatre, one who excelled in their understanding of drama was known as a 'rasajna' – which means a knower of rasa. What's interesting here is that the notion of rasa is given such a high priority. It was considered more important than the niceties of structure, or the potency of the idea. These could be applauded for their perfections but equally forgiven the occasional flaw. Rasa, on the other hand, had to be right, not just present but well blended in developing configurations throughout the story. The rasajna had to be able to sample a drama, as a wine taster sniffs the contents of a glass and relish its qualities.

According to scholars of the time, the primary tastes are as follows:

Shringara – Erotic – Love
Hasya – Comedic – Merriment
Karuna – Pathos – Sorrow
Vira – Heroic – Enthusiasm
Bhayanaka – Odious – Disgust
Adbhuta – Wonder – Awe

To which were added (and disputed by some):

Shanta – Peace
Vatsalya – Paternal fondness

The first word in each line gives us the Sanskrit name, the second an English equivalent, the third the inner state of which the taste is said to be an experience. Some of the nuance is lost in translation.

We may not agree with this list but it certainly opens up some fascinating territory.

The two rasa of shringara and vira are the dominant tastes from which the others derive. From shringara comes hasya, and from vira comes karuna. We are familiar enough with the love comedy and the heroic tragedy, the two masks by which drama is often represented.

The West Wing and *House of Cards* (US Version) are two dramas which explore an identical scenario, namely the goings-on at the White House in Washington. Their flavours, however, are very different. While the first is laced with bristling wit and comedic moments, the latter emphasises the dark, bitter nature of the political world. Same place, same characters, similar predicaments and machinations, very different rasa.

Like notes on the musical scale, the rasa might be few in number, but the variations in which they can be mixed, and the experiences they can generate, are limitless. Any drama will have a key flavour derived from a particular combination of rasa. It is in the hands of the writer how this extends and elaborates through the play. A funny moment might give way to a tender one. A heroic action could resolve into a sense of pathos. A good dish will toy with our palates, moment by moment, and as a whole.

In addition to the mix, there is also intensity. The rasa might be very obvious, or delicately evoked. The photography might be bright or muted. Performances could be histrionic or understated. It is all, as one might expect, a matter of taste.

Ancient as these ideas are, we can soon detect the lurking rudiments of genre. If shringara is the root of the romantic comedy, vira is the heart of a thumping action movie. Bhayanaka is an obvious candidate for grand-daddy of the horror flick. Blend a teaspoon of vira with a sprinkling of bhayanaka and you're a long way into the feel and tone of a thriller.

Genre, then, is much to do with the dominant style. Just as a combination of rasa can guide our decisions about setting, character, structure, pace, motif, etc, so these begin to conglomerate into identifiable types. In the finished piece, rasa will determine the lighting, costume, delivery of dialogue and manner of acting; in other words, every detail.

It can help us, sometimes, to have a genre in mind when establishing our flavours. On other occasions we might just find the story naturally slipping into certain conventions. We can resist that or not as we wish. What matters is that we find a style that remains consistent and palatable. Too many tastes mixed together can result in no taste. Too much of one particular taste might be overbearing. An erratic movement of rasa from one moment to the next, never quite lingering enough to have an effect, nor develop with any sensible progression, will feel ragged and inept. The culturally sophisticated viewer might point to structural flaws, or implausibility in the characters. The general audience will simply turn their noses up.

There is no creative necessity to think of genre in advance of exploring the story. In many ways, genre is simply a marketing afterthought. Just as we might contemplate our dining options (Indian, Italian, Chinese), so we might feel in the mood for a comedy, family drama or thriller. Labelling helps the viewer to choose. There are few restaurants which simply declare the provision of 'food'. Mostly, their name is an attempt to convey the sense of a dominant taste (Raj Paradise, Luigi's, Bamboo Dragon). While we might be startled to get a poppadom in a French bistro, it doesn't follow that all the food in every French eatery is identical. The menus might be similar but the genius of the chef will vary between establishments. In the same way, identifying your genre doesn't mean you have to copy somebody else's recipe. There is plenty of room for your own personal taste, inclinations and quirks.

We've seen that rasa is familiar both as a way of experiencing story and of sampling life. We would all recognise a sweet pleasure, a sour conversation, or a bitter recollection. The notion of rasa is woven through our language, even if the concept is rarely isolated, at least in the Western cultural tradition, for analysis. The rasa of story, however, differs from that of everyday life in a crucial respect. It is detached. If we see a car crash on the streets we might be shocked, horrified, and anxious to assist. On screen we may feel much the same but are unlikely to call for an ambulance.

A good friend of mine once took up fencing lessons while staying in New York. A few weeks into her course, about which she had become passionate, she went to see a performance of *Macbeth*. When the fight scene was taking place, her eye went to the swordsmanship, evaluating and gauging the respective techniques of Macbeth and Macduff. She suddenly found herself shouting 'look out!', much to the embarrassment of her husband. We find that sort of behaviour surprising, if not hilarious. It is assumed that we are following a play, a make-believe in which nothing is real. In that spirit we can observe the most horrific events and stroll home happily. The horror or romance, fear or loathing, is of an aesthetic nature only. So why is it so enjoyable?

There is a clue in the final word of each line of the grid. According to the theory of rasa, these are latent emotional states (or a way of describing them), integral to all our experiences. If you take a moment to ponder this, you might find that every object in the room around you, every item in your pockets, every photograph you upload for your friends, every moment of every waking day, has some kind of emotional content. Sometimes that content is potent, even overpowering, in both positive and negative ways. Much of the time, however, the mixture is so haphazard, and so mercurial, that we feel only a generalised sense of emotional texture. We're a little bit sad, a little bit worried, a little bit disgusted by something. I once wrote a line for a character in which he said that he was 'almost happy'. My editor said that was a terrible line. I said I thought it rather good, actually. She said 'No, no, I mean it's just a terrible thing for anyone to say'. Nietzsche wrote of a 'miserable ease', and Pink Floyd of 'comfortably numb'. This is a way of living, not living itself.

Rasa tasted through the medium of drama allows us to harmonise and intensify those emotional states. We can relish them again. We can re-connect with our emotional perceptions. We can feel, quite simply, alive. While this is enjoyable in the moment of experience, it has a restorative effect on our general condition. This is akin to the principle of catharsis, a concept largely attributed to Aristotle, by which negative emotions are cleansed or purified. The Indian approach is a little more subtle. Through drama, our emotional states are untangled, reactivated, and balanced. The result is much the same, and might go some way to explaining why theatre and medicine were so profoundly connected in the culture of ancient Greece.

Rasa is the result of all the elements working together. Your structure should be strong enough to stand straight, and flexible enough to jump and run without falling over. The story world should be a rich integration of its components, every object and action emerging naturally from its tones and textures. The territory of experience which the story explores, which is to say your themes, should be recognisable but fresh, familiar in principle, but expressed in some unique way. The characters must be of the world, properly formed from the inside out, as real in their attributes as you or I. The dialogue should be perfectly measured to express their thoughts, feelings and rationale, linking thereby to the thoughts, feelings and rationale of the story. But if rasa is the end product, the culmination of your all efforts, it is also at the beginning.

It is the sense by which you know you've got Stuff. It will guide your exploration of that Stuff through every detail of the unfolding script by which it finds expression.

As we've seen, rasa is not a mechanical device, nor literary technique. It is the emotional experience of your story. You may tweak and nudge your elements to get the flavours just so, but this will be according to your personal tastes and what they tell you as you dip the spoon. Every writer will have a unique taste. We might write very different pieces over the years, exploring different themes and flavours, but there's usually that individual spark which makes us recognisably us. You know an Elmore Leonard novel from a quick glance at any page. You can recognise Laurie Lee in every paragraph of a Laurie Lee book. There is that Harold Pinter feeling nobody else can ever quite replicate though many have tried. Scorsese, Coppola, Terrence Malick, Woody Allen, Michael Bay and Peter Weir aren't just names, they are styles that we can instantly savour.

Finding your own style, or voice, can take time. It will certainly take some writing. Bear in mind that it isn't something to be contrived but discovered and, thereafter, refined. Mechanical approaches to writing, which is to say story software, rigid schematics, grids-as-gospel, predetermined shapes and off-the-peg themes, are all very well for an audience of lawn-mowers. But we are writing for that subtle, emotional, thoughtful, rational, sensitive, and ultimately sentient entity known as the human being. They want human experiences prepared by human writers. They want you.

CONCLUSION
LAST WORDS

The simple premise of this book is twofold. The first is that story comes naturally to us. The second is that the laws of story reflect the laws of nature.

We all love stories and many love to tell them. Some of us, for whatever reason, make a decision to devote ourselves to this art. Sometimes our stories will spring spontaneously, whole and complete, into being. Sometimes we'll have to work on them. But craft is to be found in the very nature of experience. And the more we understand that experience, the more skilful we can become.

Our job is to share experience itself. It has to follow that both inspiration and execution come from the Stuff of life. What else are we trying to talk about?

The material of this book has been drawn in part from my own adventures in the trade, conversations with fellow writers, discussions with students, and a little of the rich heritage of literature in which we are privileged to participate; and in part from my ceaseless quest for an easy life.

A story that I'm bursting to tell tends to tell itself. So I'm always on the lookout for those little nuggets of circumstance, those instances and events, that force me to grab the pen and start scribbling. The stronger the impulse, the less one has to worry about who the characters are, or how it ends, or its structure and tone.

But I also know what it is to look over a draft and notice that its themes aren't fully understood, that the characters are a little woolly, the motifs imprecise and the style all over the place. That's when it helps to have a knowledge of craft as a form, or even a schematic, so that we can tuck back into that script and start fixing it. Which is where books on the subject, courses and classes, workshops and seminars, and the company of other writers come in. But unless you're writing, to be perfectly honest, they're not much use. They're just answers to questions you don't have. By all means, absorb all the knowledge you can from all the sources you can get hold of, but only to help the writing that you're already engaged in. The cutting edge of your development as a writer can only happen, in the end, where the pen meets the page.

All the writers that I know are passionate about writing. If I haven't written for a few days, apparently, I become ratty and irritable. I still get a little thrill from buying a new pot of ink, or a pad of paper. I will run my fingers over all those empty lines, waiting for story, as a stamp collector might relish a first day cover. Sometimes, midway through a third rewrite, a little of that enthusiasm might have dimmed, but that's when it's most crucial to remember why you write, and why you wanted to write this.

Not all writers are concerned about the form. Some just get on with it. Personally, I find the art itself almost as fascinating as that which emerges from it. What is a story? What is character? How does plot unfold and why? These are questions that have entertained me for years – and still do. A few days ago I showed a clip from *Hana-bi* to a group of undergraduate students. I've watched that scene over and over but one of the students pointed something out to me that I hadn't noticed before. I love that. But, as I said, some writers aren't fussed about the how's and why's; they just want to get that story out.

Since I remain convinced that story is a natural attribute of the human psyche, I am wary, as you might have gathered, of schemes that seek to mechanise the creative act. Check-box charts of 'what happens when' are a lazy way for those who know nothing of drama to gauge whether or not a script is working. If I have attempted to unearth the shape and dynamic of the elements of drama, it is always with one eye on their relevance to the innate knowledge of real experience. This approach is harder in some ways, since your writing has to be true and passionate. But it's far easier if you have a nose for truth and the passion to speak of it. You just have to look for that truth and its natural means of expression. It's all there, in your Stuff.

So enjoy the world. Live it. Experience it. Suffer it. Dig into it. Scribble down what you find. And then share that insight, and the unique delight of its essential flavour with others. That, in brief, is the job.

Good luck!

About Us

In addition to Creative Essentials, Oldcastle Books has a number of other imprints, including No Exit Press, Kamera Books, Pulp! The Classics, Pocket Essentials and High Stakes Publishing > **oldcastlebooks.co.uk**

Checkout the kamera film salon for independent, arthouse and world cinema > **kamera.co.uk**

For more information, media enquiries and review copies please contact Frances > **frances@oldcastlebooks.com**